*W*oolf *S*tudies *A*nnual

Volume 22, 2016

PACE UNIVERSITY PRESS • NEW YORK

Copyright © 2016 by
Pace University Press
41 Park Row, Rm. 1510
New York, NY 10038

All rights reserved
Printed in the United States of America

ISSN: 1080-9317
ISBN: 978-0-9619518-3-2 (pbk: alk.ppr.)

Member

Council of Editors of Learned Journals

☉ Paper used in this publication meets the minimum requirements of
American National Standard for Information
Sciences–Permanence of Paper for Printed Library Materials,
ANSI Z39.48–1984

Editor

Mark Hussey   Pace University

Editorial Board

Tuzyline Jita Allan	Baruch College, CUNY
Eileen Barrett	California State University, East Bay
Morris Beja	Ohio State University
Kathryn N. Benzel	University of Nebraska-Kearney
Pamela L. Caughie	Loyola University Chicago
Wayne K. Chapman	Clemson University
Patricia Morgne Cramer	University of Connecticut, Stamford
Beth Rigel Daugherty	Otterbein College
Louise DeSalvo	Jenny Hunter Endowed Scholar for Literature and Creative Writing, Hunter College, CUNY
Anne Fernald	Fordham University
Amanda Golden	New York Institute of Technology (Book Review Editor)
Sally Greene	Independent Scholar
Leslie Kathleen Hankins	Cornell College
Suzette Henke	Thruston B. Morton, Sr. Chair of Literary Studies, University of Louisville
Karen Kaivola	Provost and CAO, Augsburg College
Karen Kukil	Associate Curator of Special Collections, William Allan Neilson Library, Smith College
Jane Lilienfeld	Curator's Distinguished Professor of English, Lincoln University
Toni A. H. McNaron	University of Minnesota
Patricia Moran	London City University
Vara Neverow	Southern Connecticut State University
Annette Oxindine	Wright State University
Beth Carole Rosenberg	University of Nevada, Las Vegas
Bonnie Kime Scott	San Diego State University
Brenda R. Silver	Dartmouth College
Susan Squier	Brill Professor of Women's Studies and English, Pennsylvania State University
Peter Stansky	Stanford University
Alex Zwerdling	University of California, Berkeley

In Memoriam: Jane Marcus, 1938-2015.

Many thanks to readers for volume 22: Michael Bird (Independent Scholar); Gregory Castle (Arizona SU); Marcia Day Childress (U of Virginia School of Medicine); Melba Cuddy-Keane (U of Toronto); Claire Davison (U Sorbonne Nouvelle); Jane de Gay (Leeds Trinity); Jennie-Rebecca Falcetta (Massachusetts C of Art); Jane E. Fisher (Canisius C); Diane F. Gillespie (Washington SU); Jane Goldman (Glasgow U); Cheryl Hindrichs (Boise SU); Maggie Humm (U East London); Nancy Knowles (Eastern Oregon U); Holly Laird (U of Tulsa); Alison Lewis (Drexel U); Brenda Lyons (Everest C); Jean Mills (John Jay C, CUNY); Gabrielle McIntire (Queens U, Canada); Makiko Minow-Pinkney (Independent Scholar); Suzanne Nalbantian (Long Island U); Claudia Olk (Freie U Berlin); Steven Putzel (Penn State Wilkes-Barre); Robert Sawyer (E Tennessee SU); Lorraine Sim (U of Western Sydney); Elisa Kay Sparks (Clemson U); Rod Taylor (Stanford U); Julie Vandivere (Bloomsburg U); Michael Whitworth (Merton C, Oxford U); Janet Winston (Humboldt SU); Elizabeth Wright (Bath Spa U).

Woolf Studies Annual is indexed in *Humanities International Complete, ABELL,* and the *MLA Bibliography.*

Call for papers for a special issue of the *Virginia Woolf Miscellany*

Issue #91/Spring 2017

Virginia Woolf, Bloomsbury, and the War to End War

This issue commemorates the advent of the Great War and its representation by Virginia Woolf and her friends and colleagues in Bloomsbury and beyond (even H.G. Wells, who wrote a 1914 pamphlet called *The War that Will End War*)—noncombatants, combatants, and conscientious objectors; writers of prose, poetry, and drama; fiction and memoirs; criticism, reviews, and social commentary; journalists, historians, philosophers, and humanists. Contributions need not necessarily involve work done during the war, but gauge the war's ongoing effect on a wide range of topics and perspectives: cultural, socio-economic, modernist, feminist, to name the most obvious. How did war-consciousness, for example, affect views of mass culture and consumerism? Articles on other topics (e.g., constructions of self and identity in wartime, and post-war aesthetics) are also welcome.

Please send *inquiries* to Karen Levenback at kllevenback@att.net ASAP and *submissions* of not more than 2500 words by 1 August 2016.

Contents

Woolf Studies Annual

Volume 22, 2016

	viii	Abbreviations
		ARTICLES
Emily Dalgarno	1	Virginia Woolf Reinvents the Socratic Dialogue
Christine Fouirnaies	21	Was Virginia Woolf a Snob? The Case of Aristocratic Portraits in *Orlando*
J. Ashley Foster	41	Writing in the "White Light of Truth": History, Ethics, and Community in Virginia Woolf's *Between the Acts*
Clara Jones	75	Virginia Woolf and "The Villa Jones" (1931)
		GUIDE
	97	Guide to Library Special Collections
		REVIEWS
John Young	117	*Mrs. Dalloway* by Virginia Woolf. Anne E. Fernald, ed.
Gretchen Gerzina	120	*Vanessa and Her Sister* by Priya Parmar; *Adeline* by Norah Vincent; *Virginia Woolf in Manhattan* by Maggie Gee
Lauren Elkin	125	*Contemporary Woolf/Woolf contemporaine* Claire Davison-Pegon and Anne-Marie Smith-Di Biasio, eds.

Janine Utell	128	*Virginia Woolf: Twenty-First-Century Approaches* Jeanne Dubino, Gill Lowe, Vara Neverow, and Kathryn Simpson, eds.
Amanda Golden	131	*Modern Manuscripts: The Extended Mind and Creative Undoing from Darwin to Beckett and Beyond* by Dirk Van Hulle
Matthew James Vechinski	135	*Roomscape: Women Writers in the British Museum from George Eliot to Virginia Woolf* by Susan David Bernstein
Jonathan Goldman	138	*Modernism and Autobiography* Maria DiBattista and Emily O. Wittman, eds.
Carolyn Allen	140	*A Poetics of Postmodernism and Neo-modernism: Rewriting* Mrs. Dalloway by Monica Latham
Sarah Cornish	144	*The Cambridge Companion to Modernist Culture* Celia Marshik, ed.; *The Cambridge Companion to The Bloomsbury Group* Victoria Rosner, ed.
Jane de Gay	148	*The Cambridge Companion to* To the Lighthouse Allison Pease, ed.
Jean Mills	151	*Interdisciplinary/Multidisciplinary Woolf: Selected Papers from the Twenty-Second Annual International Conference on Virginia Woolf* Ann Martin and Kathryn Holland, eds.; *Virginia Woolf and the Common(wealth) Reader: Selected Papers from the Twenty-Third Annual International Conference on Virginia Woolf* Helen Wussow and Mary Ann Gillies, eds.
Elisa Kay Sparks	157	*Critical Insights: Virginia Woolf & 20th Century Women Writers* Kathyrn Stelmach Artuso, ed.

Karen Zumhagen-Yekplé **160** *Modernist Fiction and Vagueness: Philosophy, Form, and Language* by Megan Quigley

165 International Notes

167 Notes on Contributors

169 Submission Guidelines

173 Other Woolf Titles Available

Abbreviations

AHH	*A Haunted House*
AROO	*A Room of One's Own*
BP	*Books and Portraits*
BTA	*Between the Acts*
CDB	*The Captain's Death Bed and Other Essays*
CE	*Collected Essays* (4 vols.)
CR1	*The Common Reader*
CR2	*The Common Reader, Second Series*
CSF	*The Complete Shorter Fiction*
D	*The Diary of Virginia Woolf* (5 vols.)
DM	*The Death of the Moth and Other Essays*
E	*The Essays of Virginia Woolf* (6 Vols.)
F	*Flush*
FR	*Freshwater*
GR	*Granite & Rainbow: Essays*
JR	*Jacob's Room*
L	*The Letters of Virginia Woolf* (6 Vols.)
M	*The Moment and Other Essays*
MEL	*Melymbrosia*
MOB	*Moments of Being*
MT	*Monday or Tuesday*
MD	*Mrs. Dalloway*
ND	*Night and Day*
O	*Orlando*
PA	*A Passionate Apprentice*
RF	*Roger Fry: A Biography*
TG	*Three Guineas*
TTL	*To the Lighthouse*
TW	*The Waves*
TY	*The Years*
VO	*The Voyage Out*

Virginia Woolf Reinvents the Socratic Dialogue
Emily Dalgarno

Although Woolf's lifelong interest in Plato has been widely noted, we have yet to explore the kinds of tension that arise in her work when she reads a text by Plato in the context of contemporary culture.[1] Woolf's attention to the vocabulary and argument of the dialogues, which reflects her early training as a student/translator, distinguishes her from Matthew Arnold and others who read the Platonic dialogues as a univocal philosophical treatise. Her untraditional reading makes better sense in the context of recent interpretations of Plato that focus on the artistic structure of the dialogues. They stress the element of play, in which a fictional Socrates is less an authoritative figure than a voice that in concert with his friends demonstrates how a mode of talk becomes a mode of thought inviting the participation of the reader. In other words the dialogues demonstrate how the play of voices among non-philosophers turns a social interaction into a philosophical inquiry, with a consequent displacement of intentional control from the figure of Socrates.[2] Harry Berger Jr. writes of the dialogues as "a text that 'speaks' against Socrates as well as through him," in a field of textual play that empowers the reader (84-85). Rather than a treatise on philosophy the dialogues demonstrate, as Charles Griswold argues, Plato's attempt to justify philosophical inquiry in the face of fundamental disagreements, so that the dialogues demonstrate "the origination of philosophy itself out of the medium of opinion" (153). The argument against univocal interpretation has had a far ranging impact on the study of Plato among European philosophers. Max Statkiewicz for instance studies the interaction of philosophers from Nietzsche to Derrida with the texts of Plato in order to validate modes of thinking "that chal-

---

[1] Andrew McNeillie writes that Plato "was the philosopher Woolf read far more enthusiastically and extensively than ever she read Moore or any other philosopher" (14). Molly Hoff characterizes Lady Bruton's luncheon as "a topos derived from Plato and Horace" (96). Theodore Koulouris's *Hellenism and Loss in the Work of Virginia Woolf* studies Woolf's "Greekness" from a variety of perspectives, and concludes that she saw Greek "as a rich repository of literary paradigms" (117). Regina Fowler observes that "in *To the Lighthouse* Woolf conducts her own dialogue with Plato" (227). Brenda Lyons concludes in her study of *Jacob's Room* that Woolf's arguments do not engage with Plato's, but rather draw from the dialogues to inspire, complicate, and support her own aesthetic ends" (290). Melba Cuddy-Keane studies Woolf's dialogic discourse as a distant reflection of Platonic dialogue: "Woolf's reading of Plato stands as a possible description of her own technique . . . as a process of settling and unsettling, as we are urged simultaneously to form opinions and never to allow opinion to harden into truth" (135). Ruth Vanita studies motifs from the *Symposium* in *A Room of One's Own*.
[2] Derrida first suggested that the dialogues complicate the figure of Socrates, in "Plato's Pharmacy," *Dissemination*, trans. Barbara Johnson (Chicago: University of Chicago Press, 1981), 61-173.

lenge the dominance of univocal interpretation, as well as the corresponding treatise format, in the modern philosophical tradition" (4). For my purposes I focus on two of Woolf's essays, "On Not Knowing Greek" (1925) and "On Being Ill" (1926), where she signals her strategy by gesturing towards the dialogues, and then posits a reading that is modeled not on listening but on the reader's willingness to transform personal experience into philosophical inquiry. In *Three Guineas* her strategy is more aggressive yet tacit, a reference to Socrates merely hinted at the end.

Aporia as it is defined in classical studies is a device that questions the boundaries of received opinion and opens the discussion to other speakers/readers. Although it has always been understood as referring to the impasse that occurs when at the end of a dialogue no agreement has been reached, Vasilis Politis defines it as a means to reach a second stage. Aporia begins "as the mental state of perplexity and being at a loss in the face of the Socratic demand for definitions; and leads to aporia as the puzzlement about particular puzzles and problems." In the first stage Socrates seeks by means of extended interrogation, or *elenchus*, to establish definitions; a second phase concerns the moment when he turns impasse into the impetus for the search for knowledge (89). In this second phase the etymology of aporia sheds light on an impasse that disrupts accepted views on the subject-object relationship, and leads the reader into what Woolf figured in "On Being Ill" as those "wastes and deserts of the soul" (*E4* 317).

Feminist scholars have shown how deeply Woolf engaged her historical moment. This study amplifies the reach of that research by suggesting that her translations brought to bear on historical questions aporia and an ancient mode of discourse. As a lifelong student of ancient Greek she was both the reader who admires the thoughts expressed in a Socratic dialogue, and the writer whose questions led to the realization that the definitions that are the first step in aporia are historically contingent, and thus subject to change. In three essays Woolf adapts *Socratic* aporia as a means to convert received opinion into philosophical inquiry, a project that grants the reader new authority. Her reading notes on the *Symposium* privilege Diotima, who argues that love can lead to a kind of philosophical procreation, but the omission of her name from "On Not Knowing Greek," where the dialogue figures, suggests how the attitude of the British government and the public towards homosexuality complicates attempts to sort out Woolf's position on gender identity. In "On Being Ill" Woolf focused on Socrates' image in the *Phaedo* of the mortal body of bones and sinews that feels pain and fears death. She translated the debate about the impact of Socrates' impending death on the relationship of soul to body into a test of the limits of representation. In *Three Guineas*, where Woolf turns the question of how to prevent war into a redefinition of Fascism, aporia becomes the vehicle for locating divergent views not only in text and photographs but also in semantics. By structuring her essays as replies to the very Greek texts that were the foundation of British university education Woolf asserted the authority not of the philosophical treatise but of the question. All three works converted the Socratic question into a question about the function of language that freed her to assume a position astride the impasse of the aporetic essay.

Woolf's emphasis on the *question* distinguishes her study of Plato from that of Matthew Arnold. Her early training in Greek grammar with Janet Case meant that she encountered Greek texts as a challenge to her skill as a translator that oriented her focus on semantics and structure. Case in her turn introduced Woolf to Jane Harrison, who took Woolf into a wider world of scholarship. Jean Mills, in *Virginia Woolf, Jane Harrison and the Spirit of Modernist Classicism*, argues for the importance of these mentors: Case and especially Harrison not only taught Woolf about the ancient Greeks, but also suggested alternative models of gender relationships and power.[3] The structure of the Platonic dialogues, in which a question has the power to advance an argument, thus granting authority to the questioner, proved fertile ground in Woolf's search for a language in which women's writing might counterbalance public discourse.

The title and language of "On Not Knowing Greek" mimic passages from Matthew Arnold's "Literature and Science" (1895): "when we talk of endeavoring to know Greek and Roman antiquity, as a help to knowing ourselves and the world, we mean endeavoring so to know them as to satisfy this ideal, however much we may still fall short of it" (X: 58). Rather her essay stresses the strangeness of "the wish to know Greek, try to know Greek, feel forever drawn back to Greek…" and relies instead on the question (*E4* 38). Arnold's knowledge of the Platonic dialogues was broader and more professional, but his image of Socrates and Plato was shaped by Victorian attitudes that she resisted. As M. W. Rowe observes, Arnold's was the Socrates of Xenophon and of Benjamin Jowett, which is to say a Socrates notable as a good citizen and more identified with Christian values than the figure who is studied today (242-256). Although Arnold's colleagues had noted that he identified himself with Socrates, the end of "Culture and Anarchy" makes it explicit: " . . . in his own breast does not every man carry about with him a possible Socrates, in that power of disinterested play of consciousness upon his stock notions and habits" (V: 57-58). By contrast Woolf's idea of knowing as provoking a series of questions—"who shall say?"—brings her closer to Montaigne and to a more radical and contemporary Socrates (*E4* 39). In a passage of the *Charmides* where he considers the inscription "know thyself" as "a sort of salutation" from the god, he reassures Charmides: "You come to me as though I professed to know about the questions

---

[3] Mills, chapter one. Henry M. Alley makes a similar point in "A Rediscovered Eulogy: Virginia Woolf's 'Miss Janet Case: Classical Scholar and Teacher.'" *Twentieth Century Literature* 28 (1982), 292.

which I ask, and as though I could, if I would, agree with you. Whereas the fact is that I enquire with you into the truth of that which is advanced from time to time, just because I do not know, and when I have enquired, I will say whether I agree with you or not" (Jowett 20). Although she shared Arnold's spiritual longing, Woolf's position was more subversive: her goal was to appropriate for her own purposes a vocabulary and an epistemology that remained in the hands of the professors. The struggle with herself is closer to Andrea Nightingale's recent study of Socrates and self knowledge: "Ultimately, however, he attains self-knowledge by moving back and forth between his contemplating soul and his earthly person: it is the interplay between these two that generates self-knowledge in the Platonic philosopher" (26).

In "On Not Knowing Greek" Woolf remained in one respect close to Arnold: she stressed the poetry and drama of the dialogues, while, like Plato she made a particular use of philosophy without asserting it in her own name. Seeing the ancient Greeks at a tremendous distance from English language and culture, the essay accepts an idealized Socrates and reader. Woolf touches lightly on *elenchus*, "an exhausting process," and cites without comment the image of Socrates in Alcibiades's speech in the *Symposium*, which praises "the divine images of his mind . . . [so that] everything which Socrates commands surely ought to be obeyed even like the voice of a God" (*E4* 46). Woolf's attribution of "dramatic genius" to Plato, and her focus on the dialogues as drama, is consistent with a Socrates who is the mouthpiece of wisdom and a reader who experiences that "exultation of mind that can only be reached when all the powers are called upon to contribute their energy to the whole" (*E4* 47). In Berger's words, "The aesthetic decision to read the text as drama, and the ethical decision to idealize the Platonic Socrates to the status of a quasi-mouthpiece, seem reciprocally to reinforce each other" (95). In addition the idealized Socrates would seem to demand an Arnoldian reader, who turns to the Greeks when "sick of the vagueness, of the confusion, of the Christianity and its consolations, of our own age" (*E4* 51). Until Woolf engaged the dialogue on its terms, to accept an image of the god-like Socrates left her a spectator on the sidelines.

Woolf's essay begins with a citation of the argument between Socrates and Protagoras in the *Protagoras*: "Can virtue be taught? Is virtue knowledge?" (*E4* 46). In the dialogue the two discuss whether virtue can be turned into knowledge, and whether *techne* (craft, art, or performance) can be used to question the purity of philosophical argument.[4] Socrates asks whether Protagoras means to "teach the art of politics, and that you promise to make men good citizens," and when Protagoras agrees that is his profession, rejoins, "I have a doubt whether this art is capable of being taught" (Jowett 132). Yet after persuading Protagoras to speak more briefly, and to "argue" rather than "wrangle," by the end of the dialogue no

---

[4] For a more detailed definition of *techne* see Martha Nussbaum, *The Fragility of Goodness* (Cambridge: Cambridge University Press, 2001), 94-9 and 443-44, n.10.

agreement has been reached. Martha Nussbaum provides historical perspective: Protagoras is the older, a man who has lived through the glorious past of Athenian political culture, and naturally resists Socrates's attempts to "measure" as a way to counter "appearance . . . that deceiving art" (187-88). Socrates is searching for "a standard or measure that will render values commensurable, therefore subject to precise scientific control. The need for measurement motivates the search for an acceptable measure" (110). The question is urgent, for the reader knows, as the speakers do not, that the dialogue occurs three years before the outbreak of the Peloponnesian War, and before a plague that devastated Athens. He is aware that "the moral consensus is soon to be unhinged by external pressures, by the pull of conflicting obligations . . . that among the dialogues' characters some will soon be dead and others will soon be killing" (91).

At the end of the dialogue the two leave their disagreement unresolved, a passage that gave some Victorian translators, John Stuart Mill for instance, an opportunity to misrepresent its philosophical importance by suppressing its aporetic structure. Alexandra Lianeri cites the Taylor translation (1976), in which the dialogue ends with an aporia: "It seems to me that the conclusion we have just reached is jeering at us like an accuser. And if it could speak, it would say 'How absurd you are, both of you'" (172). She argues that Mill's translation of the lines "Socrates finally remarked what a whimsical turn their discussion had taken," occludes Socratic irony, and with it a debate about "the inseparability of philosophy and democratic politics. It involved the collective and critical mode of sifting opinions carried out by free and equal interlocutors, none of whom is in firm possession of knowledge" (172).

Mill's translation suppresses the *elenchus* that is central to Woolf's reading of the dialogues, and to her sense of aporia. She identifies on humane grounds with the speaker whose inconsistencies of opinion are revealed by Socrates's "remorseless" questioning: "It is an exhausting process; to contract painfully upon the exact meaning of words; to judge what each admission involves; to follow intently, yet critically, the dwindling and changing of opinion as it hardens and intensifies into truth" (*E4* 46).[5] More importantly Woolf values aporia in its second sense, in which it names not simply the speechless confusion of the interlocutor, but a kind of searching for the answer to the puzzle that arises specifically from that state of confusion (Politis 89). In 1921, contemplating the coincidence of a friend's risky marriage and the premature death by drowning of another, she wrote of her sense

---

[5] Whether *elenchus* establishes Socrates's ideas in positive terms is a question. The literature is large, but see George Grote, *Plato and the Other Companions of Sokrates* (London, 1875), who believed that it is purely destructive, and for a historical overview Hugh H. Benson, "The Dissolution of the Problem of the Elenchus," *Oxford Studies in Ancient Philosophy* 13 (1995): 45-112.

of powerlessness: "And sometimes I suppose that even if I came to the end of my incessant search into what people are & feel I should know nothing still. I mean I go on thinking in the belief that if one thinks about it enough one comes to some conclusion. That I begin to judge doubtful" (*D2* 119). The doubts that were aroused by her search for a link between desire and death are a continuing theme. In the essay we see her preference for the argument that is kept in play by *elenchus*: "For as the argument mounts from step to step, Protagoras yielding, Socrates pushing on, what matters is not so much the end we reach as our manner of reaching it. That all can feel—the indomitable honesty, the courage, the love of truth which draw Socrates and us in his wake to the summit where, if we too may stand for a moment it is to enjoy the greatest felicity of which we are capable" (*E4* 46). If we read this passage together with Woolf's satiric portrait of Mr. Ramsay as a man who when others yield pushes on to stand at the summit, we can observe Woolf on both sides of an argument about the difference between philosophy as end or means.

The *Protagoras* makes the two senses of aporia and its relationship to *elenchus* especially clear. Protagoras prefers the extended speech as the means to persuasion, Socrates question and answer, and questioner and respondent as two roles that can be exchanged: "If Protagoras is not disposed to answer, let him ask and I will answer" (Jowett 153). In a further attempt to disarm Protagoras he cites a line from the *Iliad* that helps to define aporia. Socrates says of himself, "Do not imagine, Protagoras, that I have any other interest in asking questions of you but that of clearing up my own little difficulties. For I think Homer was very right in saying that 'When two go together, one sees before the other'" (*Iliad* X: 224). If the disagreement with Protagoras were diachronic, or historical as Nussbaum argues, the visual image suggests that it is synchronic as well, and that aporia occurs at the intersection of the temporal and the visual. As a result of the disagreement between Socrates and his respondents *elenchus* advances the dialogue beyond definitions into the exploration of virtue and knowledge that is left unresolved at the end. David Sedley comments on a method that "creates a double confrontation, one within the dialogue, the other between the dialogue and the reader, who is forced by a complex interaction with the text to reflect on the philosophical issues which it addresses" (4-5). Woolf's preference for *elenchus* made it possible for her to sidestep the idealized Socrates apparent in well-known Victorian translations/interpretations, in order to make a different use of dialogue: since perspective requires coordinates and hence divergent views, the reader is ineluctably drawn into the argument.

Seven pages of Woolf's notes survive from her reading of the *Symposium* with Janet Case. Several are now illegible, but enough remains to reveal her enthusiasm for the dialogue, and especially for Diotima's speech on philosophical procreation which Socrates reports: "A truly instructed lover will go on from better to [word illegible] loving bodies then souls till he gets finally a glimpse of absolute beauty, which is more beautiful than any of the vessels in which it takes lodging."[6] The speech, she concludes, was "one of the most beautiful I have read. It is an entire expression of something often hinted at in the other dialogues" (MHP 59). Since much of Woolf's youthful enthusiasm for the *Symposium* survived, the absence of Diotima from "On Not Knowing Greek" is surprising, but consistent with the essay's reticence about homosexual behavior. Woolf limited the debate about love to two men, Alcibiades and Socrates, who among all the figures in the dialogue represent opposing ideas of truth. No sooner has Socrates finished recounting the discourse about love that he has heard from Diotima, in which she has argued that loving the beautiful boy leads to true virtue (212a), than Alcibiades bursts in, drunk, with a love story to tell about the behavior of Socrates.[7] In her notes Woolf terms the ensuing exchange "a strange little scene [two words illegible] half in earnest" (MHP 58). Alcibiades's speech is delivered "as though on the stage . . . . He feels all Socrates' grandeur—yet wishes the man dead sometimes . . . The end is almost tragic, for Socrates is above it all—not to be moved, and acts with a kind of delicate chill irony which must have maddened" (MHP 59). Reading the dialogue like a drama suggests that as though like Diotima and the flute girl, she views from offstage a debate of concern only to men.

How then does the dialogue resolve the vast difference between a Socrates instructed by Diotima and the drunken speech of Alcibiades? Nussbaum explores Alcibiades's postulate, in which "sexual and epistemological need are joined and, apparently, inseparable," which characterizes as well his attitude towards Socrates, who is revealed as closed and indifferent (190). Each man has a version of truth: Socrates believes what he has been told by Diotima; and Alcibiades, without any apparent metaphysical understanding, tells the lover's truth about Socrates. Nussbaum's conclusion is compelling in the context of a *Symposium* that for the sake of Woolf's argument contains only these two: "We see two kinds of value, two kinds of knowledge, and we see that we must choose. One sort of understanding blocks out the other . . . The *Symposium* now seems to us a harsh and alarming book . . . . for it does make a case for that conception of value, but it shows us also, all too clearly, how much that conception requires us to give up."[8]

---

[6] Monks House Papers, Reel 1, MHA 21. Citations are from pages numbered in Woolf's hand as 58 and 59, identified as MHP. And see Silver, *Reading Notebooks* 168.
[7] *The Symposium*, trans. M. C. Howatson, eds. M. C. Howatson and Frisbee C. C. Sheffield (Cambridge: Cambridge University Press, 2006). Subsequent references are to this text.
[8] *Ibid.*, 198. David Gribble replies to Nussbaum, that "it is the speech of Socrates in praise of a real, philosophical *eros* and way of life that provides the context which allows us to see through the superficial attractiveness of Alcibiades . . . the *Symposium* is not a dialogue where figures are straightforwardly condemned, but one where the weaknesses in people and their positions are suggested, through more implicit and oblique means" (253).

David M. Halperin's essay, "Why is Diotima a Woman?" explores the contradictions of gender implicit in Socrates's receiving advice from a prophetess who argues that men can become pregnant. As a female, Diotima's authority was owing in part to her access to divine wisdom, and to her disinterested position on pederasty. Her specifically gendered vocabulary of erotic desire helped Plato to avoid an appearance of "Socratic approval for a social practice for which Plato himself entertained the liveliest mistrust" (116-17). Given the position of women in Athenian society, Diotima was part of the social reproduction of male culture, since she "represents a woman's perspective in a form recognizable by men" (146). Halperin argues that Diotima is fictional, a projection of male fantasy, indeed a mask designed to be worn by men, suggesting a femininity that is defined by reference to masculinity. In the larger project of the *Symposium*, to represent the institutional conditions for the practice of philosophy, Diotima may be said to rival Alcibiades (150). Together they put in question modes of access to philosophy: whereas Alcibiades refers to his experience in bed in an attempt to claim intimacy, Diotima gestures in a dream towards an imaginary experience of gender in which males give birth. The question of Diotima is consistent with a feminism that in Rachel Bowlby's *Virginia Woolf: Feminist Destinations* "lies precisely in her insistence on the sexual inflection of all questions of historical understanding and literary representation" (15). Gender in the *Symposium* seems, to use Bowlby's term—the "destination" of various socially conflicted desires as they are inflected by Plato's representation.

As though to accommodate contradiction, Woolf chose in her essay to cite Shelley's version of Alcibiades's speech in his translation of the *Symposium*, "The Banquet," a work that owing to its explicit language could not be published in his lifetime. Woolf's choice literally translated the *Symposium* into an era when there was a political reason to prefer an aporetic argument about the love between men. Citing Shelley's translation of a speech by Agathon, " . . . for everyone even if before he were ever so undisciplined, becomes a poet as soon as he is touched by love," serves to distract the reader from the drunkenness and sexuality of Alcibiades (*E4* 49). Rather, Woolf's "Truth is various" served an important political function, to keep at a distance questions of sexuality and gender identity that at the time she wrote were harshly treated under British law. Clive Bell wrote in a memorial volume on Proust that "he wrote of certain relations of which British writers may not treat freely" (88).[9] In 1934 Woolf wrote to Quentin Bell that she was writing of sodomy: "In French yes; but in Mr Galsworthys English no" (*L5* 273). In fact homosexuality remained a criminal act in Britain until the Sexual Offences Act of 1967. In these circumstances to include Diotima might have pointed to a complexity

---

[9] See chapter four of my *Virginia Woolf and the Migrations of Language*, in which I discuss the difficulties of naming or writing about homosexuality in Britain.

in the heterosexual/homosexual distinction that was better kept offstage, as though Woolf anticipated readers who shared the attitude of an earlier generation towards what Linda Dowling describes as "the perilously equivocal space between Platonic relations and spiritual procreancy on the one hand, and Greek love and the Socratic corruption of youth on the other" (103). As Sue Roe observes, Woolf lacked "in the final analysis a fixed and dependable reference point for the construction of gender"(6). In the dialogues she found a culture like hers in which the plurality of discourses reflects controversy about actual legal and historical conditions.

In "On Being Ill" we see more clearly the hermeneutic tension that arises around the body when an ancient text is translated into contemporary culture. In it we see the translator's sense of the "incomprehensible" phrase, coupled with the illness and frustrated desire that fueled her anger. The essay was written during a period of personal crisis, when Woolf faced illness and separation from Vita Sackville-West. After fainting at a party in the summer of 1925, her letters for September report lying in bed for weeks, "comatose with headaches. Cant write" (*L3* 208). Although her ill health persisted, the essay was completed in November. As Hermione Lee observes, it is one of Woolf's "most daring, strange and original essays." A new edition (2012) reprints the essay along with Julia Stephen's *Notes from Sick Rooms*, thereby combining two works that deal with illness from the dual perspective of patient and nurse (Woolf, *On Being* xiii). But it makes a different kind of sense when read alongside the *Phaedo*, a dialogue that was among the assignments for the Greek class at King's College London in which Woolf enrolled in 1898. (Jones and Snaith 19). Lorraine Sim, who has studied Woolf's essay in the context of contemporary social attitudes, reads it as an exploration of minor illness in an era when new technologies of health had become a national preoccupation. She acknowledges the Platonic dimension of Woolf's argument: "In 'On Being Ill' the Platonic view of the body as an ethically corrupt creature that must be ruled over by sovereign mind is reversed" (92).[10] But an exclusive focus on biographical or ethical themes obscures the view of an essay that "speaks against Socrates as well as through him" as it brings into play the doubts expressed by his interlocutors. By incorporating the views of Simmias and Cebes Woolf brings to the fore the event that haunts the dialogue, the imminent demise of Socrates, in order to question the capacity of language to represent the mortal body in the context of illness and death.

"On Being Ill" begins with a discussion of the *soul* (a term that neither Socrates nor Woolf ever defines) that her diaries from the 1920s suggest she derived from her study of Russian as well as Greek literature. She attacks a philosophy that elevates *soul* at the expense of body, and thus assumes that "the body is a sheet of plain glass through which the soul looks straight and clear" (*E4* 317f.).

---

[10] See Sim 89-92. For a review of the literature on the essay see Coates 1n.

The moment when "the body smashes itself to smithereens, and the soul (it is said) escapes," refers to one of the most problematic aspects of the *Phaedo*, in which the survival of the soul after death is mixed in with an inconclusive debate on suicide. Socrates responds to Cebes: "we human beings are in a sort of prison and that one must not release oneself from it or run away, that seems to me a weighty saying and one that is not easy to penetrate" (62b).[11] Since Socrates's friends are waiting with him for his execution, and their discussion is interrupted by instructions from "the man who will give you the poison" (63d), in these circumstances questions about the immortality of the soul remain in the background.

Unlike other Socratic dialogues the *Phaedo* presents what Christopher Bobonich calls "a strand of Greek ethical and political reflection that is disturbing and profoundly alien to us," in its insistence that "only a philosopher can genuinely live well and only a philosopher can lead a truly happy and flourishing life" (1). Non-philosophers suffer from a fundamental cognitive defect that forbids them from understanding virtue or from valuing the well-being of others. After his friends agree that food, drink and sex are bodily distractions from the work of the soul, Socrates concludes that "if we are ever to have pure knowledge of something, we must be separated from the body and view things by themselves with the soul by itself" (66e). The philosopher in search of truth must be "separated as far as possible from eyes and ears and virtually from his entire body, for the reason that the body disturbs his soul and, whenever it associates with it, doesn't let it acquire truth and wisdom" (66a).[12] Much of the dialogue studies the ways that the soul can lose its way, in particular the motivations of the non-philosopher. Human beings live in a kind of prison (62b), from which the philosopher understands that death brings release: "Well, other people have probably not realized that the sole pursuit of those who correctly engage in philosophy is dying and being dead" (64a). The non-philosopher's attention to the body prevents her acquiring wisdom, which comes "when it [the soul] is being troubled neither by hearing nor by sight nor by pain, nor by a certain sort of pleasure either" (65c). The philosopher seeks to be alone, "separated as far as possible from eyes and ears and virtually from his entire body, for the reason that the body disturbs his soul and, whenever it associates with it, doesn't let it acquire truth and wisdom" (66a).

In "On Being Ill" Woolf joins those critics of Socrates who as George Grote expressed it, saw "the error . . . of dwelling exclusively on the intellectual conditions of human conduct and omitting to give proper attention to the emotional and volitional as essentially cooperating or preponderating in the complex meaning of

---

[11] *Meno* and *Phaedo*, tr. Alex Long, ed. David Sedley (Cambridge: Cambridge University Press, 2010). Subsequent references to the *Phaedo* are to this text.

[12] Sandra Peterson lists Socrates's involvement with the body, for instance his having spent the night with his wife, as evidence that he does not fulfill the role of "true philosopher," as Simmias and Cebes understand it (191).

ethical attributes" (399-400). Woolf in effect reversed the emphases of the *Phaedo*: that is, while parenthetically granting its concern with the survival of the soul after death, she heeded the admonition in her 1923 diary, "never forget to begin with the state of the body" (*D2* 228). "On Being Ill" draws attention to two passages in which Socrates briefly notes the problem of the sick body: "should certain diseases attack it, they impede our hunt for reality" (66c). A second passage explores the division between "the sensible and seen" and "the intelligible and visible." In it Socrates makes allowance for illness: "the soul of the true philosopher abstains from pleasures and desires and pains, so far as it can, reckoning that when one feels intense pleasure or fear, pain or desire, one incurs harm from them not merely to the extent that might be supposed—by being ill for example . . . but one incurs the greatest and most extreme of evils, and does not take it into account" (83c). The "greatest of evils" is that the soul takes for real whatever the body declares to be so: "Because each pleasure and pain rivets and pins it [the soul] to the body as if with a nail, and makes it corporeal, since it believes to be real the very things that the body says are real" (83e). The fact that the dialogue ends with the death of Socrates renders his argument against the corporeal constraints of the soul poignant, but forces into the background the apparent contradiction between a philosophy that disdains illness as incapacitating, but whose "sole pursuit . . . is dying and being dead" (64a).

Those moments that Socrates seems determined to keep parenthetical are the high points of "On Being Ill." They furnished Woolf with a discussion of body and soul that invites us to explore the philosophical problem of illness as it bears on the Socratic distinction between the philosopher and the non-philosopher.[13] Woolf began by querying the vocabulary of "the wastes and deserts of the soul [that] a slight attack of influenza brings on" (*E4* 317). Although she makes an exception for Proust and de Quincey:

> literature does its best to maintain that its concern is with the mind; that the body is a sheet of plain glass through which the soul looks straight and clear, and save for one or two passions such as desire and greed, is null, negligible and non-existent. On the contrary, the very opposite is true. All day, all night the body intervenes; blunts or sharpens, colours or discolours, turns to wax in the warmth of June, hardens to tallow in the murk of February . . . But of all this daily drama of the body there is no record. (*E4* 318)

Reasoning against the asceticism of the *Phaedo* she in effect reverses its emphases by parenthetically granting the premise that the soul survives the death of the body, while entering an urgent claim for the primary role of the "drama of the body"

---

[13] Jane Marcus reads "On Being Ill" as an exploration of the willed passivity that can lead a writer into new territory (109-110).

in knowing. Perhaps Woolf had in mind the passage in which Socrates limits the weaknesses of the body to food, drink, and sex (64d), and rebelled against the passage in which he likens body and soul to the slave and his master (80a). But in the heat of her argument she takes no notice of Platonic nuance: the soul "reasons best when it is being troubled neither by hearing nor by sight nor by pain, nor by a certain sort of pleasure either, but when it as much as possible comes to be alone by itself" (65c).

Although Woolf challenged Socrates's arguments about illness, her emphasis on the drama of a body that responds to change shifts the focus of her essay to a question that runs like a thread throughout the *Phaedo*. The two most skillful thinkers, Cebes and Simmias, express the doubt and fear of death that create aporia in the dialogue. Cebes, who Simmias says is "more resolute than anyone in not believing arguments" (77a), tells Socrates, that "the matter of the soul causes people to have strong doubts and to worry that once separated from the body it no longer exists anywhere" (70a). Socrates acknowledges that "Simmias has doubts and fears" that the soul "may perish first" (91cd), "for anyone of any intelligence should be afraid, if they do not know that it is immortal and cannot offer an argument to show as much. This is the sort of thing, Cebes, that I think you're saying" (95bc). Nevertheless doubt in the *Phaedo* does not have the same resonance as in a post-Cartesian world. Mary McCabe marks Plato's position: "his account of the coherence of the person is not set against a background of doubt . . . It is the absence of doubt, therefore, that marks Plato off from Descartes, not a deficiency of what it is to be a person" (280). Although the statement may be historically true of Plato, Socrates is unable to satisfy Simmias, and their disagreement holds open a question to which there can be no final answer. But whereas in the *Phaedo* Socrates keeps the fear and doubt that create aporia on the plane of abstract philosophical argument, in the twentieth century "On Being Ill" translates fear into the context of a "Nature . . . [that] in the end will conquer; the heat will leave the world; stiff with frost we shall cease to drag our feet about the fields; ice will lie thick upon factory and engine; the sun will go out." *Woolf's* aporia recognizes a world which "divinely beautiful . . . is also divinely heartless" (*E4* 321), where the language of health and "that tyrannical 'I'" (*E4* 323) are countered by a recognition of the "'incomprehensibility'" of "some phrase in Latin or Greek" (*E4* 324). The doubts expressed by Simmias and Cebes as fear of the incomprehensible become in Woolf's essay a problem of translation.

The etymology of aporia sheds light on Woolf's elusive image of the solitude of illness as "a snow field of the mind, where man has not trodden" (*E4* 322). Sarah Kofman identifies the linguistic roots of aporia in the speech of Diotima, which traces the lineage of Love, the son of Poros, himself the son of Metis, the word for wily intelligence. "One speaks of a *poros* when it is a matter of blazing a trail where no trail exists, of crossing an impassable expanse of territory. An unknown, hostile and boundless world, an *apeiron* which it is impossible to cross from end to end . . . a space where any way that has been traced is immediately obliterated, which transforms any journey into a voyage of exploration which is always unprecedented, dangerous and uncertain" (10). Kofman cites the *Phaedrus* to argue that philosophical "fecundity constantly gives birth to the divine part of the soul: thought," which has the power "to release men from that most fearful aporia of all: death" (34). As a philosopher who experienced illness herself, Woolf tests Socratic wisdom at a point where the values of health and death suggest a contradiction which the dialogues address only indirectly.

In "On Being Ill" illness is an "undiscovered country . . . [of] wastes and deserts" (*E4* 317). The transition from a familiar to a terrifying state is framed by the contrast that she noted in *A Room of One's Own*, where "the beauty of the world, . . . has two edges, one of laughter, one of anguish, cutting the heart asunder" (15). These two "edges" are marked by the opening and closing paragraphs of the essay. It starts with laughter, in the scene of the narrator in the dentist's chair, where "we go down into the pit of death and feel the waters of annihilation close above our heads and wake thinking to find ourselves in the presence of the angels and the harpers when we have a tooth out and come to the surface in the dentist's chair and confuse his 'Rinse the mouth' with the greeting of the Deity stooping from the floor of Heaven to welcome us" (*E4* 317). At the end of the essay the scene of comic boundary crossing is balanced by the somber image of the Marchioness of Waterford clutching the curtain in agony as she watches through the window the hearse that contains her husband's body. In Woolf's hands the aporetic essay is structured by the "unprecedented" exploration afforded by illness: it is framed by death figured in a comic image and a death that inspires a moment of speechless grief. In the *Phaedo* Simmias and Cebes join with others who experience both pleasure and pain, and are "sometimes laughing, but at other times in tears" (59a). In "On Being Ill" their doubts become a problem of representation: death anticipated in the unconscious mind and death mourned remain incomprehensible while both lack a language.

The advent of Fascism in the 1930s offered a new challenge to ancient texts. As war approached, British intellectuals invoked the name of Socrates to stimulate public resistance to Fascism. Perhaps the best-known work was written by a Labour MP, Robert Crossman. His *Plato Today* (1937), comprised of a dozen half-hour broadcasts that he had delivered on the BBC, included the chapter, "Plato looks at Fascism," and concludes: "It is Socrates, not Plato, whom we need" (187). Woolf's friend, G. Lowes Dickinson, did something similar. In *After Two Thousand Years: A Dialogue Between Plato and A Modern Young Man* (1930) he devotes a long section to the discussion of war between Plato and Philalethes. His Swiftian description of trench warfare and gas attacks prompts Plato to conclude that such warfare "might seem the best end that could come to a race so incurably base and foolish" (89). Apparently Philalethes recognizes no incongruity between that pronouncement and the image of Socrates as an adored martyr, "so humorous, so sane and so divinely charitable; so free not only from hypocrisy and hatred, but also from the righteous indignation that clouds even the noblest souls," an image that Plato seconds (105). Far from engaging discrepant views, the two maintain their distance from conflict. *Plato and his Dialogues* (1932) reproduced Dickinson's broadcast talks in which the author interrogates Socrates on modern political problems. He represents again the serene and confident Socrates of Arnold, and defines a dialogue that elides *elenchus*: where "it is possible to give full weight to different points of view by actually putting into the mouths of a character views which he passionately holds" (74).

Woolf was not impressed. She confessed her "novelists prejudice . . . about the dialogue form. I am always rather bothered by it. If you bring in people, then I want to know quantities of things about them . . . Thence, perhaps, what I used to feel with Goldie's dialogues—something too restricted, too formed" (*L5* 293). Although neither Woolf's notebooks nor her footnotes reference Socrates or Plato, *Three Guineas* tests a more ambitious if tacit use of *elenchus* and aporia to transform public discourse. The narrator is asked to respond to a letter in which "an educated man asks a woman" how war can be prevented. Her reply is impeded by the imprecision of language: "But is there no absolute point of view? Can we not find somewhere written up in letters of fire or gold, 'This is right This wrong?'" (124). Questions abound and they provide the occasion to explore "the meaning of these rather abstract words" (213) and to redefine "dead words" (228). The word *influence* has changed, and so too have *patriotism, free, feminist, adulterate, poverty, chastity*, and *outsider*. Other words are considered in conflicting historical contexts: *house, think, bridge*, and *fear*. The call for "further definitions" marks the first stage of Woolf's aporia.

"Craftsmanship" (1937) suggests that vocabulary is contingent on "the living body." The essay, originally a talk on the BBC, redirects the question that Socrates asked in the *Protagoras*, whether virtue can be taught, to the concern of the essay, "if you could teach, if you could learn, the art of writing" (*E6* 95). What is at stake for both writers is *truth*, perhaps the most vexed word in her vocabulary. After dismissing the analogy with teaching pottery or carpentry, Socrates adduces the example of an ode by Simonides, in which one line, "Hardly can a man be truly good," suggests semantic contradictions that, Socrates suggests, might stem from an ancient philosophy of Crete. Woolf, too, brushes aside the idea of the writer's craft as making useful objects. Old words come to us, she suggests, in "sunken meanings," that become available after the writer's death, "purified of the accidents of the living body" (*E6* 94). Perhaps the phrase distinguishes the ancient text that is referenced, from one whose vocabulary—"truth" and "beauty" for instance—has been assimilated. She leaves the problem unresolved: "How can we combine the old words in new orders, so that they survive, so that they create beauty, so that they tell the truth? That is the question" (*E6* 95).

To focus on Woolf's Socratic semantics suggests that dialogue in her work is more than a pedagogic exchange of ideas, in particular because dialogue is constructed out of the historical contradictions inherent in vocabulary.[14] From the perspective of postmodernism Pamela Caughie argues that "What Woolf wants to preserve is the plurality of discourses making up any one society; she does not seek to reinstate some organic relation through increased homogenization. What is needed, on the contrary, is increased diversification" (188). Brenda Silver, who notes "dialogues within dialogues" in *Three Guineas*, and witnesses who "speak for themselves within skillfully orchestrated dialogues," builds her analysis of anger on Woolf's redefinitions of words (343-45). Anger, "whether explicitly named or notable for its elision, marks the contested site of the text's authority" (347). She argues for the philosophical power of Woolf's text: far from merely redefining certain terms, it "claims the authority of anger as the site of a discursive stance," in which form becomes "a means of altering the truths by which we live" (342). In effect she seconds Sedley's interpretation of *elenchus* as a "double confrontation, one within the dialogue, the other between the dialogue and the reader." In both eras the stakes are high because armed conflict is about to erupt. If there is a nod towards the "sunken" vocabulary of Socrates, it may come at the end of *Three Guineas*, when the narrator refuses to sign a form, and apologizes three times over "for writing at all" (272).[15]

Woolf's adaptation of Socratic *elenchus*, far from merely prompting an exchange of ideas, manifests emotion felt in the living body as the source of philosophical questions about a world in the absence of an ideal model or an authoritative interpreter. It confers on local social and historical questions an urgency that, if we read the letters sent to Woolf about the book, has always attracted readers (Snaith). Michael Frede has argued that the aporetic dialogue depends on the particular relationship established by *elenchus* between Socrates and his respondents. He does not refute the respondent's claim, but rather the authority of the respondent: "By asking the right questions he shows that the respondent, given his own beliefs, has reason to claim exactly the opposite of what he had claimed at the outset"

---

[14] For instance Melba Cuddy-Keane writes, "Dialogic discourse defines a space for exchange and negotiation . . . Conversation does not give the victor's crown to the dominant view; its aim is to expose the complexities of the situation and to provoke further thought" (135). Randi Saloman concludes that: "The refusal of *Three Guineas* to make a final statement or to offer a moral imperative is its most frustrating feature—and its greatest triumph" (104); Rod C. Taylor reads Woolf's letter to the barrister as her attempt "to dialogue with her correspondents [in order] to engage her readers in the critical thinking process" (74).

[15] Woolf read the *Apology* in 1899 with Janet Case (*L*1 26).

(211). In the exchange between them "it is crucial . . . that the premises reflect the respondent's belief" (212). Woolf's narrator seizes the unanswered question as an opportunity to challenge not the question posed in the letter—how to prevent war, but the authority of her correspondent. In response to the request to sign a manifesto, she attacked the failure of universities: "That, however, is a question for you to answer" (212). Posing in turn her questions, she shapes the course of the argument by attacking the premises of her correspondent, "the authorities . . . [who] said that God was on their side, Nature was on their side, Law was on their side, and Property was on their side" (190).

Woolf redesigned Socratic aporia to address the intractable questions of life and death and the prevention of war. She stands among the philosophers of her generation whose thinking on these matters was grounded in the study of Plato. As a translator of Greek she gained the freedom to move between the roles of the reader who yields to the pleasure of the text, and the writer who questions its language. Unlike her Victorian contemporaries she rejected Socratic wisdom, instead opting for questions that by accommodating her own sometimes conflicting opinions make apparent the historical conditions of aporia. Laura Marcus observes that the tendency to inconsistency and contradiction in Woolf's work affected her feminism: "Her alternating loyalty to and deviation from the familiar positions of the feminist movement produced contradictions in her thought which late twentieth-century feminisms have found it difficult to accept, tending to opt for one pole rather than another, instead of recognizing and negotiating inconsistencies" (211). Such contradictions are particularly in evidence in Woolf's work of the 1920s, which is "substantially concerned with the relative fixities or mutabilities of sexual and gender identities" (222). Feminist studies of Woolf have long noted her criticism of the constrictions of gender identity, but her philosophical concern with the mortal body that is imperiled by illness and war, and the historical dimension of vocabulary, shifts the emphasis. The question substitutes for the authority of stable positions a perspective that I read in the context of Homer's "When two go together one sees before the other," where fundamental disagreements cannot be reconciled, since they both acknowledge historical fact, and that philosophical change begins with language.

Works Cited

Alley, Henry M. "A Rediscovered Eulogy: Virginia Woolf's 'Miss Janet Case: Classical Scholar and Teacher.'" *Twentieth Century Literature* 28 (1982): 290-301. Print.

Allen Judith. "Virginia Woolf, 'Patriotism,' and 'our prostituted fact-purveyors.'" *Virginia Woolf's Bloomsbury, vol 2. International Influence and Politics.* Eds. Lisa Shahriari and Gina Potts. New York: Palgrave Macmillan, 2010. 17-33. Print.

Arnold, Matthew. *Complete Prose Works of Matthew Arnold.* Ed. R. H. Super. Ann Arbor: U of Michigan P, 1974. Print.

Bell, Clive. "A Foot-note." *Marcel Proust: an English Tribute.* Ed. C. K. Scott Moncrieff. London: Chatto & Windus, 1923. 83-89. Print.

Benson, Hugh. "The Dissolution of the Problem of the Elenchus." *Oxford Studies in Ancient Philosophy* 13 (1995): 45-112. Print.

Berger, Harry Jr. "Levels of Discourse in Plato's Dialogues." *Literature and the Question of Philosophy.* Ed. Anthony J. Cascardi. Baltimore and London: Johns Hopkins UP, 1987. 75-100. Print.

Bersani, Leo. *Homos.* Cambridge and London: Harvard UP, 1995. Print.

Bobonich, Christopher. *Plato's Utopia Recast: His Later Ethics and Politics.* Oxford: Oxford UP, 2002. Print.

Bowlby, Rachel. *Virginia Woolf: Feminist Destinations.* Oxford and New York: Blackwell, 1988. Print.

Caughie, Pamela. *Virginia Woolf and Postmodernism: Literature in Quest & Question of Itself.* Urbana and Chicago: U of Illinois P, 1991. Print.

Coates, Kimberly Engdahl. "Phantoms, Fancy (and) Symptoms: Virginia Woolf and the Art of Being Ill." *Woolf Studies Annual* 18 (2012): 1-28. Print.

Crossman, Robert. *Plato Today.* Oxford: Oxford UP, 1937. Print.

Cuddy-Keane, Melba. *Virginia Woolf, The Intellectual and the Public Sphere.* Cambridge: Cambridge UP, 2003. Print.

Dalgarno, Emily. *Virginia Woolf and the Migrations of Language.* Cambridge: Cambridge UP, 2012. Print.

Derrida, Jacques. "Plato's Pharmacy." *Disseminations.* Trans. Barbara Johnson. Chicago: U of Chicago P, 1981. 61-173. Print.

Dickinson, G. Lowes. *After Two Thousand Years: A Dialogue Between Plato and A Modern Young Man.* London: George Allen & Unwin Ltd., 1930. Print.

———. *Plato and His Dialogues.* New York: W. W. Norton & Company, Inc., 1932. Print.

Dowling, Linda. *Hellenism and Homosexuality in Victorian Oxford.* Ithaca and London: Cornell UP, 1994. Print.

Fowler, Regina. "Moments and Metamorphoses: Virginia Woolf's Greece." *Comparative Literature* 51 (1999): 217-42. Print.

Frede, Michael. "Plato's Arguments and the Dialogue Form." *Oxford Studies in Ancient Philosophy: Supplementary Volume 1992.* Eds. James C. Klagge and Nicholas D. Smith. Oxford: Oxford UP, 1992: 201-219. Print.

Gribble, David. *Alcibiades and Athens: A Study in Literary Presentation*. Oxford: Clarendon P, 1999. Print.
Griswold, Charles L., ed. *Platonic Writings/Platonic Readings*. New York and London: Routledge, 1988. Print.
Grote, George. *Plato and the Other Companions of Sokrates*. London: J. Murray, 1865. Print.
Halperin, David. *One Hundred Years of Homosexuality and other Essays on Greek Love*. New York and London: Routledge, 1990. Print.
Hoff, Molly. "A Feast of Words in *Mrs. Dalloway*." *Woolf Studies Annual* 1 (1995): 89-105. Print.
Howatson, M. C. and Sheffield, C. C. eds. Trans. M. C. Howatson. *The Symposium*. Cambridge: Cambridge UP, 2008. Print.
Jones, Christine Kenyon, and Snaith, Anna. "'Tilting at Universities': Woolf at King's College London." *Woolf Studies Annual* 16 (2010): 1-44. Print.
Jowett, Benjamin. Trans. *The Dialogues of Plato Translated into English*. 2nd edition. Vol. 1. Oxford: Clarendon P, 1875. Print.
Kofman, Sarah. "Beyond Aporia?" *Post-Structuralist Classics*. Ed. Andrew Benjamin. London and New York: Routledge, 1988. 7-44. Print.
Koulouris, Theodore. *Hellenism and Loss in the Work of Virginia Woolf*. Surrey: Ashgate, 2011. Print.
Lianeri, Alexandra. "Effacing Socratic Irony: Philosophy and techne in John Stuart Mill's Translation of the Protagoras." *Socrates in the Nineteenth and Twentieth Centuries*. Ed. Michael Trapp. Aldershot: Ashgate, 2007. 167-185. Print.
Lyons, Brenda. "Virginia Woolf and Plato: The Platonic Background of *Jacob's Room*." *Platonism and the English Imagination*. Eds. Anna Baldwin and Sarah Hutton. Cambridge: Cambridge U P, 1994. 290-297. Print.
Marcus, Jane. *Virginia Woolf and the Languages of Patriarchy*. Bloomington: Indiana UP, 1987. Print.
Marcus, Laura. "Woolf's Feminism and Feminism's Woolf." *The Cambridge Companion to Virginia Woolf*. Eds. Sue Roe and Susan Sellers. Cambridge: Cambridge UP, 2000. Print.
McCabe, Mary. "Irony in the Soul: Should Plato's Socrates be Sincere?" *Socrates from Antiquity to the Enlightenment*. Ed. Michael Trapp. Aldershot: Ashgate, 2007. 17-32. Print.
———. *Plato's Individuals*. Princeton: Princeton UP, 1994. Print.
McNeillie, Andrew. "Bloomsbury." *The Cambridge Companion to Virginia Woolf*. Eds. Sue Roe and Susan Sellers. Cambridge: Cambridge UP, 2000. 1-28. Print.
Mills, Jean. *Virginia Woolf, Jane Ellen Harrison, and the Spirit of Modernist Classicism*. Columbus: Ohio State UP, 2014. Print.

Nightingale, Andrea. "Plato on Aporia and Self-knowledge." *Ancient Models of Mind: Studies in Human and Divine Rationality*. Eds. Andrea Nightingale and David Sedley. Cambridge: Cambridge UP, 2010. 8-26. Print.

Nussbaum, Martha. *The Fragility of Goodness*. Cambridge: Cambridge UP, 2001. Print.

Peterson, Sandra. *Socrates and Philosophy in the Dialogues of Plato*. Cambridge: Cambridge UP, 2011. Print.

Politis, Vasilis. "Aporia and Searching in the Early Plato." *Remembering Socrates: Philosophical Essays*. Eds. Lindsay Judson and Vassilis Karasmanis. Oxford: Oxford UP, 2006. 88-109. Print.

Roe, Sue. *Writing and Gender: Virginia Woolf's Writing Practice*. New York: St. Martin's P, 1990. Print.

Rowe, M. W. "Arnold, Plato, Socrates." *Platonism and the English Imagination*. 242-256. Print.

Saloman, Randi. *Virginia Woolf's Essayism*. Edinburgh: Edinburgh UP, 2012. Print.

Sedley, David. *The Midwife of Platonism: Text and Subtext in Plato's* Theaetetus. Oxford: Oxford UP, 2004. Print.

—— and A. Long. Ed. Trans. *Meno and Phaedo*. Cambridge: Cambridge UP, 2011. Print.

Silver, Brenda. "The Authority of Anger: *Three Guineas* as Case Study." *Signs* 16 (1991): 340-70. Print.

——, ed. *Virginia Woolf's Reading Notebooks*. Princeton: Princeton UP, 1983. Print.

Sim, Lorraine. *Virginia Woolf: The Patterns of Ordinary Experience*. Surrey: Ashgate, 2010. Print.

Snaith, Anna. "Wide Circles: The *Three Guineas* Letters." *Woolf Studies Annual* 6 (2000): 1-168. Print.

Statkiewicz, Max. *Rhapsody of Philosophy: Dialogues with Plato in Contemporary Thought*. University Park: Pennsylvania State UP, 2009. Print.

Taylor, Rod C. "Narrow Gates and Restricted Paths: The Critical Pedagogy of Virginia Woolf." *Woolf Studies Annual* 20 (2014): 55-81. Print.

Vanita, Ruth. "Plato, Wilde, and Woolf: The Poetics of Homoerotic 'intercourse' in *A Room of One's Own*." *Journal of Lesbian Studies* 14 (2010): 415-430. Print.

Verity, Andrew. Trans. *The Iliad*. Oxford: Oxford UP, 2011. Print.

Woolf, Virginia. *The Diary of Virginia Woolf, Vol 1*. Ed. Anne Olivier Bell. New York: Harcourt Brace Jovanovich, 1977. Print.

——. *The Diary of Virginia Woolf, Vol 2*. Eds. Anne Olivier Bell, Andrew McNeillie. New York and London: Harcourt Brace Jovanovich, 1978. Print.

——. *The Essays of Virginia Woolf*. Vol 4. Ed. Andrew McNeillie. New York: Harcourt, Inc. 1988. Print.

———. *The Letters of Virginia Woolf*. Eds. Nigel Nicolson and Joanne Trautmann. Vols. 1-6. New York and London: Harcourt Brace Jovanovich, 1975-1980. Print.

———. *On Being Ill. With Notes from Sick Rooms* by Julia Stephen. Ashfield: Paris Press, 2012. Print.

———. *A Room of One's Own and Three Guineas*. Ed. Michèle Barrett. London: Penguin, 1993. Print.

———. Monks House Papers, Reel 1, MHA 21. Microfilm.

Was Virginia Woolf a Snob? The Case of Aristocratic Portraits in *Orlando*
Christine Fouirnaies

When Virginia Woolf introduced the idea of *Orlando* (1928) to Vita Sackville-West, whose life was the basis for Orlando, she explained that Sackville-West's "excellence as a subject" arose largely from her "noble birth," adding teasingly: "(But whats [*sic*] 400 years of nobility, all the same?)" (*L3* 429). Even before she contemplated *Orlando*, Woolf wrote of Sackville-West in her diary: "Snob as I am, I trace her passions 500 years back, & they become romantic to me, like old yellow wine" (*D2* 235-36). From the outset, Woolf thus tied her interest in Sackville-West to her own snobbishness. This was a character trait that had great interest for Woolf, who made it a theme for introspection in one of the papers she read to the Bloomsbury Memoir Club in 1936. In this paper, entitled "Am I a Snob?," she juxtaposes her desire to engage with members of the upper class with her indifference toward meeting writers, intellectuals, and scientists—she would rather meet the Prince of Wales than Einstein—and concludes that she is "a coronet snob," confessing: "I want coronets; but they must be old coronets; coronets that carry land with them and country houses; coronets that breed simplicity, eccentricity, ease" (186). Although there are no coronets on display in the portraits that illustrate *Orlando*, the photographs of Sackville-West, a famous aristocrat at the time, and the historical paintings of her aristocratic ancestors portray the coronet-wearing segment of society in a visually convincing and enticing manner. The historical paintings, used to illustrate Orlando as a man, and the photographs, used to illustrate Orlando as a woman (the portraits show Orlando first as a boy in the Elizabethan age and lastly as a thirty-six-year-old woman in 1928) thus accord with Woolf's craving for "coronets." However, the illustrations express more than Woolf's "attraction to aristocracy, to Englishness, to wealth," which Suzanne Raitt identifies as part of Woolf's attraction to Sackville-West as a lover (Raitt 160). The illustrations also articulate the ambivalence to these "social privileges" that Woolf, according to Raitt, later demonstrated in *Three Guineas* (1938). The illustrations thus anticipate Woolf's most political works, beginning with *A Room of One's Own* (1929), and they involve Sackville-West directly in a critical exposition of the aristocracy.

The element of class critique in *Orlando*'s illustrations may seem incongruous with Woolf's reverence for the aristocracy, but it is in line with her politically charged pictorial practice in *Three Guineas*. Diane F. Gillespie has argued that the photographs of a general, heralds, participants in a university procession, a judge and an archbishop are used in *Three Guineas* "to exemplify and to challenge the kinds of masculine values she indicts as causes of war" (136). Likewise, Maggie

Humm has analyzed how the photographs become "timeless dead icons of patriarchy" (227), while Merry M. Pawlowski has read them as "illustrations of the masculine spectacle of public space" (725). Most recently, Rebecca Wisor has shown the relevance of the identities of the men in the photographs for Woolf's anti-patriarchal stance. Although a visual representation of the aristocracy is manifest in *Orlando*'s illustrations, the relevance of this for Woolf's class politics has not received critical attention. Studies have shown how Woolf maintained her relationship to Sackville-West by involving her in the production of the images (Gillespie 136, Humm 217), and some scholars have focused on how the images relate to Orlando's change from man to woman (Erika Flesher, Talia Schaffer). As we will see below, both Woolf's relationship to Sackville-West and Orlando's gender have an important class dimension. Elizabeth Hirsh has drawn attention to how Woolf's inclusion of the Sackville portraits functions as a way of taking possession of Sackville-West, de-privatizing her life, heritage and estate (171-75). However, Woolf not only takes ownership of Sackville-West's life, heritage and estate via the Sackville portraits, she also uses the portraits to debunk Sackville-West's class, and she additionally couples them with photographs that parody those same portraits. That the illustrations demonstrate negative aspects of the aristocracy is interesting in relation to Woolf's class politics, which Patricia McManus has shown continues to be a source of contention for critics.[1] *Orlando* has been read specifically by Sean Latham as an uncritical celebration of the aristocracy (90-117). Careful attention to the illustrations offers a more nuanced perspective on *Orlando*'s politics and reveals that Woolf's ambivalence to the aristocracy started earlier and was more critical than customarily thought.

This article first expounds Woolf's pictorial strategy by providing new and more accurate information about the identities and histories of the portraits. It then demonstrates how Woolf uses the Sackville portraits to paint the aristocracy as ridiculous, menacing and decadent. Finally, the rest of the illustrations are revealed to show Orlando, the fictional figure, and Sackville-West, the model, as deviating from the upper class, in the process showcasing qualities that are presented as admirable but adverse to the aristocracy. The illustrations are thus shown to scrutinize the institution of aristocracy, the foundation for "coronet" snobbery. Woolf's question "Am I a Snob?" echoes a question Orlando asks near the end of the novel, when she seeks out "what people call the true self": "'What then? Who then?' she said.

---

[1] Feminist studies have done much to challenge the conception that Woolf was apolitical, mostly through focusing on Woolf's essays, diaries and later works. See, for example, the works by Jane Marcus, Anna Snaith and Alice Wood. Much scholarship on Woolf's class politics has centered on her relationship to the lower classes. John Carey includes Woolf among those modernists who felt threatened by the lower classes; Alison Light writes about Woolf's ambivalent and fraught relationship with her servants; and Alex Zwerdling attributes the absence of the lower classes in Woolf's fiction to her "middle-class guilt" (98).

'Thirty-six; in a motor-car; a woman. Yes, but a million other things as well. A snob am I? The garter in the hall? The leopards? My ancestors? Proud of them? Yes!'" (279). Orlando's question—"A snob am I?"—is affirmed by the final exclamation, as well as her evocation of the garter in the hall and the leopards, which according to Sackville-West's *Knole and the Sackvilles* (1922) can be found at Sackville-West's ancestral home, Knole (2-3, 29). Inserted for immediate ocular inspection, the illustrations incorporate Sackville-West, Knole and the Sackvilles (her ancestors) into *Orlando* in an even more obvious way than the garter and the leopards. However, the illustrations are not used to champion aristocratic pride. Rather, as Woolf's ironical stance in "Am I a Snob?" similarly implies, being a "coronet snob" is deplored.

The Origins of *Orlando*'s Illustrations Revisited

Except for the portrait on the original dust jacket, *Orlando* does not provide the sources for its illustrations. The illustrations' titles, which double as their captions, only indicate whom the portraits portray in the narrative (mainly Orlando). However, Sackville-West can be recognized in most of the photographs, while research reveals that most of the paintings are Elizabethan paintings of Sackvilles. The first Sackville portrait is a late-sixteenth-century portrait of Thomas Sackville, Lord Buckhurst, 1st Earl of Dorset (1536-1608), reproduced on the Hogarth Press jacket (Figure 1).[2] The illustration is not given a title in Orlando, but below the list of illustrations it is stated that the "*Illustration used on the jacket is reproduced by kind permission of the Worthing Art Gallery.*" J. H. Stape has researched this portrait, finding that the original was destroyed in an air raid on February 23rd 1944 in London, where it had been sent for repair ("Man at Worthing" 5-6). The rest of the Sackville portraits, three in all, were chosen at Knole on October 18th 1927 with Sackville-West (Nicolson 32). Woolf wrote to Sackville-West only a few days after beginning *Orlando* asking to visit Knole for that purpose (*L3* 430). The portraits are still held at Knole, and the original identities of the subjects, as well as the period and the painters, can thus be ascertained. A painting by Marcus Gheeraerts the Younger of Mary Curzon, the Countess of Dorset (1585-1645), who was married to Edward Sackville, 4th Earl of Dorset (1589-1652), is used to portray "Archduchess Harriet," Orlando's suitor. "Orlando as a Boy" is illustrated by a double portrait by Cornelius Nuie of Edward Sackville (?-1646) and Richard Sackville, 5th Earl of Dorset (1622-1677)—although the painting is cropped in *Orlando* so that only Edward Sackville is shown. And Gerard Soest's painting of Richard Sackville, the Richard left out of "Orlando as a Boy," is used for the "Orlando as Ambassador" illustration. This last illustration has previously been thought to be a painting of

---

[2] The first American editions by Harcourt, Brace and Company, and Crosby Gaige were published with no illustration on their jackets.

Lionel Sackville, 1st Duke of Dorset (Gilbert xlviii; Stape, Notes 196). However, Richard Sackville's name is written in the lower right-hand corner on the canvas of the original painting (outside the scope of the section that Woolf used for her illustration in *Orlando*). The Sackvilles used to illustrate Orlando are thus not distant relatives, but brothers, and Mary Curzon, used to illustrate the Archduchess Harriet, is in fact their mother. The similarity of the portraits in their sitters' physical traits as well as in their conspicuous embedding in aristocratic culture and symbols enables Woolf to mount a critique of the aristocracy.

Figure 1. Orlando. *London: Hogarth Press, 1928. Courtesy of the Mortimer Rare Book Room, Smith College.*

There are three photographs of Sackville-West as Orlando. "Orlando on her return to England" is often assumed to be by the Lenare studio in London, but the Lenare photograph that is similar to this illustration located with the Monk's House Albums at Houghton Library is slightly different—both in composition and quality.[3] It is more likely that the illustration was produced in the studio shared by Vanessa Bell, Woolf's sister, and Bell's partner, Duncan Grant. In a letter to Sackville-West, Woolf wrote: "You'll lunch here at *one sharp* on Monday wont [*sic*] you: bringing your curls and clothes. Nessa wants to photograph you at 2, that is if she thinks the Lenare too bad. I'm not sure" (*L3* 435). Nigel Nicolson and Joanne Trautmann write in a footnote to this letter that "Orlando about the year 1840," the second photograph of Sackville-West, resulted from this session (435). However, it seems that the Lenare photograph for "Orlando on her return to England" was indeed deemed "too bad," so both photographs could have been taken in Bell and Grant's studio. There is also another photograph that looks like "Orlando on her return to England," a blurry one that Madeline Moore gives the caption "Vita Sackville-West posing as a lily in Vanessa Bell's studio, 1928" (98-99). "Orlando at the present time," the last photograph of Sackville-West and the last illustration in *Orlando*, was most likely taken by Leonard Woolf at Long Barn, the home Sackville-West shared with her husband, Harold Nicolson. Writing to Sackville-West, Woolf explained that "I wanted to ask if it would be convenient should we call in on Sunday on our way back; at Long Barn. It has now become essential to have a photograph of Orlando in country clothes in a wood, to end with. If you have film and a camera I thought Leonard might take you" (*L3* 488). Apart from historical paintings of Sackvilles and photographs of Sackville-West, there is a photograph depicting the Russian Princess Sasha, Orlando's Elizabethan lover, and a painting used to illustrate Marmaduke Bonthrop Shelmerdine, who becomes Orlando's husband at the end of the novel. Woolf asked Bell to photograph Angelica Garnett, Woolf's niece and Bell's daughter, for "The Russian Princess as a Child," whilst "Marmaduke Bonthrop Shelmerdine, Esquire" is a portrait of an unknown man by an unknown artist, which was bought from a London dealer by Sackville-West because she thought it looked like her husband, Harold Nicolson (*L3* 484, note 2). Both illustrations, along with the photographs of Sackville-West, capture and accentuate qualities that oppose those on display in the historical paintings of the Sackvilles.

Historical Paintings of the Sackvilles: The Anti-Aristocratic Element

The Sackville paintings that Woolf selected to illustrate *Orlando* display ridiculous, violent and decadent characteristics of the aristocracy. Gheeraerts's car-

---

[3] Virginia Woolf's Monk's House Albums, ca. 1867-1967 (MS Thr 564), Harvard Theatre Collection, Houghton Library, Harvard University, folder 94.

icature-like portrait of Mary Curzon, which illustrates the Archduchess Harriet, is the Sackville portrait most obviously used satirically. In *Knole and the Sackvilles*, Sackville-West refers to another portrait of Curzon, describing her in this instance as "severe, uncompromising, but impeccable" (86). In the portrait used in *Orlando*, Curzon also comes across as severe and uncompromising with her stern expression and rigid pose, but she seems more ridiculous than impeccable. She is excessively accessorized with a massive farthingale, several sleeves, a cartwheel ruff, jewels, a headpiece, a fan and a mirror, and her facial and bodily features are simplified and exaggerated. Her torso, no wider than her sleeves, makes her look impossibly slender and tall. Intriguingly, the portrait is reproduced in a 1934 survey of Elizabethan dress. The two quotations that accompany the portrait in this survey attest to the extremity and vanity that Curzon's appearance exudes: in the first, Montaigne ridicules the slender waists achieved through measures such as swallowing gravel, ashes, coals, dust, tallow, and candles; in the second, Fynes Moryson remarks upon the strange practice of wearing a mirror at one's girdle (Morse 59). In *Orlando*'s text, the bumptious behavior and amorous advances of the Archduchess (who turns out to be an Archduke, thus adding another farcical layer to Curzon's portrait) repel Orlando. With his comic height, bulging eyes, lank cheeks, and high headdress—qualities that can all be observed in the portrait—the Archduke is repeatedly compared to a hare. This comparison nods to the harebrained demeanor of the Archduke, but may also playfully refer to Henry Lascelles, 6th Earl of *Hare*wood (1882-1974), Sackville-West's unsuccessful suitor. As the Archduke, Lascelles eventually married "a very great lady," Mary, the Princess Royal, and the official photographs of him from this wedding reveal, much like Gheeraerts's portrait of Curzon, elongated body proportions, a rigid stance, and ornate garb (Figure 2). By compounding the identities of Curzon and Lascelles in the illustration of the Archduke, Woolf ridicules them both, and sets up a pathetically pompous aristocratic type to be scorned, as Orlando does when she laughs at the Archduke and refuses the title and fortune that he offers her.

The portrait on *Orlando*'s jacket offers a more concrete critique of the ruling classes, and a more personal one, for Thomas Sackville was instrumental to the self-understanding and self-fashioning of Sackville-West and her immediate family. The first Sackville that Sackville-West describes in *Knole and the Sackvilles* is Thomas Sackville, and she concludes by describing her grandfather, Lionel Sackville-West, 2nd Baron Sackville (1827-1908), who "bore a really remarkable resemblance" to Thomas Sackville (219). Moreover, Sackville-West's father, Lionel Edward Sackville-West, 3rd Baron Sackville (1867-1928), visually emulated the first Lord of Knole by dressing up as him for a photograph in 1911 (Figure 3). Woolf plays upon the way the Sackville-Wests venerated and pictorially celebrated Thomas Sackville by placing a portrait of him on the cover of *Orlando*.

Figure 2. Henry George Charles Lascelles, 6th Earl of Harewood; Princess Mary, Countess of Harewood by Vandyk. Whole-plate glass negative, 28 February 1922. © National Portrait Gallery, London.

The reader, however, is not likely to recognize Thomas Sackville in the portrait, encountering instead a nameless, middle-aged, Elizabethan man of wealth, wielding a sword and a shield, wearing armor, jewelry, and black paint on his naked upper body. The martial ardor, decadent privilege, and gauche, blackened body of Thomas Sackville segue into the opening line of *Orlando*, which pits Orlando "in the act of slicing at the head of a Moor which swung from the rafter." The origin of the head can be traced back to the imperial violence committed by Orlando's forefathers: "Orlando's father, or perhaps his grandfather, had struck it from the shoulders of a vast Pagan who had started up under the moon in the barbarian fields of Africa" (15). Orlando's inheritance, captured visually in the portrait of Thomas and textually in the opening line, is one of colonial arrogance and aggression. There are many less absurd and more dignified portraits of Thomas Sackville, for example the one of him in his role as diplomat reproduced in Sackville-West's *Knole and the Sackvilles*, but Woolf's choice of a Sackville depicted as outlandish and aggressive ensures that injustices of the aristocracy are forcefully portrayed and denounced.

Figure 3. Lionel Edward Sackville-West, 3rd Baron Sackville as Thomas Sackville, Earl of Dorset by Speaight Ltd, published by Hudson & Kearns Ltd. Photogravure, 20 June 1911, published 1912. © National Portrait Gallery, London.

Like the other Sackvilles represented in *Orlando*'s illustrations, the Sackvilles chosen to depict Orlando are described in *Knole and the Sackvilles*. As a young man, Edward Sackville, the boy in "Orlando as a Boy," was "murdered in cold blood" by Parliamentarians—a story, which, together with Nuie's portrait, served as inspiration for the "enormous novel" that Sackville-West wrote when she was thirteen (82, 106). Richard Sackville, the man in "Orlando as Ambassador," has no particular interest according to Sackville-West, "save that he translated *Le Cid* into English verse and wrote a poem on Ben Jonson" (112). It seems, however, that Woolf chose Edward and Richard Sackville to portray Orlando not for their life stories, but because they as brothers with similar traits can be easily compounded, and also because Richard Sackville looks remarkably like Sackville-West. In fact, Richard Sackville and Vita Sackville-West look so alike that Talia Schaffer mistakes "Orlando as an Ambassador" for a photograph of Sackville-West (27, 55-56). The resemblance of Edward Sackville, Richard Sackville and Vita Sackville-West in these portraits facilitates the transition from painted Orlandos to photographed Orlandos, from historical Sackvilles to Sackville-West, from male Orlando to female Orlando.

The Sackville portraits selected to portray Orlando are not as farcical and hyperbolic as either the Archduchess illustration or the jacket illustration, but they are aristocratic in a traditional way, impressing upon the viewer the subjects' inherited wealth and authority.[4] The facial expressions of Edward and Richard Sackville are content and placid, their features refined, and their hair luscious. Edward stands self-assuredly on a checkered floor with one hand placed on his hip; the other handles some dice laid out on a table. In the background one can see a draped curtain and a painted landscape. Edward's garments include an elaborately embroidered collar, a textured and scalloped vest, frill sleeves, breeches with bows, and narrow shoes with gargantuan pom-poms. Only Richard's upper body can be seen in his portrait, but like Edward's dress and surroundings his jewel-embellished collar and silken cloak also indicate leisure and extravagance. The Sackville brothers' attire makes its way into the text: when Orlando rushes to greet Elizabeth I at his home, he thrusts on "crimson breeches, lace collar, waistcoat of taffeta, and shoes with rosettes on them as big as double dahlias"—a precise description of Edward's ornate dress (22). The "long Turkish cloak" in which Orlando wraps himself whilst reveling in the Constantinople morning from his balcony emulates the rich, shiny material that envelops Richard (111). The material lavishness depicted in the portraits is thus directly incorporated into the narrative, and the portraits provide an actual view of the splendor.

Descriptions of portrait galleries in the narrative, however, add a decadent dimension to the opulence of the illustrations. When Orlando is abandoned by the Russian Princess Sasha, he takes to "pacing the long galleries and ballrooms with a taper in his hand, looking at picture after picture as if he sought the likeness of somebody whom he could not find." The portraits function as a hall of mirrors, reflecting Orlando's loss. They nourish his "strange delight in thoughts of death and decay"—thoughts that are developed when his moody nocturnal perambulations lead him to the house's sepulcher:

> It was a ghastly sepulchre; dug deep beneath the foundations of the house as if the first Lord of their family, who had come from France with the conqueror, had wished to testify how all pomp is built upon corruption; how the skeleton lies beneath the flesh; how we that dance and sing above must lie below; how the crimson velvet turns to dust; how the ring (here Orlando, stooping his lantern, would pick up a gold circle lacking a stone, that had rolled into a corner) loses its ruby and the eye which was so lustrous shines no more. "Nothing remains of all these Princes," Orlando would say, indulging in some pardonable exaggeration of their rank, "except one digit," and he would take a skeleton hand in his and bend the joints this way and that. (67)

[4] For the distinction between aristocratic and non-aristocratic portraiture see Woodall 1-25.

The sense of doom the gallery portraits inspire extends to the house and to Orlando's ancestry. A metonymic as well as a symbolic connection is established between the macabre ancestral portrait galleries, Orlando's house, the dissolution of Orlando's lineage, and the portraits of Sackvilles used as illustrations of Orlando. The authority of aristocratic portraits is usually accentuated when these portraits are placed in galleries (such as Orlando's or those at Knole), as they visually construct the genealogical lineage that gives the subjects in the portraits their power. Galleries in *Orlando*'s narrative, however, signify waste, ruin and doom. Yet, although Orlando is the last in his line, and despite the fact that he defeats death just as a portrait uncannily preserves its sitter for eternity, Orlando is not an eerie or morose figure, and *Orlando* is not a Gothic or Decadent novel. Aristocratic portraits and portrait galleries are instead used to give a moribund tint to the aristocratic heritage in which Orlando revels. The portraits of Orlando make a subtle but nonetheless denigrating critique of the aristocracy—despite the fact that the figure of Orlando is tied to Sackville-West, Woolf's friend and lover.

The Sackville portraits used as illustrations in *Orlando* exhibit the morbidity that Woolf detected at Knole in general and in the paintings of its galleries in particular. As she wrote in her diary after her first visit in 1924: "the extremities & indeed the inward parts are gone dead. Ropes fence off half the rooms; the chairs & the pictures look preserved; life has left them" (*D2* 306). Woolf comments not only on the sense of death that the house and its contents give her, but also their vastness: "You perambulate miles of galleries; skip endless treasures—chairs that Shakespeare might have sat on—tapestries, pictures, floors made of the halves of oaks; & penetrate at length to a round shiny table with a cover laid for one" (*D2* 306). The contrast between endless objects and their sole owner, Sackville-West's father, becomes even sharper as she finds herself looking out of the window on her train journey home to London:

> But its [*sic*] the breeding of Vita's that I took away with me as an impression, carrying her & Knole in my eye as I travelled up with the lower middle classes, through slums. There is Knole, capable of housing all the desperate poor of Judd Street, & with only that one solitary earl in the kernel. (*D2* 307)

It seems that Woolf took away with her two impressions: Sackville-West's aristocratic distinction and the social inequalities that accompany such a distinction. By selecting outrageous and extravagant Sackville portraits, and incorporating their ridiculous, offensive and decadent properties in her text, Woolf expresses the critical attitude that in her diary moderates the awe that she experienced when she visited Sackville-West at Knole for the first time.

The Sackville portraits provide a material foundation and a direct connection to the Sackvilles, whom Woolf later used in a draft of a 1940 letter to Sackville-

West's son, Benedict Nicolson, as a metonymy for the upper classes. In her letter to Nicolson, Woolf distances herself from Roger Fry's statement, "I understand nothing of humanity in the mass," explaining that with the *Common Reader, A Room of One's Own* and *Three Guineas* she had done her "best to destroy Sackvilles and Dufferins" (*L6* 419-20). The illustrations are proof that Woolf's attack on "Sackvilles," meaning the upper classes, was already begun in *Orlando*. Similarly to how she would use photographs in *Three Guineas* of men in official garb to expose their dress as preposterous and underpin the analogy she makes between patriarchy and Fascism, Woolf uses Sackville portraits as visual-rhetorical weapons employed against the institution the subjects represent—in *Orlando*'s case, the aristocracy. In *Three Guineas*, the female narrator asserts that a man in official dress is not to women "a pleasing or an impressive spectacle. He is on the contrary a ridiculous, a barbarous, a displeasing spectacle" (39-40). The same could be said about the pompous, haughty, spoiled aristocrats on exhibition in *Orlando*. Orlando is proud of his rank and wealth, but petty exaggerations reveal that pride to be pathetic: for example, when in the sepulcher Orlando claims his ancestors are princes, or later, when Orlando sighs that four hundred and seventy-six bedrooms mean nothing to the gypsies, when she has stated earlier in their discussion that the number of bedrooms in her castle is three hundred and sixty-five (137)—the same number of bedrooms (the number of days in a year) that Sackville-West claims Knole has (*Knole and the Sackvilles* 4). In *A Room of One's Own*, when the narrator derides the "pathetic devices" that make people feel superior, she cites as examples "wealth, or rank, a straight nose, or the portrait of a grandfather by Romney" (52-53). The implication is similar in *Orlando*: a fancy painting of one's ancestor is an erroneous source of superiority.

Orlando's Deviation from the Aristocracy: Photographs of Vita Sackville-West

That the illustrations in *Orlando* deal with Sackville-West's aristocratic background accords with the social awareness that Woolf saw as central to life-writing. In "A Sketch of the Past," Woolf stresses that life-writing must analyze how society, including class, has influence on the subject:

> Consider what immense forces society brings to play upon each of us, how that society changes from decade to decade; and also from class to class; well, if we cannot analyse these invisible presences, we know very little of the subject of the memoir; and again how futile life-writing becomes. (80)

While the paintings of Sackville-West's ancestors depict not only Orlando's aristocratic background, but also Sackville-West's, the photographs of Sackville-West on the other hand demonstrate that Orlando's (and Sackville-West's) identity is not completely conditioned by the aristocracy on display in the paintings. Unlike the "preserved" and "dead" paintings from Knole, the photographs of Sackville-West do not originate in the aristocracy. Since the photographs are produced specifically for *Orlando*, they offer a commentary tailored to Orlando and Sackville-West. That at least two versions of "Orlando on her return to England" were discarded, including one taken in Lenare's studio, suggests the precedence of creative vision in the photographs. Woolf could have chosen paintings of Sackville-West to illustrate Orlando. The portrait by the society portrait painter Philip Alexius de László de Lombos (1910) would have provided a natural continuation of the aristocratic vein of the Sackville portraits. Woolf instead chose a medium that she could control and which furthermore is considered cheap, modern and egalitarian. With its easy and widespread production, photography as a medium is considered less prestigious than painting as well as an instigator of the "democratization" of portraiture (Tagg 16, 34-59). The lower and more democratic status of photography seems to be echoed in the illustrations' titles, which unlike "Orlando as a Boy" and "Orlando as Ambassador" are written with lower-case letters: "Orlando on her return to England," "Orlando about the year 1840" and "Orlando at the present time."

In the 1920s, many people could not afford to have their portrait painted, but most people could have their photograph taken. Photography is thus not as rooted in social status as painting. Moreover, social indicators are easily and cheaply imitated in photographs, making them more mutable and unreliable. This is exemplified in the photography of Woolf's great-aunt Julia Margaret Cameron, whose subversion of class in the production of her photographs Woolf emphasized:

> Boatmen were turned into King Arthur; village girls into Queen Guinevere. Tennyson was wrapped in rugs: Sir Henry Taylor was crowned with tinsel. The parlour-maid sat for her portrait and the guest had to answer the bell . . . She cared nothing for the miseries of her sitters nor for their rank. The carpenter and the Crown Prince of Prussia alike must sit as still as stones in the attitudes she chose, in the draperies she arranged, for as long as she wished. ("Julia Margaret Cameron" 6-7)

"Orlando on her return to England" and "Orlando about the year 1840" are especially reminiscent of Cameron's photographs. Woolf turns a present-day aristocrat into an aristocrat of the past rather than a village girl into royalty, or a knight into a pauper, but the act of posing is made explicit. "Orlando on her return to England" deliberately imitates "Orlando as an Ambassador" with Sackville-West's pose and guise, but the photograph appears fraudulent and insincere. According to the narrative, Orlando returns to England during the Reformation, thus with its title, "Orlando on her return to England," the photograph would have to predate the invention of photography. "Orlando on her return to England" was supposedly made to look like a painting by Sir Peter Lely (1618-1680) (Glendinning 205), who painted many of the portraits at Knole (Sackville-West, *Knole* 41), but it is obviously a photograph. "Orlando about the year 1840" is also anachronistic. It feigns to be a Victorian photograph ("about the year 1840")—but as Victoria Glendinning has observed, Sackville-West does not look "1840 in the least" (205). The clash and clutter of patterns and accessories in Sackville-West's attire correspond to the metaphorical way in which the Victorian period is described in the text, especially in Orlando's vision of the Victoria Memorial as "a conglomeration . . . of the most heterogeneous and ill-assorted objects, piled higgledy-piggledy," but the kimono-style top and checkered skirt diverge from what was worn in the Victorian era as well as the bombazine skirt, bassinette, and crinolines that Orlando buys in the narrative (209-13). The pretension of "Orlando on her return to England" and "Orlando about the year 1840" is thus flaunted, dissociating Sackville-West from her aristocratic guise, distancing her from the Sackvilles, and preventing her from becoming conflated with her aristocratic identity. Furthermore, whereas the Sackvilles in the historical portraits are subsumed into one aristocratic type (it is only with this article for example that the true identity of the subject in "Orlando as Ambassador" is revealed), Sackville-West has an indexical presence in the photographs that in her role as a public figure was and is recognizable. In these photographs that imitate the Sackville portraits, but which parade their own artifice, Sackville-West is shown to be not quite like her ancestors and Orlando not uniformly a Sackville-like character. They assert Orlando's aristocratic heritage by emulating the Sackville paintings, but they also mark Orlando and Sackville-West's difference from the aristocracy and the Sackvilles.

Unlike the photographs that show Sackville-West as Orlando in the past, "Orlando at the present time" possesses a snapshot aesthetic with associations of spontaneity, immediacy and intimacy. The photograph appears near the end of the novel, when Orlando is her "single self, a real self" and also the same age as Sackville-West at the time of *Orlando*'s publication. Although Sackville-West is posing, her demeanor and dress are relaxed, and the setting is informal, outside in nature (all characteristics of the snapshots Woolf took privately of friends and family). Among unleashed dogs, wild-growing grass and heavy foliage, Sackville-West seems at ease and content, resting her arm on a rustic gate. Although the "country clothes" that Sackville-West wears do not match the "whipcord breeches and leather jacket" that Orlando changes into "in less than three minutes" in the narrative—the sight of which is claimed to ravish the viewer with "the beauty of movement"—they do not seem different from everyday and everyman's clothes (282). Movement is also apparent in the photograph, not only with the blurry outlines of the dogs rummaging in the grass, but also

Sackville-West's walking stick indicates recent activity. This photograph, in which Sackville-West seems to pose as herself, thus seems less stilted, elevated and preserved and more lively, down-to-earth, and free-spirited than the Sackville portraits and the photographs pretending to be from the Restoration and Victorian period.

Read in conjunction with the text, "Orlando at the present time" likely depicts Orlando on the path that leads to the oak tree, Orlando's favorite place on her estate. The photograph can thus be interpreted to show Orlando and Sackville-West as landowners. The photograph, however, was taken at Long Barn, which, unlike Knole, is a house with limited land and not a castle with vast grounds. More importantly, it shows Orlando "in a wood" as Woolf writes in her letter. For nature, and in particular the oak tree, inspired Orlando to write "The Oak Tree," which, like Sackville-West's 1926 poem "The Land" (also a celebration of rural nature), wins a prize. In the narrative, Orlando is described as "a nobleman afflicted by the love of literature," as if literature and nobility are incompatible; he suspects that he "was by birth a writer, rather than an aristocrat"; and his liking for literature translates into "a liking for low company, especially for that of lettered people whose wits so often keep them under, as if there were the sympathy of blood between them" (29). The allusion to pastoral poetry in the photograph thus also distances Orlando from her aristocratic birth, associating her instead with literature, depicted in the text as belonging to the lower classes. In her essay "Lady Dorothy Nevill" (1925), Woolf compares the aristocracy to a cage with bars that limited Nevill's potential; the photographs of Sackville-West depict someone who, if not wholly freed, has at least to some extent roamed outside aristocracy's cage, delving into literature and, in the first two photographs of Sackville-West, yielding to jesting transmutations of her identity.

Gender as Class: Photographs of Vita Sackville-West, Angelica Garnett, and Portrait of an Unknown Man

One obvious way in which Sackville-West differs from her ancestors in the illustrations is her gender. Although Orlando cross-dresses in the text, and Sackville-West was known for her masculine attire, Sackville-West is consistently shown as a woman in women's clothes in the photographs produced for *Orlando*. In a discussion of whether sex affects identity, the narrator compares "Orlando on her return to England" to "Orlando as Ambassador." First Orlando's portraits are used to "prove" that Orlando's face has remained "practically the same"; later, they are used to reflect "certain changes": "The man has his hand free to seize his sword, the woman must use hers to keep the satins from slipping from her shoulders. The man looks the world full in the face, as if it were made for his uses and fashioned to his liking. The woman takes a sidelong glance at it, full of subtlety, even of suspicion" (171). As already discussed, the faces are in fact not very different, but rather strikingly similar. With female and male portraits that look alike the illustrations construct an androgynous ideal. The "strength of a man and grace of a woman" that characterize Orlando in the text can be detected in both the male and female portraits (126-27). The portraits thus question the strict separation of male and female gender identities, not their essential and inherent nature. Rather than claiming that sexual identity is either irrelevant or constructed, Woolf sets up an androgynous ideal and casts gender difference in relation to status.

Perhaps because the narrator-biographer directly implicates the illustrations in a discussion of gender identity, the connection that the text makes between gender and class, and its relevance to the illustrations, has been overlooked. Returning to England as a woman Orlando reflects:

> I shall never be able to crack a man over the head, or tell him he lies in his teeth, or draw my sword and run him through the body, or sit among my peers, or wear a coronet, or walk in procession, or sentence a man to death, or lead an army, or prance down Whitehall on a charger, or wear seventy-two different medals on my breast. (144)

This is a decidedly patrician picture of the male sex: Orlando bemoans that, as a woman, she has lost status and privileges, such as wearing a coronet. It is worth noting that the uproar in Constantinople happens just as Orlando is crowned with a ducal coronet, and that he turns into a woman immediately after he has been robbed of it. Orlando's change to a woman thus also marks a change of class, which anticipates the way in which Woolf casts gender difference as class inequality in *Three Guineas*, the female narrator addressing the opposite sex:

> Your class possesses in its own right and through marriage practically all the capital, all the land, all the valuables, and all the patronage in England. Our class possesses in its own right and not through marriage practically none of the capital, none of the land, none of the valuables, and none of the patronage in England. (33)

Not only does Woolf substitute gender with the word "class," she conceptualizes the difference between the two in terms of wealth (capital, land, valuables, patronage) usually associated with the upper class.

In *Orlando*, the narrator's gender discussion is centered around women's clothes, and these clothes act as visual metaphors in the illustrations for how Orlando as a woman is "clothed with poverty and ignorance, which are the dark garments of the female sex" (146). On her voyage back to England, Orlando cannot explain to the Captain, who acts as a guardian to her, that she, who has now been "lapped like a lily in folds of paduasoy," had once been a Duke, an Ambassador, had "hacked heads off, and lain with loose women among treasure sacks in the holds of pirate ships" (148). The way Sackville-West is lapped like a lily (or a Lely) in "Orlando on her return to England" is thus contrasted not only to her former masculine identity, but also to the titles and actions of the ruling class. Sackville-West herself felt a victim during the photographic session for "Orlando on her return to England"; as she told Nicolson, she was miserable "draped in an inadequate bit of pink satin with all my clothes slipping off" (qtd. Glendinning 182). She looks equally uncomfortable in "Orlando around the year 1840," propped up and weighed down by an excess of clothes and accessories. Orlando enjoys being a woman, but her dress reflects that there are certain constraints that distance her from her former rank. For example, when she returns to England as a woman her right to her wealth and possessions is contested. In the end Orlando wins her case; Sackville-West, on the other hand, did not as a woman inherit her beloved Knole when her father died in January 1928.

The liberties of cross-dressing described in the text lead Schaffer, with the help of Judith Butler's theory of gender performativity in *Gender Trouble*, to read the illustrations as masquerades that in their imperfection reveal maleness and femininity to be artificial constructs. However, none of the illustrations shows Orlando cross-dressing. The illustrations instead demonstrate the oppression of dress rather than the liberties of cross-dressing. Only the Archduke is portrayed as cross-dressing in the illustrations, but both he and Curzon's portrait are denounced as aristocratic and repulsive. The portraits of Sasha and Shelmerdine, on the other hand, demonstrate that Orlando is attracted to feminine and not aristocratic types. Although the titles indicate that Sasha is a princess and Shelmerdine an esquire the portraits do not signal their rank, but rather their feminine and childlike qualities. Garnett is a child, although Sasha in the narrative is an adult, and the innocent expression and soft features of the unknown man in the portrait used to illustrate Shelmerdine resonate with the descriptions of Shelmerdine as a "boy (for he was little more)" and as "strange and subtle as a woman" (227). Furthermore, unlike the colossal, dense and solid Sackville portraits, these portraits are modest. The photograph of Garnett is similar to the many photographs that Bell took of Garnett: as a child Garnett's "favourite vice was dressing up," and Bell, like her great-aunt Cameron, favored "quite extravagantly 'artistic' poses" in her photographs (Bell and Garnett 11, 81). The portrait expresses this playful, domestic, dress-up atmosphere, and it also has a homemade quality with paint applied to its foreground and background. The portrait of an unknown man is lightly painted in a soft, demure, and fluid style. The portraits of Sasha, who was modeled on Violet Trefusis, with whom Sackville-West had an affair, and Shelmerdine, based on Sackville-West's husband Nicolson, thus offer an alternative to stale aristocracy with their feminine, childlike qualities and informal aesthetic. There is no illustration in *Orlando* depicting Woolf, who also attracted Sackville-West, but the portraits used to illustrate Orlando's lovers reflect Woolf's feminine gender and lower class.

Reflections of the Aristocracy and Pauses for Reflection

The illustrations in *Orlando* serve a function that has been hitherto underappreciated. Using a pictorial strategy similar to the one she would later use in *Three Guineas*, Woolf utilizes paintings of the Sackvilles to challenge the institution of aristocracy. Changing medium, she uses photography to distinguish Orlando from Sackville-West's ancestors. Thematically, gender is cast as class, thus further distinguishing Orlando from the aristocracy. In the text, the poet Nicholas Greene, whose visit to Orlando's country estate makes Orlando "unaccountably ashamed of the number of his servants and of the splendour of his table" (80), writes a "spirited satire" on his return to London:

> It was so done to a turn that no one could doubt that the young Lord who was roasted was Orlando; his most private sayings and doings, his enthusiasms and follies, down to the very colour of his hair and the foreign way he had of rolling his r's, were there to the life. And if there had been any doubt about it, Greene clinched the matter by introducing, with scarcely any disguise, passages from that aristocratic tragedy, the Death of Hercules, which he found as he expected, wordy and bombastic in the extreme. (88-89)

In this *mise en abîme*, the way Greene "roasts" Orlando mirrors Woolf's pictorial treatment of Sackville-West in *Orlando*. No one can doubt that Orlando is Sackville-West, especially not when the photographs are taken into consideration. Just as Greene incorporates material from Orlando's *Death of Hercules*, Woolf incorporates material not only from Sackville-West's *Knole and the Sackvilles*, which also contains a reproduction of Nuie's portrait of Edward and Richard Sackville, but many paintings associated with Knole and the Sackvilles. With her illustrations, Woolf breaches what could have been a self-enclosed, self-contained, autonomous work. *Orlando* reaches outside itself, beyond the text, establishing a direct material link to the aristocracy, adding a concreteness and pertinence that the narrative alone could not have achieved.

At one point in the novel, when Orlando thinks about Sasha, the mental image of her face suddenly gives way to another of a "shabby man." Orlando is uncertain of the man's identity, but finally concludes: "Not a Nobleman; not one of us ... a poet, I dare say." The narrator describes how these two images, which in Orlando's mind lie on top of each other like lantern slides, cause Orlando to pause, and how these pauses disrupt his life:

> But Orlando paused. Memory still held before him the image of a shabby man with big, bright eyes. Still he looked, still he paused. It is these pauses that are our undoing. It is then that sedition enters the fortress and our troops rise in insurrection. Once before he had paused, and love with its horrid rout, its shawms, its cymbals, and its heads with gory locks torn from the shoulders had burst in. (75-76)

The images of Sasha and the shabby poet are connected and united in their power to arrest Orlando's conventional life and ignite in him his twin rebellions of unlicensed love and literary ambition. Like the images that *Orlando* sees, the illustrations in Orlando function as pauses in the narrative, pauses that interrupt the progression of reading; and like Orlando's pauses, they function as occasions for rebellious reflection. Woolf may have had snobbish tendencies, but the illustrations in *Orlando* are not just aristocratic portraits to be gleefully and uncritically consumed.

I would like to thank Rebecca Beasley and Laura Marcus for their helpful comments and Robert Sackville-West for showing me around Knole.

Works Cited

Carey, John. *The Intellectuals and the Masses: Pride and Prejudice among the Literary Intelligentsia, 1880-1939*. London: Faber, 1992. Print.

Flesher, Erika. "Picturing the Truth in Fiction: Re-visionary Biography and the Illustrative Portraits for *Orlando*." *Virginia Woolf and the Arts*. Ed. Diane F. Gillespie and Leslie K. Hankins. New York: Pace University Press, 1997. 39-47. Print.

Gilbert, Sandra M. A Note on the Illustrations. *Orlando*. By Virginia Woolf. London: Penguin, 1993. xlvii- xlviii. Print.

Gillespie, Diane F. "'Her Kodak Pointed at His Head': Virginia Woolf and Photography." *The Multiple Muses of Virginia Woolf*. Ed. Diane F. Gillespie. Columbia and London: U of Missouri P, 1993. 113-47. Print.

Glendinning, Victoria. *Vita: The Life of V. Sackville-West*. London: Weidenfeld and Nicolson, 1983. Print.

Hirsh, Elizabeth. "Virginia Woolf and Portraiture." *The Edinburgh Companion to*

Virginia Woolf and the Arts. Ed. Maggie Humm. Edinburgh: Edinburgh UP, 2010. 160-77. Print.
Humm, Maggie. "Virginia Woolf and Visual Culture." *The Cambridge Companion to Virginia Woolf*. Ed. Susan Sellers. Cambridge: Cambridge UP, 2010. 214-30. Print.
Latham, Sean. *"Am I a Snob?" Modernism and the Novel*. Ithaca and London: Cornell UP, 2003. Print.
Light, Alison. *Mrs Woolf and the Servants*. London: Fig Tree, 2007. Print.
Marcus, Jane. "'No More Horses': Virginia Woolf on Art and Propaganda." *Women's Studies* 4.2-3 (1977): 265-89. Print.
McManus, Patricia. "The 'Offensiveness' of Virginia Woolf: From a Moral to a Political Reading." *Woolf Studies Annual* 14 (2008): 91-123. Print.
Moore, Madeline. *The Short Season Between Two Silences*. Boston: George Allen and Unwin, 1984. Print.
Morse, H. K. Elizabethan *Pageantry: A Pictorial Survey of Costume and its Commentators from c. 1560-1620: Special Spring Number of The Studio*. London and New York: The Studio, 1934. Print.
Nicolson, Harold. *Harold Nicolson: Diaries and Letters 1930-39*. Ed. Nigel Nicolson. London: Collins, 1966. Print.
Pawlowski, Merry M. "Virginia Woolf's Veil: The Feminist Intellectual and the Organization of Public Space." *Modern Fiction Studies* 53 (2007): 722-751. Print.
Raitt, Suzanne. *Vita and Virginia: The Work and Friendship of Vita Sackville-West and Virginia Woolf*. Oxford: Clarendon Press, 1993. Print.
Sackville-West, Vita. *Knole*. London: National Trust, 1954. Print.
———. *Knole and the Sackvilles*. London: William Heinemann, 1922. Print.
Schaffer, Talia. "Posing *Orlando*." *Sexual Artifice: Persons, Images, Politics*. Ed. Ann Kibbey, Kayann Short, and Abouali Farmanfarmaian. New York: New York UP, 1994. 26-63. Print.
Snaith, Anna. *Virginia Woolf: Public and Private Negotiations*. New York: Macmillan/St. Martin's P, 2000. Print.
Stape, J. H. "'The Man at Worthing' and the Author of 'The Most Insipid Verse She had Ever Read': Two Allusions in Orlando." *Virginia Woolf Miscellany* 50 (1997): 5-6. Print.
———. Notes. *Orlando*. By Virginia Woolf. Oxford: Blackwell for the Shakespeare Head Press, 1998. 191-196. Print.
Tagg, John. *The Burden of Representation*. Minneapolis: U of Minnesota P, 1988.
Wood, Alice. *Virginia Woolf's Late Cultural Criticism: The Genesis of 'The Years,' 'Three Guineas' and 'Between the Acts.'* London: Bloomsbury Academic, 2013. Print.

Woodall, Joanna. *Portraiture: Facing the Subject*. Manchester: Manchester UP, 1997. Print.
Woolf, Virginia. *A Room of One's Own*. London: Hogarth Press, 1929. Print.
———. "A Sketch of the Past." *Moments of Being: Unpublished Autobiographical Writings of Virginia Woolf*. Ed. Jeanne Schulkind. London: Hogarth Press, 1978. 64-137. Print.
———. "Am I a Snob?" *Moments of Being: Unpublished Autobiographical Writings of Virginia Woolf*. Ed. Jeanne Schulkind. London: Hogarth Press, 1978. 182-98. Print.
———. *The Diary of Virginia Woolf*. Ed. Anne Olivier Bell and Andrew McNeillie. 5 vols. London: Hogarth Press, 1977. Print.
———. "Julia Margaret Cameron." *Victorian Photographs of Famous Men and Fair Women by Julia Margaret Cameron*. London: Hogarth Press, 1926. 1-8. Print.
———. "Lady Dorothy Nevill." *The Common Reader*. London: Hogarth Press, 1925. 248-54. Print.
———. *The Letters of Virginia Woolf*. Ed. Nigel Nicolson and Joanne Trautmann. 6 vols. London: Hogarth Press, 1975-1980. Print.
———. *Orlando*. London: Hogarth Press, 1928. Print.
———. *Three Guineas*. London: Hogarth Press, 1938. Print.
Zwerdling, Alex. *Virginia Woolf and the Real World*. Berkeley and London: U of California P, 1986. Print.

Writing in the "White Light of Truth": History, Ethics, and Community in Virginia Woolf's *Between the Acts*
J. Ashley Foster

I am now & then haunted by some semi mystic very profound life of a woman, which shall all be told on one occasion; & time shall be utterly obliterated; future shall somehow blossom out of the past. (D3 118)

Now is life very solid, or very shifting? I am haunted by the two contradictions. This has gone on for ever: will last for ever; goes down to the bottom of the world—this moment I stand on. Also it is transitory, flying, diaphanous. I shall pass like a cloud on the waves. Perhaps it may be that though we change; one flying after another, so quick so quick, yet we are somehow successive, & continuous—we human beings; & show the light through. But what is the light? (D3 218)

Virginia Woolf expresses deep ambivalence concerning things of a religious nature throughout her *oeuvre*. On the one hand, she most certainly scorned the patriarchal, conventional, transcendent Judeo-Christian God.[1] In *Three Guineas* (1938), Woolf criticized openly and acutely the Anglican Church for its complicity in war-making systems, capitalism, imperialism, and the oppression of women. On the other hand, all of Woolf's writings, including her diaries, criticism, letters, fiction, and essays, are, in her own words, "haunted" by mystical speculations, ruminations on the greater nature of "life or spirit, truth or reality, this, the essential thing" ("Modern Fiction" 8) and question the "pattern" "behind the cotton wool" (*MOB* 72) of daily existence. Woolf's own standpoint is described by Jane Marcus, using Woolf's Quaker aunt's words, as "agnosticism with mystery at the heart of it" (qtd. Marcus, "Nun" 129). Woolf's complicated relationship, indeed, "troubled" "relation to religion" (Smith and Andrés Cuevas 1) has generated much academic discussion. This essay contributes to current scholarship on Woolf and spirituality by reading Quaker traces in *Between the Acts* (1941), showing that Woolf's spirituality opens onto a radical politics that issues a powerful call for building peace. Through this reading, Woolf's mysticism[2] and materialism[3] come

---

[1] Christine Froula, addressing Woolf as "St. Virginia" and reading *Three Guineas* as her "gospel," asks: "How could the Woolf who wrote, 'O you Christians have much to answer for!' to a correspondent about Christina Rossetti, who feared that her friend T. S. Eliot's religious conversion would render him 'dead to us all from this day forward,' who cheerfully roared 'I hate religion' into the composer Ethel Smyth's deaf ear after a performance of her Mass—how could this apparent hereditary and lifelong atheist, daughter of the eminent agnostic Leslie Stephen, write anything but an agnostic gospel ...?" (262).
[2] For a discussion of definitions of "mystical," see note 11.
[3] Derek Ryan undertakes a rich and highly nuanced engagement with the term "materiality" and "new materialisms" that are burgeoning in academic discourse today. Ryan makes some

together, forging an ethical cry for the individual to take action in the construction of a peaceful society.

Even though many critics describe Woolf as an "avowed atheist,"[4] scholarship on her spirituality claims that her writing calls for a consideration of mystical, religious, or sacred themes. The *Virginia Woolf Miscellany* special issue on spirituality seeks to explore how she "engages with religious forms in unorthodox ways" (1). Authors such as Annette Allen, Julie Kane, and Jui-hua Tseng present Woolf as a mystic, whose "novels exhibit a profound longing, a tending toward the numinous coupled with recognition of the transcendent embedded in reality" (Allen). While I agree that Woolf's work exhibits a "profound longing," it is not a longing for the transcendent, but for an immanent sense of communal "emotion" (or energy) that "fill[s] the emptiness" (*BTA* 101). We can find an example of metaphysical longing represented in *Between the Acts* in the passage: "From cow after cow came the same yearning bellow. The whole world was filled with dumb yearning. It was the primeval voice sounding loud in the ear of the present moment" (101). This "dumb yearning" originates deep from the guttural space of the drives. We see from this quote one example of how Woolf's spirituality is ensconced materially, "grounded in embodied being-in-the-world" (Hussey, "After Lives" 20). The primeval voice, the "yearning" of the "world" flows through the cows, manifested physically in the most common and basic of country scenes: the cows mooing, reaching through to

---

important points outlining the work that "new materialisms" are doing to "view matter as itself having agency, a view that is tied to posthumanism; the status of 'life'; and related bioethical and biopolitical issues; and a 'nondogmatic' critical reengagement with 'the material of everyday life'" (13). Though the *différance* of the terms "materiality" and "materialism" leave room for Ryan's theoretically variegated usage, and I do at moments explore the energetic relation between nature and human, here I use "materialism" and "materiality" to emphasize Woolf's engagement with embodied being, the corporal forms of existence, her concern with the physical, lived, everyday world, and the set of material, social, and historical conditions in which people are intertwined and in turn contribute to who they become and what they produce. Woolf's relationship to materialism has also been explored in the 2014 special issue of the *Miscellany*, "Woolf and Materiality." Like Jane Goldman in her contribution to this issue, I acknowledge that there are "many layers of contingent materialities" that are "entangled" in Woolf's writing (in the instance cited, Goldman is reading a postcard that Woolf sent to Duncan Grant from Skye and highlights a "strand" of historical materialism [14]). Operating on a parallel track to a discussion of how immanent spirituality is predicated on embodied being and the material nature of existence, a historical materialism is also inherent in my reading here of history and *Between the Acts*, where Woolf critiques the cycles of cultural production that iterate a set of material conditions that lead to war and stages the narration of history as a form of intervention in this process. This is a line of reasoning reinforced by Jane Marcus's likening of Woolf to Walter Benjamin in "Niece of a Nun" (120-121) and other writings, including "Thinking Back Through Our Mothers" (77-79).
[4] See, for example, Sim 139; Groover 11; and de Gay, who writes: "[Woolf] has often been described as an agnostic like her parents; more recently, she has been regarded as an atheist" (35).

the human audience watching a country pageant.[5] The problem that critics often encounter, however, in a study of Woolf's mysticism is that the material aspect of her belief system and writing, so very essential and constitutive for Woolf's philosophy, gets lost in the discussion. We must remember that for Woolf, the "material and the spiritual" worlds are "inseparably connected" (*TG* 169) and that we cannot consider one without the other.

Quakerism, I argue, offers a belief system that is commensurate with Woolf's expressions of spirituality deeply rooted in the materiality of existence and offers us a way to account for both aspects of her philosophy. In order to illustrate that Quaker thought can be used as an entrance into Woolf's texts, I first develop a frame of Quaker philosophy and ethics from the theological writings of Caroline Emelia Stephen, the pamphlets that the Hogarth Press published, and the writings circulating in the cultural milieu in which both Virginia and Leonard operated. I demonstrate that a convergence of these mystical and material philosophies informs what I call Woolf's ontology of literature. Ultimately, I argue that Woolf's spirituality is political through applying a Quaker frame to a reading of *Between the Acts*. This reveals how writing for Woolf becomes a sacred act that can bridge the spiritual and material worlds, merging her luminescent ontology of being with a call-to-action for a pacifism predicated on individual ethical participation in the global community.

Quaker Thought, Ethics, and Action in the Modernist Era

The Quaker emphasis on an immanent spirituality, the belief in a highly personal relationship with God, the interconnectedness of being, and the insistence on enacting belief through social justice and pacifist activism relates particularly well to Woolf's concerns with expressing "life" and "reality" in her writing, her idea that there is a larger "pattern" of life, her non-traditional, distinct set of personal beliefs, and the feminist, socialist pacifism that drives her work. For these reasons in particular, I argue that, even if Woolf was not a Quaker herself, Quaker thought provides an important philosophical frame through which Woolf's writings can be read.

Scholars have explored the relationship between Woolf and her Quaker mystic aunt Caroline Emelia Stephen, who was a great author in her own right, over the years since Jane Marcus's groundbreaking essay, "The Niece of a Nun." Marcus is the first to make the argument that "From Caroline Stephen, Virginia Woolf learned to speak the language of the light" (129). In "Virginia Woolf, Quaker Pacifist?," Kathy Heininge begins the work of exploring the two women's nuanced and dif-

---

[5] Ryan's analysis that seeks to "unsettle anthropocentrism and to foreground the mutual interdependence of culture and nature, human and nonhuman, meaning and matter" (12) becomes pertinent here with the image of the energetic exchange between the cows and human audience members of the pageant.

fering pacifist philosophies, and in her *Miscellany* article demonstrates that Woolf read Stephen's books *Quaker Strongholds* and *Light Arising* and annotated them with interest. Hermione Lee emphasizes the tension and exasperation that Caroline Emelia sometimes inspired in Woolf, but does trace Woolf's comments about Caroline's funeral to scenes in *Three Guineas* (66-68). Alison Lewis's work outlines Woolf and Stephen's relationship. Jui-hua Tseng contends that Caroline and Leslie Stephen, along with Walter Pater, converged as major influences on Woolf. These critics, in addition to Frances Spalding, show Caroline Emelia Stephen to be an essential influence for Woolf as a developing writer.

Caroline Emelia Stephen, though maybe the most significant, was not the only Quaker in Woolf's life. The Quakers (also known as the Society of Friends) of the early twentieth century (actually referred to as "modernist Friends"[6] by Quaker Studies historians), are in direct conversation with and ensconced in the networks of artistic production of the era, including Woolf's own Hogarth Press.[7] The Quakers were a large part of the Aid Spain relief movement, with which many modernist artists and authors were connected and involved, including Paul Robeson, Pablo Picasso, Virginia and Leonard Woolf,[8] Aldous Huxley, and Vanessa Bell.[9]

Jane Goldman,[10] however, is "not convinced" that there is a "quasi-

---

[6] The "modernist Friends" are also known as "Liberal Friends." For historians who use the term "modernist Friends," see Frost and Mendlesohn.

[7] For more information on the Quakers and the Hogarth Press see Foster.

[8] Brenda Silver's "Are You A Quaker?" recounts meeting Leonard Woolf, who asked if she was a Quaker, attesting to the familiarity between the Woolfs and the Quakers. Silver mentions that she suspected the question was intended to obfuscate Woolf's real question, which she supposed was "Are you Jewish?" but it is clear from the question that Woolf had a strong association with Quakers, as they were the first group that came to mind for him to ask about. Silver, from Philadelphia, also points out that Woolf "certainly would have known about the connection between Philadelphia and Quakerism, his sister-in-law Karin Costelloe Stephen being the descendant of a prominent Quaker family from Philadelphia and the surrounding areas in New Jersey" (13).

[9] See Foster in collaboration with the students of the "Peace Testimonies in Literature & Art" Spring 2015 Writing Seminar, *Testimonies in Art & Action: Igniting Pacifism in the Face of Total War Exhibition Catalogue*.

[10] Donna J. Lazenby offers a sustained analysis of Marcus and Goldman, criticizing both their opposing sides in the scholarly debate on mysticism and Woolf. While Lazenby makes some interesting points, arguing that they each depart from limited definitions of mysticism, she fails to contextualize Goldman's argument within the context of materialism or Marcus's argument within the logical framework of the Quakers. Lazenby takes Marcus to task for calling upon "visions and voices" (22), ignoring the Quaker emphasis on the inner light as the voice of God. Thus, when Lazenby outlines the mystic's "goal" as "union with God" and the mystic as "occupied by the soul's living relationship, in love, with the divine" (24), she does not realize how close she has gotten to Stephen's own definition of the mystic. Stephen claims, "To bear witness from first-hand experience to the possibility and the blessedness of actual communion with God is the special office of the mystic" (*Light* 12). That being

Quakerism or mysticism in her writing" (Goldman, *Feminist Aesthetics* 24) because it does not contend enough with the materialist side of Woolf, emphasizing that a "sense of material intervention (rather than a retreat into isolation)… is central to an understanding of Woolf's luminous moment" (5). Goldman here is pointing out something very important to which we must pay attention and that many of the scholars who discuss Woolf in relation to Quakerism have not emphasized enough: the Quakers provided that material intervention in their activism and ethics.[11] Because Quaker thought emphasizes the material so thoroughly, Caroline Emelia did not only lay a foundation for Woolf's sense of herself as a writer, or for her spiritual outlook. She introduced Woolf to a spiritual outlook that necessitated a fierce, defiant politics that dared to think "against the current" and engage in "mental fight" (Woolf, "Thoughts" 217), something that Woolf repeatedly did through her writing and publishing.

Given the importance of the material aspects of the world to Woolf's politics and spirituality, the terms "transcendent" or "transcendental" become dangerous, then, when considering Woolf's thought because they distort, depoliticize, and de-radicalize her writing. The Oxford English Dictionary identifies "transcendence" as "The attribute of being above and independent of the universe," whereas Woolf's spiritual theories, as this paper argues, are immanent, or as the OED specifies, "Existing or operating within; inherent; *spec.* (of God) permanently pervading and sustaining the universe." As Lorraine Sim argues, "For Woolf and many of her contemporaries, a secular form of spirituality and the sacred stemmed from, or was intimately connected to, the ordinary, material world" (139). In analyzing the famous passage from *Moments of Being* where she identifies that "behind the cotton wool is hidden a pattern; that we—I mean all human beings—are connected with this," Derek Ryan uses the term "non-transcendent interconnectivity" (2) to describe Woolf's theory. I particularly like this formulation because it speaks to Woolf's interconnectedness without separating her thinking from the world. Both these critics emphasize Woolf's existential, material point of departure. From the epigraph above, we can see that, in stating "we human beings [...] show the light through" (*D3* 218), the light shines *through* the human, not above, beyond, or outside of it.

The image of light here speaks to the influence that Caroline Emelia Stephen had on Woolf's spirituality and ontological language. When Woolf seeks to

---

said, Woolf's mysticism, though informed by, is not identical with Stephen's. The mysticism Woolf constructs, as this article will show, is one that gestures towards an immanently spiritual interconnection of being and the ethics that this interconnection implies.

[11] Juliet Dusinberre is an exception here. In writing on Woolf and Stephen, she briefly mentions that, "Quakers, with their strong tradition of social reform, do not hold that practical life should or can be separated from spiritual life" (28).

find a way to describe "life," or the "pattern" "behind the cotton wool," she often turns to metaphors of light, which is part of the unique language of the Society of Friends. The Society of Friends' very particular rhetoric, based on a belief that there is a "Divine light" (*Strongholds* 126) living and inherent in us all, and the pacifist, social justice, and humanitarian actions caused by this core belief, provide a theoretical framework that proves to be an especially appropriate lens through which to explore Woolf's writings. Like Woolf, the Society of Friends constructed a theory of being based on an immanent spirituality. The Society of Friends does not see their religion solely as a matter of private contemplation; theirs is "a religion of works not words" (Mendlesohn 7). To have faith is not enough for the friends; faith must be lived, enacted, and manifested in the world. The Quaker idea that the divine light exists in everyone translates to an ethical imperative to take actions in the world to preserve, protect, and facilitate the flourishing of the light; therefore they have an adamant social justice and pacifist activism that has a strong history of civil dissent and fighting for egalitarian human rights, an ethics argued in all of Woolf's works, but especially so in her later writings.

Quakerism originated as a mystical branch of Christianity established in the latter half of the seventeenth century. It should be noted that there are now different branches of Quaker practice, and that one of the current defining aspects of its thought is the respect for an individually-constructed theology.[12] This essay is based on the modernist "silent Meeting Friends," and is about the tradition of "unprogrammed Meetings" (Frost 78) that practice "a unique form of corporate worship on the basis of silence and obedience" (Steere 5). Though its roots are Christian, today's Quakers have a wide range of theological underpinnings. As William Frost writes: "In 1900 all Friends wanted to be Christian; today a substantial minority are uncomfortable with this label and there is a small group of atheists in Liberal Quakerism" (91). Based on the work of Quaker Studies scholar Pink Dandelion, Frost notes that in today's Quakers, "The diversity in theological beliefs was so great that Quakerism had become a manner of behaving rather than a matter of similarity of beliefs" (91). Foundational to this "manner of behaving" are the Quaker testimonies: actions that manifest the values and beliefs one holds true. The testimonies historically are simplicity, peace, integrity, equality, community (and, more progressively in the twenty-first century, sustainability)—values based on the sanctity of life and a concern for creating good in the world.

---

[12] Douglas Steere writes in his Introduction to *Quaker Spirituality*, "a large group of American Quakers ... have included the appointment of paid pastors and the conducting of the season of worship in a way that, apart from a brief period of silence and the absence of the sacraments, would differ very little from that of any plain and simple Protestant service" (4). He notes that these changes and the diversification of Quaker practices have spread globally through "missionary outreach" (4).

Emphasis on creating the kind of world that could sustain peace, the social justice component of the testimonies, and social activism grew in Quaker thought during the modernist era.[13] Caroline Emelia Stephen, a "convinced" (converted) Friend, and a great author in her own right, was on the cusp of a movement that laid the ethical and philosophical foundations for an increasingly emphasized mode of activism for the Quakers. And, though Stephen's pacifism was of a much more personal and less radical nature than either Woolf's or the later modernist Friends, her contributions to Quaker thought helped to lay the groundwork for an increasingly activist pacifism. In her theological writings, *Quaker Strongholds* (1890), *Light Arising* (1908), and *Vision of Faith* (1911),[14] Stephen describes the central tenets of Quaker faith, including a belief in that "light which glows at the heart of life" (*Vision* 18). The "inner light"[15] is often thought of as that seed of God, good, or life present in every person. Stephen writes: "there is given to every human being a measure, or germ, of something of an illuminating nature—something of which the early Friends often spoke as 'a seed of life'—a measure of that 'light, life spirit and grace of Christ' which they recognized as the gift of God to all men" (*Light* 2). Among the important phrases to note from Stephen's description of the inner light are that it is a "seed of life" that "illuminates," and that there is a lived relationship between the universal and the individual. The inner light glows inside one as it glows inside all—it is the manifestation of a *living* God within one. In her chapter "The Inner Light," Stephen notes that throughout the text she has "been speaking of 'light,' 'voice,' 'guidance,' as almost equivalent and interchangeable expressions for our consciousness of the presence of God with us and in us" (*Strongholds* 49), showing her belief that not only is there a divine presence inherent within one, but

---

[13] This is a central argument throughout Farah Mendlesohn's *Quaker Relief Work in the Spanish Civil War.* See also Frost, 78, 81, 83.

[14] The obituary that ran in the *Friends Historical Society* calls Stephen, "one of its ablest writers and most distinguished members" ("Caroline" 95) and asserts that "No one of our generation has written more clearly, more forcibly, or more sanely on the 'Inner Light'" (98). Thomas Hodgkin credits *Quaker Strongholds* with reviving the faith of the Friends and the message of the mystic George Fox (xl-xliii).

[15] Stephen was of the generation that started employing the term "inner light" in a ubiquitous manner. Pink Dandelion notes the shift from the traditional "inward light" to "inner light" "is mainly a twentieth-century invention along with much of normative Liberal Quakerism" (133), and I would contend that, along with theologian Rufus Jones, Stephen's writings helped to establish this shift. Dandelion also points out that Rufus Jones used "inward light" and "inner light" interchangeably. Similarly, Caroline Stephen uses "inner light," "light within," and "inward light" as synonymous terms throughout her work. Interestingly, there are a wide variety of conventions in the capitalization of "inner light." While it is common in Quaker Studies to capitalize the term, sometimes a reader finds only "light" capitalized and not "inner." Caroline Emelia Stephen uses a range of capitalizations in her work. Due to this inconsistency, and for the sake of simplicity, I have chosen to leave the term in lower case here.

that this presence communicates with and guides one. This comment demonstrates how the figure of the light is an elastic metaphor, sometimes signifying the voice of the inner soul, the voice of God, "inspiration" (one of Stephen's key images to which she repeatedly returns), or divine presence itself. Important here, too, is the extended metaphor of light that defines Quaker rhetoric—light is the Quaker way of envisioning and discussing divine presence, a rhetoric which Woolf adopts and to which she returns throughout her textual corpus.

This light, as Stephen emphasizes in *Light Arising*, early Friends thought about as the light of Christ's spirit as a living presence within one (44). Though most Friends in the modernist era identified themselves as Christian, it was a very personal, particular brand of Christianity that understood God in more experiential than biblical terms.[16] For the Friends, "Christianity was not a set of doctrines; it was an unmediated life-transforming experience of a living Christ" (Frost 79). This emphasis on the *experience* of a *living* Christ demonstrates the integration between the material and spiritual. It is also important to understand, in this context, that the Quaker formulation of God as light is highly individualized and personalized: the entirely personal nature of one's relationship to God means that there are theological differences among Quaker mystics and ideological shifts through the years.[17] While one of the particular aspects of the faith is the emphasis on a *living, dynamic*, and *immanent* divine light within one, that light can be understood in many ways. Feeling "that the Bible must gain by being dealt with in the same manner as all other books" (*Light* 33), many Quakers, including Stephen, rely on metaphors to gesture towards the "central unseen and eternal things," which are, according to Stephen, "Goodness, Truth, Beauty; above all, the One of whom we must think as

---

[16] The personal relationship and communion with God is also central to the early Friends. George Fox records in his journal, "as I had forsaken all the priests, so I left the separate preachers also, and those called the most experienced people; for I saw there was none among them all that could speak to my condition. ... I heard a voice which said, 'There is one, even Christ Jesus, that can speak to thy condition,' ... And this I knew experimentally" (Steere 65-66).

[17] While the notion of an immanent, present, living God within one is a foundation of Quaker thought, some do maintain that this spirit also contains a transcendental component, but interestingly, one that can not be thought of as separate from life. Rufus Jones speaks out directly against a "distinctly transcendent conception of God" and calls for a "modern emphasis on the immanence of God" (9). However, he coins the phrase "*transcendence in immanence*," arguing that "'Transcendence in immanence' appears wherever self-consciousness appears. Every aspect of our deeper life is embedded in more life than we are aware of" (36-37). We can tell from Jones's language here that thought, consciousness, and the ability to exceed one's own finite limitations by engaging in relations larger than oneself, being a part of "the total life-system" (37), is what facilitates his ideas of *transcendence in immanence*. Yet the fact that the eternal *lives* and the infinite is *in* and flows through the finite makes this theory, in the final analysis, immanent.

their source, God himself" (*Vision* 18). We can see here how Stephen draws upon Platonic forms to understand her relationship with God; these are ideals that allow for a very open, very individualized understanding of the divine.

The Quaker idea of the personal relationship with an inner light that infuses every part of life allows for an entrance into philosophical considerations of the part to the whole, or the self to the society, and dictates the Society of Friends' mode of worship. In silent Meeting Friends, of which type Caroline Emelia and the Friends in Great Britain were practicing in Woolf's time, no minister or priest administers services. Friends gather together in silence waiting for divine inspiration, waiting on a message from the inner light. When one has a message, one stands up to deliver it to the Meeting. Quakers believe that the relationship with the divine cannot be mediated.

The individual, then, becomes sacrosanct in Quaker thought. Rufus Jones, one of the great theologians of the modernist era, calls for a universal and highly political recognition of the importance of the individual. He writes: "The democracy I want will treat every human person as a unique, sacred, and indispensable member of a spiritual whole, a whole which remains imperfect if even one of its 'little ones' is missing; and its fundamental axiom will be the liberation and realization of the inner life which is potential in every member of the human race" (53). This valuation of each human being is essential to Quaker thought, as it is within the individual that a manifestation of the divine is kindled, and it is also essential to combatting totalitarian and fascist politics. This Quaker emphasis on each and every human, then, opens onto a demand for an ethical imperative of protection and responsibility. It is precisely what keeps the unity of the light from becoming a totalizing discourse.

Though each and every individual is profoundly important, for Jones and other Quakers, people are members of a web of being and society that signifies their interrelatedness; a metaphysical, social, intellectual, international, and even economic interrelatedness. The Quaker Hoyland writes about the ecstasy of mystical experiences in nature, and discusses the organic unity of the world when he writes, "We shall see the fair external world as a living whole, as a Face through which there shines to us in unmistakable certainty and splendor the Light of the beauty of God" (58). Here, Hoyland expresses the immanent, grounded, embodied spirituality of Quakers, the value of individual life, and the non-transcendental nature of a spiritual connection between the self and the community.

The immanence of the spiritual world is why, for Quakers, testimonies and political activity are so intertwined with prayer and faith—the way one lives within the world is the greatest homage that can be paid to the light that is within all. Living itself becomes a form of worship. For the Quakers, testimonies are lived actions that testify to the communal beliefs. The *Historical Dictionary of the Friends (Quakers)* defines testimonies as "the public witness of actions, beliefs, and behaviors that Friends hold to be consistent with **Truth**" (340). They are most often listed as "integrity, **simplicity**, community . . . , **peace** and **equality**" and, in some Meetings of the twenty-first century, "stewardship" (340). Quaker thought, like Woolf's philosophy, opens onto an ethic that necessitates radical social change. If the world is the "Face" of God, as Hoyland avers, then to desecrate that "Face" is sacrilege; conversely, to preserve and protect that "Face" is a sacred act and a testament to the light of life.

The Quakers, therefore, during and after the Great War, increasingly emphasized the role of peace, social justice, friendship, international cooperation, and equality in the world. Quaker activists worked within modernist networks to help promote the League of Nations, to move away from an imperialist world structure, to fight for racial and gender equality, and to maintain an absolutist pacifist stance in the wake of the First World War, the Spanish Civil War, and the progression into the Second World War. Their social conscience had won them a name in activist circles, and Quaker networks became essential and completely integrated with the movements of the time, particularly with the causes of the Friends' Ambulance Unit in World War I and the vast relief that was administered during the Great War, the Spanish Civil War, and the Second World War.[18] David Garnett and Olaf Stapledon volunteered with the Quakers during the Great War and recounted their experiences in *We Did Not Fight* (1935), Julian Bell's anthology of war resisters' stories. Roger Fry, born into an old Quaker family, went to France with the Friends and wrote a little-known vignette called "The Friends' Work for War Victims in France" and an article that was published in *War and Peace* in September of 2015 called "A Visit to France"[19] about his journey during wartime conditions.

The Friends promoted their ethics, politics, and causes through writing and distributing literature; for this, presses like Hogarth became essential.[20] The literature written by Quakers that Leonard and Virginia Woolf published covers topics such as the wrongs and atrocities of colonialism, racial equality, anti-fascism, the League of Nations, global co-operation, how to establish peace, and forging a world in which peace can thrive. All of these themes find their way into Virginia's textual corpus. As I have written elsewhere, it is clear that she was engaging in pacifist

---

[18] Thomas Kennedy observes that, "One of the remarkable features of the post-war period was the fact that, almost as soon as the guns fell silent, this minuscule religious community, despite their proscribed condition as supposedly unpatriotic pariah, began to manifest a remarkable moral influence" (9).

[19] Jane Lilienfeld published Fry's *War and Peace* article as an appendix to her essay "'Success in circuit lies': Editing the War in *Mrs. Dalloway*." *Woolf Studies Annual* 15 (2009):113-33.

[20] Helen Southworth argues that small presses should be studied as entrance points into modernist networks. As Mark Hussey has pointed out, "Publishing ... is always a collaboration" (Introduction lxii), and Gayle Rogers shows that Leonard and Virginia used their press as a form of political activism, a way to put topics that were important to them in circulation (144-145).

conversations at a time when Quaker thought and action were in dynamic interplay with modernist thought, and that the two networks fed the theories of each other (see Foster). Kathleen Innes, a prolific Quaker author highly active in the promotion of international feminism, the League of Nations, and peace, published four books on the League of Nations with Hogarth Press, which were collected into a fifth volume, *The League of Nations: The Complete Story Told for Young People* (1936).[21] These books frame the League of Nations and international cooperation as a means to lasting peace. Written as educational tracts for school children, they emphasize the value of transnational friendships and the relationship between social justice and peace. Like Woolf's *A Room of One's Own* and *Three Guineas*, Innes's work also shows a materialist concern for women, the equal distribution of wealth, fair working conditions, and a pacifism predicated on social justice.[22]

Innes had been introduced to Leonard Woolf through intersecting social and activist networks. Correspondence between Kathleen Innes and Leonard Woolf refers to them having met when Innes was Secretary of the Women's International League.[23] She became the Secretary of the Peace Committee of the Society of Friends[24] and collaborated with the Hogarth Press on the publication of the annual lecture series founded in 1926 called the *Merttens Lectures on War & Peace*.[25] The Woolfs published eight of these lectures, consisting of issues such as *Justice Among Nations* (1927), *War and Human Values* (1928), *The Danger Zones of Europe* (1929), *Britain and America* (1930), *The Race Problem in Africa* (1931), *The Roots of Violence* (1934), *Politics and Morals* (1935), and *Economic Policies and Peace* (1936). *The Race Problem in Africa*, *The Danger Zones of Europe*, and *Justice Among Nations* all advocate for racial and ethnic equality amongst peoples. They emphasize the role of the individual in the greater whole.[26]

---

[21] These titles include: *The Story of the League of Nations, Told for Young People* (1925), *How the League of Nations Works, Told for Young People* (1926), *The League of Nations and the World's Workers: An Introduction to the Work of the International Labour Organisation* (1927), and *The Reign of Law: A Short and Simple Introduction to the Work of the Permanent Court of International Justice* (1929).

[22] For a close reading that juxtaposes Innes's *Women and War* with Woolf's *Three Guineas*, or an analysis of the Hogarth Quaker pamphlets, including Kathleen Innes's works, that emphasizes the internationalist pacifism of the Quakers alongside the modernists see "Quakers in Modernism and the Hogarth Press" in Foster.

[23] Letter from Kathleen Innes to Leonard Woolf, October 1, 1924 (University of Reading, Special Collections. MS 2750/192).

[24] According to Innes's biographer, Kathryn Harvey, Innes became Secretary of the Peace Committee of the Society of Friends in 1926, and remained Secretary for ten years.

[25] Correspondence between Innes and the Hogarth Press confirms that Innes was in active negotiations with the press to have the Merttens Lectures published (University of Reading, Special Collections. MS 2750/ 357; 370; 465).

[26] This article does not provide an exhaustive list of the Hogarth publications that were writ-

The Hogarth Press Quaker publications stress the importance of individual consciousness, public opinion, and personal action in the creation of peace, themes which are emphasized in Woolf's *Three Guineas* with the creation of the "Society of Outsiders," where the "daughters of educated men" can work "by their own methods for liberty, equality and peace" (126). In *Defense of the Weak* (1935?) (which was not published by Hogarth), Innes proclaims that "energies must be directed to building up a constructive peace" and that "this war method of settling disputes is in human choice. It is deliberately planned by human brains, and could be avoided by human decision" (5). This theme appears in *The Story of the League of Nations*, where Innes argues that the greatest thing individuals can do is to show interest in the League and support it through cultivating an international spirit (57-59). Emphasis on public opinion is found in the other Hogarth Quaker materials as well, as Horace Alexander asks in *Justice Among Nations*, "Is not public opinion the final arbiter of all law" (25)? Francis Pollard, in *War and Human Values,* argues, "that human beings are answerable for their actions is surely the very criterion of their humanity. In no ultimate sense can they shift the responsibility on the Secretaries of State or commanding officers. They are capable of choice" (29), thus illustrating that it is the individual, and the individual alone, that can choose either to fight or to abstain. It is the responsibility of the individual to build the kind of world that ought to be.

For the modernist Friends, this individuality opens onto an ethics through the acknowledgement of one's participation with and responsibility towards the larger whole. For Pollard, responsibility occurs when we "feel in our bones that we are members one of another" (9). Pollard calls for each member of society, in their "responsibility as a citizen of the world," to enact a "threefold" pacifism; one that is "critical, constructive, resistant" (16) to create "a community that is conscious of its oneness" (18). This is a kind of pacifism, we shall see, commensurate with Virginia Woolf's writings, especially in *Between the Acts*. A Quaker theoretical frame, then, is one that roots politics in a deep spirituality, an immanent spirituality of living light and goodness that demands an ethics of respect for the individual while realizing humanity's existential unity and interrelatedness. Quaker thought offers a way of understanding a spirituality embedded in a rich materialism, a spirituality that insists upon social justice and human rights within-*this*-world, and a philosophy that can at once think the part to the whole.

---

ten by Quakers or have Quaker connections. For example, Hogarth also published work by Philip Noel-Baker, a British Quaker who cofounded the Friends Ambulance Unit and eventually won the Nobel Peace Prize. Diane Gillespie also mentions a number of Quaker connections in "'Woolfs' in Sheep's Clothing: The Hogarth Press and 'Religion.'"

Towards an Ontology of Literature

Quaker transmissions, both from Caroline Emelia Stephen and the Hogarth pamphlets, find their way into Woolf's own theories about writing and what it means to take action in society, transmissions that are further echoed in *Between the Acts*. From the aforementioned scholarship on Woolf and Stephen, it becomes apparent that Stephen influenced Woolf at a crucial moment in her life as a writer and helped to start her writing career.[27] Therefore, I argue, Stephen's Quaker thought has been woven into Woolf's own notions of authorship, notions of authorship which integrate her deep spirituality and vivid materiality in a way consistent with Quaker beliefs. This is significant on two levels: first, when Woolf articulates mystical notions of being, she does so in Quaker terms. Secondly, these Quaker terms are repeated and reiterated when she discusses the role of the writer in society. For Woolf, the task of the writer is precisely to forge a bond between the mystical and the material, showing the "spirit" captured within everyday life. With the feminist, socialist pacifist text of *A Room of One's Own*,[28] the essay "Modern Fiction," her memoir "Sketch of the Past" and her drafts of the unfinished "Anon," it is clear that writing for Woolf is not only a way of expressing the spiritual and material modes of existence, but these modes, in similar logic to the Quakers, insist upon an ethics of interrelatedness that is highly political, arguing for peace and social justice throughout the world. Writing, for Woolf, becomes her mode of action, a sacred action that can bridge the material and spiritual and convey the political ramifications of the interplay between them.

In "Modern Fiction," Woolf addresses how there must be an essence of the spiritual within the material for a work to succeed, for literature to live. Describing material reality only, no matter how skillfully executed, fails to capture "life." Dubbing the authors who fail to capture "life" "materialists," Woolf describes them as "spend[ing] immense skill and immense industry making the trivial and the transitory appear the true and the enduring" ("Modern Fiction" 8). Woolf seeks to reverse these proportions, and maintains that the authors who "come closer to life" (9) are the ones that "reveal the flickerings of that innermost flame which flashes its messages through the brain" (10). These writers, juxtaposed with the material-

---

[27] Tseng argues, "Writing ... became a ritual of mystical transmutation for the writer. Under Leslie Stephen's and Walter Pater's influence, Woolf established a certain knowledge of the world; under Caroline Stephen's, her soul was opened up to the spirits and to the inner light; but it was only through the act of *writing*... that Woolf was able to penetrate to the core of life's wholeness" (223-224). For how Stephen more materially helped launch Woolf's career, see Spalding 56-57.

[28] In "'No More Horses,'" Marcus writes, "*Three Guineas* is a socialist, pacifist, feminist polemic" (267), and I feel this characterization of Woolf's philosophy applies equally to *A Room of One's Own*.

ists, are "spiritual" (10). When Woolf wants to articulate the ability of writers to grasp at something deeper and more profound about existence, she conceives of a writerly project in Quaker terms. Invoking the "flickerings of that innermost flame" pulls upon the Quaker metaphor of the inner light and conception that there is the spark[29] of a divine presence living within every human being.

Woolf's own literary mission, as stated within "Modern Fiction," is to convey the spiritual essences that permeate life—spiritual essences, might I add, that are most often articulated by Woolf in terms that echo Quaker rhetoric. For Woolf, writing is about expressing and upholding the nature of being. When we unpack her images, both on writing and on being, what we find is an ontology of literature rooted in the Quaker tradition of light, with direct traces to Stephen's writings. This connection between Quaker thought, ontology, and writing is made particularly and explicitly clear when, in "Modern Fiction," Woolf says: "Life is not a series of gig lamps symmetrically arranged; life is a luminous halo, a semi-transparent envelope surrounding us from the beginning of consciousness to the end. Is it not the task of the novelist to convey this varying, this unknown and uncircumscribed spirit…?" (9). Here one can see that the "task" of the novelist is to capture some essence of "life," that essence which in *A Room of One's Own* is figured as "truth," or in other places "reality" that moves within the material and harkens at existence itself. That existence, "life," the "proper stuff of fiction," (9) "everything" (12), is formulated as a *luminous halo*, a metaphor that invokes not only illumination, but an encircling, all-encompassing, permeating force. Woolf's enveloping force of light also resonates deeply with Stephen's description of divine light as "central, unbounded, radiating" (*Light* 55), a unifying force that connects us all and one which is present *within* the material nature of existence. This luminous halo is not transcendent, but immanent in the material.

In a brilliant reading that deconstructs the image of the "luminous halo" and the criticism surrounding it, Jane Goldman demonstrates that "'Modern Fiction' explores both the outer, material and the inner, spiritual as dialectical positions out of which will emerge Woolf's 'perpetual marriage of granite and rainbow'" (*Modernism* 70). Goldman reads another passage from "Modern Fiction" to show that Woolf "points up a distinctly English tradition in a heady mix of dissent, rationalism, humour, materialism, pleasure and sensuousness" (71). Indeed, Woolf writes: "English fiction from Sterne to Meredith bears witness to our natural delight in humour and comedy, in the beauty of earth, in the activities of the intellect, in the splendour of the body" ("Modern Fiction" 12). Taken with Woolf's earlier statement that "Our

---

[29] George Fox likens the "seed" of God to a "spark" when he writes, "I felt the Seed of God to sparkle about me like innumerable sparks of fire" (*An Autobiography*, Chapter XI, "In the Home of the Covenanters"). (I have chosen to quote the edition edited by Rufus Jones because of Jones's status as preeminent modernist Quaker theologian.)

quarrel, then, is not with the classics" (6), and that modern writers' "interest" "lies very likely in the dark places of psychology" (11), a new and burgeoning field, when Woolf calls on "the infinite possibilities of the art and remind[s] us that there is no limit to the horizon" (12), it becomes clear, as Goldman points out, that Woolf is not abandoning the notion of material existence for an internal realm. In my reading, and taking into account the "oppositional energies at work in 'Modern Fiction'" (Goldman, *Modernism* 70), Woolf proposes a more holistic view towards writing: the spiritual essences embodied in the material need to be illuminated, allowed to breathe, for a work of art to flourish. Indeed, situated materially, at her present historical moment, Woolf points out that the concern with psychology is a modern phenomenon, and that the writers who place "the emphasis ... upon something hitherto ignored" ("Modern Fiction" 11) are operating contextually within their contemporary moment. The immanent nature of the halo insists on a materiality as it does a spirituality because, for Woolf, the spiritual is embedded in the material.

This coupling of luminous language mixed with a rigorous historical materialism is likewise carried forth into *A Room of One's Own*. *A Room of One's Own* immediately situates itself as a historical materialist document, concerned with the conditions of artistic production, when Woolf opens with the assertion that "a woman must have money and a room of one's own if she is to write fiction" (4). The essay then explores the effects of poverty and discrimination on the mind. However, it also traces the importance of being able to hear and reach internal truths in order to produce "a work of genius" (51), and gestures towards the concerns of "Modern Fiction" with the spiritual. Read in the context of Quaker thought, Woolf's metaphors of light and truth in relation to a creation of art unfold an ontology of literature rooted in the internal truths unveiled by the human mind connecting with the spirit, a spirit that is both universal and individualistic. It is this language of light Woolf employs throughout *A Room of One's Own* to formulate her ontology of literature, or to formulate under what conditions a work of genius can come into being. There is a difference between a work of writing and a work of genius. Engaging Quaker imagery of illumination and light, a work of genius for Woolf is written in the "white light of truth" (*AROO* 32), as opposed to a piece of writing that shows the author's anxieties, grudges, and bitterness of mind, written in "the red light of emotion" (32). Genius, for Woolf, allows the truth to shine through unimpeded.

Caroline Emelia Stephen, in *Quaker Strongholds*, unpacks the *différance* of the terms "light within" and "the inner light" revealing that these terms signify *both* inner truth *and* inspiration: "Light is the most obvious and the most eternally satisfying figure for Divine truth. It is, however, hardly more obvious or more satisfying than the other figure so commonly, and almost interchangeably, used by the same teachers, of breath—inspiration" (*Strongholds* 26). Like the impetus for Woolf's "works of genius," the Quaker light illuminates the truth *and* proffers inspiration. Shakespeare's mind, according to Woolf "the state of mind most favourable to poetry that there has ever existed" (*AROO* 50), was "incandescent" (56). After asking what state of mind facilitates works of genius, Woolf answers with the image of "incandescence," which is defined as "free" and "unimpeded" (56). "Freedom and fullness of expression are," for Woolf, "of the essence of the art" (76). They grant women the ability to "use writing as an art, not as a method of self-expression" (78). Here we can see that for Woolf, to write in the "white light of truth" is to reach through the material, into the spiritual. Describing Shakespeare's mind as "incandescent" demonstrates that Woolf calls upon Quaker imagery of light to formulate and express the metaphysical mission of writing—Shakespeare was receptive to, and able to express (precisely because of his historical and material conditions), the light of being.

The metaphor of the light, or Woolf's *luminous halo*, an all-pervading force that envelops everyone, that is both the aim and impetus for writing, also establishes an ontology of interrelatedness, or interconnectedness,[30] that Woolf's writing reveals. It is not just being that Woolf unveils in her work, but also how being is interconnected. Caroline Emelia Stephen formulates a similar philosophy of interconnectedness when she discusses a "living unity" (*Light* 70) and notes that "all light is one" (55), as do the other, more political Quaker writers of the modernist era.

Woolf echoes this philosophy of unity and interconnectedness most explicitly when, in "A Sketch of the Past," she writes, "I reach what I might call a philosophy; at any rate it is a constant idea of mine; that behind the cotton wool [of daily life] is hidden a pattern; that we—I mean all human beings—are connected with this; that the whole world is a work of art, that we are parts of the work of art" (*MOB* 72). Being, for Woolf, is cast against a larger backdrop and continuum of being. By proclaiming that "the whole world is a work of art" and that "all human beings" are a part of it, Woolf is making an observation about the parts to the whole, situating human beings as not just connected to a divine force, but also to each other. She grounds her metaphysics and spirituality within-the-world; the "pattern" is not a transcendent entity removed and far away, in another plane or another sphere; it is, in fact, a part of "life." This is very much like the Quaker idea of the immanence of the inner light—that there is a divine presence in every person, a "seed" or "germ" that connects us all. Woolf goes so far as to say that "There is no Shakespeare, there is no Beethoven; certainly and emphatically there is no God; we are

---

[30] Woolf's fictional characters demonstrate this interconnectivity throughout her textual corpus. Kathryn Carver uses Woolf's "philosophy" concerning the "pattern" behind the "cotton wool" of life as a lens to read her fiction, and maintains that Woolf's philosophy of "interconnectivity" can be read in conversation with Alfred Whitehead. She goes on to show how Woolf creates "a reality in which differentiated parts are integrated into a whole as a given, a fact of being" through readings of Woolf's fiction.

the words; we are the music; we are the thing itself" (72). Here, Woolf proposes an ontology of art grounded in interconnection, where no one artist can claim the rights of "Shakespeare" or "Beethoven," but each artist is a compilation of their community, of their time or place, of their being-within-the-world, an expression of that world and of that unity. When Woolf says "certainly" and "emphatically" that "there is no God," I read her as saying that there is no distant, far-off God, a God removed from being, that God, like Shakespeare, and Beethoven, exists within us all, as "we are the thing itself." Woolf "proves" the idea that "there is a pattern hid behind the cotton wool" to herself through "writing" (73). This is why, for Woolf, "I feel that by writing I am doing what is far more necessary than anything else" (73), because when writing she proves the existence of the pattern, because her writing stems from an ontology of literature that seeks to reach through to the inner light that is refracted in daily living.

Writing, for Woolf, becomes a sacred act of illuminating the relationship between the spiritual and material, the relationships between people, and the responsibility of the individual to the community—all relationships that carry political implications. In "Anon," Woolf's unfinished attempt to write a "Common History book" (qtd. Silver, "Last Essays" 356) the spiritual, material, and historical merge as Woolf tries to uncover the origin of writing and struggles to "create a form that would convey underlying forces of historical process" (Silver, "Last Essays" 359). Writing "Anon" at the outbreak of the Second World War, Woolf conceives of a primitive origin of writing that can counteract the war-making system, that can fend off the threat of extinction. Imagining that the writing impulse is a great primeval voice of glorious song that "broke the silence of the forest" (Silver, "Last Essays" 382), and expressed a "common voice" (382), harkening toward "the common belief" (384), Woolf infuses the sacred into the writing act. "Anon," indeed, sang the song "to do homage to the old pagan Gods," (383) where the "old Gods lay hidden between new" (384). The invocation of Anon as song gestures towards Woolf's notion of Beethoven and Shakespeare as communal figures. The singing of "Anon," the "common voice" of humanity, recalls the statement that "we are the words; we are the music" from "A Sketch of the Past," again merging the notion of writing-as-artistic production with an immanently spiritual interconnectedness. Through tracing the origin of writing to a song that paid "homage to the old pagan Gods," Woolf is always already developing the relationship between writing and worship, between words and a witness to being, and between the self and other.

The act of writing in "Anon" merges with history and historical catastrophe in that, as Woolf is seeking to trace but also escape and picture an alternative to her own historical moment, she harkens back to a primeval voice and finds in that voice an act of creation that will save humanity from absolute "oblivion." Stages of the working drafts read:

> The heart of this vast proliferation of printed pages remains the song. The song has the same power over the reader in the 20th century as over the hearer in the 11th. To enjoy singing, to enjoy hearing the song, must be the most deep rooted, the toughest of human instincts comparable for persistency with the instinct of self-preservation ... Only when we put two and two together—two pencil strokes, two written words, two bricks {notes} do we overcome dissolution and set up some stake against oblivion. (403)

"Anon," singing, writing, language, literature here is "self-preservation," that very thing which can offer "some stake against oblivion" (403). Writing, then, carries with it a trace of the divine, of the sacred, the original song that sang of the gods, while it simultaneously takes a stand against Woolf's contemporaneous war-ridden moment. Here we can again see how Woolf merges the spiritual and material—it is the spiritual essence of "life" which will provide fortress against the present moment. Writing, sharing the "common voice" and rooted in the instinct of "self-preservation," may give us hope, may offer us the outlet against war into a world in which peace is possible. The singing of the song allows us to "overcome dissolution." If writing is one of the ways in which humans can capture and reflect the light, if in writing the "task" of the novelist is to encompass "life," the *luminous halo* that allows us to speak and write in "truth," and "overcome dissolution," then the responsible citizen must help to facilitate and set the material conditions to make these artistic undertakings possible; in other words, the responsible citizen must help to create a peaceful world based on social and economic equality. Woolf's philosophy, rooted in her Quaker aunt and reinforced by the cultural conversations of the time (which were heavily influenced by Quakers), opens onto an ethics that calls for individuals to work together to change the world. It offers Woolf the challenge, task, and ethical imperative of her career to promote the pacifist values through her literature that a close reading of *Between the Acts* marks as profoundly important.

Quaker Thought and Ethics in *Between the Acts*

History, the sacred, writing, and ethics are entwined and explored in *Between the Acts*. Far from asserting that "the progress of Nazism would cause that pacifism [the pacifism of *Three Guineas*] to slip away as she wrote *Between the Acts*" (Mackay 29), I argue, in tandem with Alice Wood and Nancy Knowles, that *Between the Acts* carries forward Woolf's pacifist philosophy.[31] To see Woolf's internal struggle with the ethics of pacifism (a struggle all conscientious pacifists

---

[31] On *Between the Acts*' pacifism, see also Froula and Laurence; on Woolf's late pacifism, see Mills and Maggio.

undertake, especially during times of total war[32]), or her ambivalence concerning England, recorded in her diaries and letters, as a relinquishing of her political or public stance is to ignore the ethical, spiritual, and atmospheric underpinnings of *Between the Acts*. When read from the perspective of Woolf's ontology of literature, however, and the Quaker traces in the novel, a particular *kind* of pacifism opens up. *Between the Acts* issues an ethical imperative for peace based on humanity's communal integration,[33] while acknowledging that this action for peace must first occur on an individual level. Restaging, reformulating the way we narrate history, insists Woolf, can help to stop the repetitive cycle of war, and shows us, as the Quakers believe, that peace, like war, is a *choice*. Read through a Quaker lens, *Between the Acts* demonstrates that the actors of Miss La Trobe's play and audience are unified in their being; this unity opens onto an ethical imperative to end the cycles of force iterated throughout history, and the task of the writer in war time is to bridge the gap between the spiritual and material to deliver this ethical message.[34] Taking into account the deep spirituality that is tied to the ethico-politico, a Quaker reading of *Between the Acts* works on multiple registers. Quaker thought offers a way to read the ontological interconnectedness and mysticism that binds the community in the English village while also contending with the turn to the individual as responsible actor in the larger world stage.

Set in June 1939, right before Britain declared war on Germany in September of that year, *Between the Acts* takes place over one day in a small English village. The creative talent, Miss La Trobe, has written and staged the annual village pageant. Featuring "Scenes from English History" (*BTA* 59)[35] spanning the settlement, Chaucer's time, the Elizabethan era, the Age of Reason, Victorian age and Present

---

[32] See, for example, the American Friends Service Committee relief worker S. Emily Parker's diary from her time in Spain during the Civil War, where she contemplates, "The ideal of peace face to face with the fact of war seems quite a different thing than when discussed in the quite [*sic*] of a fellowship of like-minded pacifists. What do we have to say today? For those of us who believe in a way of life not based on violence this is a very real and searching question. We are called to an accounting …" (9).

[33] For more on interconnectedness in *Between the Acts* see Annette Allen; Sanja Bahun; Emily Hinnov.

[34] Alice Wood likewise maintains that *Between the Acts* "interrogates art's social role" (103) and that Woolf was convinced that "as intellectuals, artists have a duty to respond publicly to social, political and economic upheaval in times of national or international crisis" (106).

[35] All of the in-text citations to *Between the Acts* refer to Mark Hussey's Cambridge edition. While I have gained valuable insights from Melba Cuddy-Keane's introduction and annotations in the Harcourt edition of *Between the Acts*, I have chosen to cite the Cambridge edition because it removes the italics of the pageant (chosen by Leonard), and more closely resembles Virginia's typescript, which accentuates the blurring of boundaries between the play and its context. As Hussey notes, "Leonard Woolf's decision to use italics uniformly throughout the pageant has the effect of separating it from the narrative in a way the text itself undercuts" (lxvii).

Day, caricatures such as "England" and "Reason" bridge the gaps between epochs. The play, overshadowed by the war that is yet-to-come, levels a poignant critique of history in its retelling. La Trobe, a modernist artist, fragments the narrative and destabilizes the plot so that her audience leaves wondering and debating as to the meaning of the pageant, required to engage in meaning-making on an individual level.[36] The formal and experimental components of Woolf's text collapse the distinctions between artist and audience, thus making "unity out of multiplicity" (*TG* 169), expressing the ontological relationship of the part to the whole, and an ethical imperative to rewrite current narratives. Looming on the brink of war, *Between the Acts* argues "Surely it was time someone invented a new plot" (*BTA* 155) and chose "peace."[37] In illustrating the individual's responsibility to community, and in calling for "a new plot," writing *Between the Acts* can be understood as a sacred act for Woolf precisely because it calls for an engagement with ethics, a responsibility to and for the other, a responsibility that is ultimately political.[38]

The village pageant inspires the members of the community to recognize their ontological connection, to have an aesthetic experience that brings them into their interdependency while retaining their individuality.[39] Through the play, the audience feels their universal connectedness, executing Woolf's larger mission to bridge the divide between the spiritual and material, conveying the way in which the individual makes up the larger community.[40] La Trobe's pageant, fragmented, loosely organ-

---

[36] The introduction to *Communal Modernisms* observes, "Miss La Trobe attempts to give her audience a transformative, personalized performance instead of one that insists on a singular, authoritative view. Everyone participates in mutual meaning-making as the text of the play comes alive through the collaborative performance of artist and spectator" (Hinnov et al.1).

[37] The text tells us, "Peace was the third emotion. Love. Hate. Peace. Three emotions made the ply of human life" (*BTA* 67). Melba Cuddy-Keane, in her annotations to *Between the Acts*, shows that Woolf experimented with different permutations of combinations for this sentence (176). It is significant, then, that Woolf *chose* peace as she is, ultimately, asking her audience to do in the text.

[38] According to Bahun, writing is "the ethically most appropriate way to engage with a catastrophic historical moment" (156), a mode of response that allows for intervention without adding to the nightmare of history.

[39] Alternately, Zwerdling argues "The pageant can be seen as providing us not so much with a comprehensive vision of the past as with a prehistory of the present. It follows English culture through its historical states to emphasize the gradual but persistent decay of the sense of community" (317).

[40] Hinnov names these experiences "choran community," defining her term as "textual instances that communicate the possibility of genuine interface between the self and other which also implicates an awareness of the larger, interconnective community" (*part of whole*). In other words, in specific instances of *Between the Acts*, Woolf captures moments where her characters "interface" with other characters and become aware of it. While Hinnov is not operating in the Quaker tradition, the ideas of the connection amongst subjects, and an awareness of that connection, provide a reading of interconnectedness in *Between the Acts*

ized, and resistant to any one total meaning, represents a modernist drama in that every audience member questions its significance and must construct a message for themselves: "They all looked at the play; Isa, Giles and Mr. Oliver. Each of course saw something different" (*BTA* 153). With this diffusion of meaning, the play inspires meditation amongst the audience on the self's relation to the interconnected nature of being, and implicates the individual in the construction of the world.

The Reverend Streatfield, though a ridiculous figure raising money, voices and directs the audience's thoughts to these concerns of self and other when he speaks "merely as one of the audience" (137), observing that, "To me it was indicated that we are members one of another. Each is part of the whole [...] We act different parts; but are the same [...] May we not hold that there is a spirit that inspires, pervades ..." (137-138). Though his speech at the end of the play can seem bombastic—in Woolf's own words "an intolerable constriction, contraction, and reduction to simplified absurdity" (136)—and becomes a source of amusement and embarrassment for the audience, he performs an important rhetorical function at the end of the text, offering his reading as one of the audience members. He is ridiculous, yes, but with his speech, is not Woolf implying that there is something of the ridiculous about humanity? "There he stood their representative spokesman; their symbol; themselves; a butt, a clod, laughed at by looking-glasses" (137). His words cannot be dismissed, rather, they should be taken as representing one of the larger themes in the play and offering a valuable perspective on Miss La Trobe's masterpiece. The emphasis on oneness, on unity, the idea that "each is part of the whole" is consistent with the logic of the rest of the text, so when Reverend Streatfield voices his interpretation, he is articulating and offering focus to a trope that flows throughout *Between the Acts* and that the following analysis further unfolds.[41] Secondly, the way in which these statements are repeated and resound in the dispersing audience, staying in the minds of the country folk, disseminates these considerations amongst the population and facilitates the people questioning their relationship to the larger social structure. In short, La Trobe's fragmented play on English history inspires the audience, Streatfield included, to reflect upon their relationship to the universe.

Streatfield's observation that "we are members one of another" demonstrates the relationality of the part to the whole. This observation carries with it the ethical imperative of individual choice that the play reflects back upon the audience—as the existentialist Sartre has written, when one chooses for oneself, one also shapes the trajectory of the world. Streatfield's statement echoes Francis Pollard's Merttens Lecture, published by Hogarth in 1928, which anticipates Sartre's arguments, and

that is commensurate with the Quaker thought.
[41] For a reading that upholds Rev. Streatfield as bombastic and ridiculous, see Zwerdling, 312-313.

in which he avers, "we must feel in our bones that we are members one of another" (9). Because we are "members one of another" and "world unity and inner harmony stand or fall together" (12), one of Pollard's main arguments in *War and Human Values* is that the individual composes the whole, and that individuals have a *choice* in the kind of world they construct. Personal, human choice, the responsibility and complicity that implicates each individual in the world structure, is quite literally reflected to the audience in Miss La Trobe's staging of "the present moment" (133) when the audience is forced to view "Ourselves" (133). The actors, leaping out onto the stage with mirrors, shards of glass, and all kinds of reflective surfaces, confront the audience with themselves. The light that bounces from these shiny planes includes the audience as actors in the play on the world stage, collapsing the boundaries between art and life, between viewer and participant. They become part of the play as they stare at the players and instead witness themselves reflected through glittering mirrors.[42] It destabilizes the audience. It exposes them. It exposes their complicity in the larger schema of their contemporaneous moment. Aside from Mrs. Manresa, none want to look at who they are. Their discomfort is what Sartre might call "anguish": the realization that, not only are people responsible for manifesting themselves, but also for manifesting the world in which we all live (25). Anguish is the acute pain experienced in the face of the realization that *we are all responsible*, and the discomfort of the audience indicates that their own complicity in the world is dawning on them.

A voice, "Whose voice it was no one knew" (134), continues the implication of their own reflections, and calls for an acknowledgement of individual responsibility. It indicts the individual in the tragedy of war: "Consider the gun slayers, bomb droppers,—here or there. They do openly what we do slyly" (134). Here, the audience's actions (or non-actions) are paralleled with the "gun slayers" and "bomb droppers." The "voice" equates the audience's submissive refusal to stop the war with the obvious and violent gestures of war, showing that one amounts to the other. The audience's participation in the systems of war are tantamount to their support for it. It is only when the "orts, scraps, and fragments" (135) take individual responsibility and join together in a unified whole that civilization can be rebuilt. A reporter describes the next scene in his notes, showing the reader what is taking place in the pageant: "Miss La Trobe conveyed to the audience Civilisation (the wall) in ruins; rebuilt (witness man with hod) by human effort; witness also woman handing bricks" (130). Here the reporter illustrates how Miss La Trobe places responsibility on individual action to create peace—a man with a hod and a woman with a brick can reconstruct the wall that mass mobilization tore down. Human

---

[42] For a very interesting reading of the way in which *Between the Acts* aesthetically addresses patterns of violence and implicates Woolf, her cultural moment, and even "ourselves" in those patterns, see Cole's chapter "Patterns of Violence."

effort, and importantly men and women working together in their own way, can restore the wall that human effort destroyed; however, each human, on an individual, personal level must make that *choice*. The voice, by demanding the audience "look at ourselves" (135), insists that each individual must take responsibility for rebuilding the wall of civilization, a civilization which is "doomed" ("the doom of sudden death hanging over us" says William [83]) and threatened by the looming war: "Look at ourselves, ladies and gentlemen! Then, at the wall; and ask how's this wall, the great wall, which we call, perhaps miscall, civilisation, to be built by (here the mirrors flickered and flashed) orts, scraps and fragments like ourselves" (135)? The looming war haunts this text, prophesying tragedy, and the "voice" is the one that reminds us that, in Kathleen Innes's words, peace, like war, is a *choice*.

This voice, Cuddy-Keane supposes, "might be the voice of the gramophone, or of the author, or of music, or 'Was that voice ourselves'" (xlvii)?[43] For Cuddy-Keane,

> More important than identifying this voice, perhaps, is the sense of a voice without fixed location ... We are thus not always sure if a thought should be assigned to narrator or a character ... But the "other" voice might also suggest the presence of some underlying, unifying common spirit, not transcendent and elsewhere, but—if we could only hear it—immediate and here. (xlvii)

Cuddy-Keane's language here calls for a Quaker reading. The suggestion of the "voice" as a "presence" of a "unifying common spirit" that is not "transcendent and elsewhere" invokes the Quaker practice of waiting on messages from the inner light in silent Meeting for worship, so as to better hear the voice of divine guidance. Stephen describes this when she writes: "Our manner of worship is the natural ... result of the full recognition of the reality of Divine inspiration—of the actual living present sufficient fulness [*sic*] of intercourse between the human spirit and Him who is the Father of spirits" (*Strongholds* 51). Stephen emphasizes here the Quaker idea that, not only is the light present in each individual, but if one listens, the inner light will guide one's course in life and communicate how one is to behave in the world. She continues to specify: "What Friends undoubtedly believe and maintain is that to the listening heart God does speak intelligibly" (*Strongholds* 59). Here, Stephen describes the Quaker belief that God speaks directly to, and through, the individual. When Cuddy-Keane identifies the voice as the "presence" of a "unifying common spirit" that is not "transcendent and elsewhere," she gestures towards the Quaker idea of the voice of the inner light. The "voice" can be read as the "voice" of the inner light that permeates daily existence and, for the Quakers, is cultivated in Meeting for worship.

[43] For an alternative reading that sees the voice as a fascist threat, see Ellis.

It is no mistake, then, that Miss La Trobe scripts ten minutes of silent reflection directly preceding the "present moment" scene. The ten minutes can be thought of as an impromptu silent Meeting for worship, preparing the heart ("their own wild hearts") to listen and be able to hear the message of the "voice" implicating and merging the one in the many. Indeed, the area of lawn where the play is performed is described as a primeval "church":

> The other trees were magnificently straight. They ... suggest columns in a church; in a church without a roof; in an open-air cathedral, a place where swallows darting seemed, by the regularity of the trees, to make a pattern dancing, like the Russians, only not to music, but to the unheard rhythm of their own wild hearts. (*BTA* 47)[44]

Meeting for worship, held in simple, unadorned locations, sometimes outside, is the place where Friends reflect upon their behaviors in the world, their relationship to the community, and to the divine. Silent Meeting for worship is the Friends' method of listening—it is a clearing away of the noise in life to be able to hear the messages from the depths of the soul inspired by the inner light. Quakers gather in corporate worship to intensify and share this experience, allowing the felt presence of the light to grow with the community of silent worshippers. The light is therefore both communal and personal; while one hears divine messages individually, the energy of the community can strengthen and support the presence of the light. Meeting is, according to Douglas Steere, a "vessel" of divinity (14) where those gathered can "hear the rhythm of their own wild hearts" (*BTA* 47).

In other words, Miss La Trobe's spontaneous Meeting for worship, with the community gathered together, allows the villagers to sit with themselves, in the full presence of their fellow audience members, nature, and the reality of the present day. In Miss La Trobe's stage notes, "'After Vic.' she had written, 'try ten mins. of present time. Swallows, cows etc.' She wanted to expose them, as it were, to douche them, with present time: reality" (129). From Woolf's other writings, we know that "reality" is a word that also stands in for "life," not only material existence, but the "reality" that has ingrained within it a spiritual connectedness. The audience, however, fails to respond immediately, and Miss La Trobe panics: "Reality too strong" (129). The audience, implicated in the tragedy of the present moment, does not want to look at themselves—overwhelmed by the unorthodoxy, the boredom, or even what it means to sit silently for ten minutes with no stimulation, a mounting discomfort becomes palpable. It builds like humidity right before it rains.

In a writerly gesture that absorbs and signifies the interconnectedness of

---

[44] Marcus attributes this setting to Woolf's visit to Bayreuth in 1909. See "Some Sources for *Between the Acts*."

being that Woolf throughout this text conveys, nature comes in and discharges the pent up communal emotion through a burst of rain. In a movement that at once binds the world in togetherness and mourns for its contemporary moment of the historical tragedy of the Second World War, the world, nature, the audience, weep for humanity: "No one had seen the cloud coming. There it was, black, swollen, on top of them. Down it poured like all the people in the world weeping. Tears. Tears. Tears" (129). Isa understands this burst of rain as indicative of the historical moment: "Oh that our human pain could here have ending!" (129) she thinks to herself. The rain hits her cheeks, and the novel specifies that, though Isa appeared as though she were crying, "they were all people's tears, weeping for all people" (129). Weeping for all people because of the fighter planes that interrupt the end of the pageant, weeping for all people because Europe is like a "hedgehog" on the brink of war, "bristling with guns, poised with planes" (39). The timing of the text, then, is significant because Woolf sets the scene in the months before war, at the historical crossroads when there is still time to intervene. Different potential historical trajectories from the one that was taken—the possibilities of what might have been—silhouette the text.

By refusing to put the army into Miss La Trobe's play, Woolf asks us to consider what history would look like without the military. In doing so, she "baffle[s]" (113) her audience, who ask, "Why leave out the British Army? What's history without the Army, eh" (113)? In this revisionist history, then, possibly the "future shall somehow blossom out of the past" (*D3* 118). Through this historical materialist gesture, where Woolf accepts the "task to brush history against the grain" (Benjamin 257), she challenges us to think a historical narrative that relocates the military from its central, prominent position to the periphery. In doing so, she questions the values of a patriarchy upon which the play's present moment of an England bristling toward war was built.[45]

In her engagement with history, Woolf fulfills, in Alice Wood's terms, her role as cultural critic by asking her audience, and her readers, to consider their role in the pattern of design and to take responsibility for their actions that compose the larger conglomerate of the whole. Alice Wood writes that "Miss La Trobe challenges her audience's conception of history, which is, her literary-based pageant emphasizes, itself just a story" (127). Through her reframing and allegorizing of history, Miss La Trobe exposes "history" as narrative, a social construct. This construction illustrates that there is choice involved in how we, as members of various communities, tell our stories, and the way in which we construct the past

---

[45] Gillian Beer considers this radical historical materialist gesture "an extraordinary liquidation of the expected triumphalist summary" (145) and notes the "discomfiture" (145) of the audience members in response to a history that refuses to participate in the glorification of the military.

offers a trajectory for the future. As Nancy Knowles points out, the very narrative structure of *Between the Acts* critiques the systems, particularly the patriarchal systems, that allow for war to occur in the first place. In engaging in this critique of history, Woolf exposes the fallacies of the past, calling upon us (citizens in a global community) to rethink how we tell our own historical stories and how we approach the future. Just as in *Three Guineas* and "Thoughts on Peace in an Air Raid," where Woolf points out that, if we are to ever have peace, "We must compensate the man for the loss of his gun" (218) by giving "him access to the creative feelings" (219), *Between the Acts* presents "art as a faith to be believed in" (Wood 114). Woolf demonstrates art's ability to reflect back on us "ourselves" and our own complicity in and responsibility for world affairs, and thus calls for a recognition of our material contributions to the fabric of "reality" and a deliberate attempt to change the social and historical course we are on.

Through art, through writing specifically, Woolf asks us to "think peace into existence" ("Thoughts" 216) by taking up the "mental fight" of "thinking against the current, not with it" ("Thoughts" 217). Pointing out that reading Woolf is a transformative experience, Madelyn Detloff contends that her writing has the power to "change us—not because of what it says or means but because of the habits of mind that it cultivates as we experience it" (209). In similar logic, Melba Cuddy-Keane discusses Woolf's process in creating *Between the Acts* as "a *kind* of writing rather than as a *subject* about which to write; ... this particular kind of writing asserted for her a different system of values from the mentality that leads to war" (xlii), a set of values transferred and communicated to her reader. I would argue, extending Detloff and Cuddy-Keane, that the new "habits of mind" or "values" that contradict the war mentality that Woolf proposes are precisely to illuminate the way in which humans are a part of each other, the way in which being is interdependent and interrelated, "values" that take on an ethical orientation towards the other, "values" that are essentially Quaker. *Between the Acts* issues a powerful call for peace by communally weeping for the tragedy of human existence in a time of war and by asking us, the audience and readers, to rebuild the wall of society, one brick at a time, one individual choice at a time.

Between the Acts was never finished. Despite Leonard Woolf's assertion that Virginia would not have made significant changes to the draft he published, Mark Hussey convincingly points out that she almost certainly would have. In this way, "*Between the Acts* remains in process, permanently deferred" (*BTA* lxi), a text and process in becoming. One could read it as an ultimate writerly text, in Roland Barthes' language, of process and not product, of constant reformation and shaping, more pliable in the hands of readers and critics than other, more "finished" work because it lacks the authority of the "final" stages of development. It is a living text, one that speaks through the audience and through the ages to our present time, having never had its potential ever finally realized in a decisive printing, or, in a sense, its "proper" ending. Like history, the end is yet to be written, and in this way, it calls to its readers to take up its mantle and implicates us, the present day, ourselves, in the rebuilding of the wall of civilization. It is, as Charles Andrews argues about *The Years*, "literary activism" (64), calling to us in our present moment to consider history without the army and ways in which we can put an end to our communal tears.

In her critique and engagement with history, in asking us to rethink what history would look like without the military, and in casting the responsibility of restoring the wall of civilization on us, as citizens in a global world, Woolf enacts Pollard's "threefold" pacifism, a pacifism that is "critical, constructive, resistant" (16). Through her revision of England's history, Woolf critiques the patriarchal system that has inevitably led to war. She resists the traditional metanarratives of her present day in refusing to celebrate the army. And, calling for her readers to choose "peace" and to find "a new plot," by asking that we, as society, deliberately reconstruct the wall of civilization, she puts forth a constructive notion of pacifism that shows that peace is more than the absence of war—it is a human choice built on deliberate, constructive measures.

Between the Acts carries Quaker traces, then, in its coupling of deep spirituality and rich materiality, of juxtaposing individual choice with communal and ethical responsibility, and in rallying a powerful call-to-action for peace predicated on an acknowledgement of the sanctity of life. I am not arguing that Virginia Woolf was a closeted Quaker; however, accepting that Caroline Stephen was one of the "invisible presences" (*MOB* 80) in Woolf's life and that Woolf published and was writing in conversation with many Quakers, I do believe Woolf's work reflects values and concerns taken up by the Society of Friends. I think we can use Quaker philosophies as an entrance point into her texts, and as a framework for understanding her mysticism, which was oriented towards political ends and rooted very concretely within-the-world. Quaker thought allows us to bridge seemingly incommensurate elements in Woolf's writings, and helps us to understand how to reconcile spirituality and materialism, atheism and mysticism, art and action. *Between the Acts* reverberates with these concerns and, more importantly, shows us that the work of finding a "new plot" and rebuilding the wall of civilization is yet to be done.

This article has greatly benefited from the feedback of Mark Hussey and my two anonymous peer-reviewers. Many thanks for their time and suggestions. The Woolf community at large also contributed to this thought through their engagement with my work on Woolf and the Quakers at the 23rd and 25th Annual Conferences on

Virginia Woolf. My gratitude to Jane Marcus, who helped cultivate these ideas through years of discussion and mentorship.

Profound appreciation goes to Special Collections at the University of Reading, Haverford College's Quaker & Special Collections, King's College Archive Centre, and the University of Delaware Special Collections for their assistance with my research. Thank you to The University of Sussex and the Society of Authors as the Literary Representative of the Estate of Leonard Woolf for allowing me access to Kathleen Innes's correspondence with the Hogarth Press.

Works Cited

Alexander, Horace G. *Justice Among Nations*. First Merttens Lecture on War and Peace. London: Hogarth, 1927. Print.

Allen, Annette. "Virginia Woolf's Spirituality: 'We are the words; we are the music." *L&B* 24:1.2 (2004). Web. 30 Sep 2015.

Andrews, Charles. "'beauty, simplicity, and peace': Faithful Pacifism, Activist Writing & *The Years*." *Virginia Woolf Writing the World: Selected Papers from the Twenty-Fourth International Virginia Woolf Conference*. Ed. Pamela L. Caughie and Diana Swanson. Clemson: Clemson UP, 2015: 63-68. Print.

Bahun, Sanja. *Modernism & Melancholia: Writing as Countermourning*. Oxford and New York: Oxford UP, 2014. Print.

Barthes, Roland. *S/Z*. Trans. Richard Miller. New York: Hill and Wang, 1974. Print.

Bell, Julian, ed. *We Did Not Fight: 1914-18 Experiences of War Resisters*. London: Cobden-Sanderson, 1935. Print.

Buxton, Charles Roden. *The Race Problem in Africa*. The Merttens Lecture. London: Hogarth Press, 1931. Print.

Carver, Katelynn. "Behind the Cotton Wool: Process Philosophy in the Works of Virginia Woolf." *The Graduate Journal of Harvard Divinity School* (Spring 2013). Np. Web. 12 Jan 2016.

"Caroline Emelia Stephen." *Bulletin of Friends' Historical Society of Philadelphia*. 3.2 ([June] 1909): 95-98. Print.

Cole, Sarah. *At the Violet Hour: Modernism and Violence in England and Ireland*. Oxford and New York: Oxford UP, 2012: 197-286. Print.

Cuddy-Keane, Melba. "Introduction" and "Notes." *Between the Acts* by Virginia Woolf. Orlando: Harcourt, 2008: xxxvi-lxvi and 151-212. Print.

Dandelion, Pink. *An Introduction to Quakerism*. Cambridge and New York: Cambridge UP, 2007. Print.

de Gay, Jane. "Challenging the Family Script: Woolf, the Stephen Family, and Victorian Evangelical Theology." *Interdisciplinary/Multidisciplinary Woolf:*

Selected Papers from the Twenty-Second Annual International Conference on Virginia Woolf. Ed. Ann Martin and Kathryn Holland. Clemson: Clemson UP, 2013: 35-40. Print.

Dusinberre, Juliet. *Virginia Woolf's Renaissance: Woman Reader or Common Reader?* Iowa City: U of Iowa P, 1997. Print.

Ellis, Steve. "Virginia Woolf and the Theatre of War." *British Writers and the Approach of World War II.* Cambridge and New York: Cambridge UP, 2015: 188-233. Print.

Foster, J. Ashley. "Recovering Pacifisms Past: Modernist Networks, the Society of Friends, and the Peace Movement of the Spanish Civil War." *Quakers in Literature.* (Quakers in the Disciplines series, Vol. 3) Ed. James W. Hood. Philadelphia: Friends Association for Higher Education, April, 2016. Print.

——. in collaboration with students of the "Peace Testimonies in Literature & Art" Spring 2015 Writing Seminar. *Testimonies in Art & Action: Igniting Pacifism in the Face of Total War Exhibition Catalogue.* Haverford: Haverford College Libraries, 2015. 12 pages. Digital and print.

Fox, George. *An Autobiography.* Ed. Rufus Jones. Philadelphia: Ferris & Leach 1909. Reproduced by Project Gutenberg. Ebook.

Frost, J. William. "Modernist and Liberal Quakers, 1887-2010." *The Oxford Handbook of Quaker Studies.* Oxford and New York: Oxford UP, 2013: 78-92. Print.

Froula, Christine. *Virginia Woolf and the Bloomsbury Avant-Garde: War, Civilization, Modernity.* New York: Columbia UP, 2005. Print.

Fry, Roger. "The Friends' Work for War Victims in France." 1915-1917. MS The Papers of Roger Eliot Fry REF/1/22. King's College Archive Centre, Cambridge, England.

Gillespie, Diane F. "'Woolfs' in Sheep's Clothing: The Hogarth Press and 'Religion.'" *Leonard & Virginia Woolf, The Hogarth Press, and the Networks of Modernism.* Ed. Helen Southworth. Edinburgh: Edinburgh UP, 2010: 74-99. Print.

Graham, John W. *Britain and America.* The Merttens Lecture. London: Hogarth Press, 1930. Print.

Goldman, Jane. *The Feminist Aesthetics of Virginia Woolf.* Cambridge and New York: Cambridge UP, 1998. Print.

——. *Modernism, 1910-1945: Image to Apocalypse.* New York: Palgrave Macmillan, 2004. Print.

——. "Two Postcards from Skye: Virginia Woolf in the Hebrides." *Virginia Woolf Miscellany.* 85 (Spring 2014): 13-15. Print.

Gooch, G.P. *Politics and Morals.* Merttens Lecture. London: Hogarth Press, 1935. Print.

Groover, Kristina. "Enacting the Sacred in *Mrs. Dalloway*." *Virginia Woolf Miscellany*. 80 (Fall 2011): 11-13. Print.
Harvey, Kathryn. "'Driven by War into Politics!': A Feminist Biography of Kathleen Innes." Diss. U of Alberta, 1995. Web. 15 May 2015.
Heininge, Kathy. "Virginia Woolf: Quaker Pacifist?" *War and Peace as Liberal Arts: Twelfth Annual Conversation in the Liberal Arts*. Westmont College, Santa Barbara, CA. Feb. 21-23, 2013. Web: 30 Sept. 2015.
———. "The Search for God: Virginia Woolf and Caroline Emelia Stephen." *Virginia Woolf Miscellany*. 80 (Fall 2011): 20-21. Print.
Hinds, Hilary. "'Let your lives preach:' the embodied rhetoric of the early Quakers." *George Fox and Early Quaker Culture*. Manchester and New York: Manchester UP, 2011. 33-55. Print.
Hinnov, Emily M., Laurel Harris, and Lauren M. Rosenblum. "Introduction." *Communal Modernisms: Teaching Twentieth-Century Literature and Culture in the Twenty-First-Century Classroom*. New York: Palgrave Macmillan, 2013: 1-17. Print.
Hinnov, Emily M. "'Each is part of the whole: we act different parts; but are the same': From Fragment to Choran Community in the Late Work of Virginia Woolf." *Woolf Studies Annual* 13 (2007): 1-23. Web. 10 Sept. 2015.
Historical Dictionary of the Friends (Quakers), 2nd ed. Ed. Margery Post Abbott, Mary Ellen Chijioke, Pink Dandelion, and John William Oliver Jr. Lanham, MD: The Scarecrow P, 2012. Print.
Hodgkin, Thomas. "Caroline Stephen and the Society of Friends." *The Vision of Faith and Other Essays*. Cambridge: W. Heffer & Sons Ltd. and London: Headley Bros, 1911: xxxv-xlviii. Print.
Hoyland, John S. *The Light of Christ*. Swarthmore Lecture. London: The Swarthmore House, 1928. Print.
Hussey, Mark. "Introduction." *Between the Acts* by Virginia Woolf. Cambridge and New York: Cambridge UP, 2011: xxxix-lxxix. Print.
———. "Woolf: After Lives." *Virginia Woolf in Context*. Ed. Bryony Randall and Jane Goldman. Cambridge and New York: Cambridge UP, 2012: 13-27. Print.
Innes, Kathleen E. *Defense of the Weak*. London: Peace Committee of the Society of Friends, C. F. Hodgson & Son, Ltd., 1935?. Print.
———. *The Story of the League of Nations: Told for Young People*. London: Hogarth Press, 1925. Print.
Jones, Rufus. *Rufus Jones Speaks to Our Time*. Ed. Harry Emerson Fosdick. New York: The Macmillan Company, 1951. Print.
Kane, Julie. "Varieties of Mystical Experience in the Writings of Virginia Woolf." *Twentieth Century Literature* 41.4 (Winter 1995): 328-349. Print.
Kennedy, Thomas C. *British Quakerism 1860-1920: The Transformation of a*

Religious Community. Oxford and New York: Oxford UP, 2001. Print.

Lazenby, Donna J. *A Mystical Philosophy: Transcendence and Immanence in the Works of Virginia Woolf and Iris Murdoch.* London and New York: Bloomsbury, 2014. Ebook.

Lee, Hermione. *Virginia Woolf.* New York: Vintage, 1999. Print.

Knowles, Nancy. "Active Pacifism in a World at War: The Legacy of Virginia Woolf's Pacifist Theory on Narrative Structure." *The Theme of Peace and War in Virginia Woolf's Political Philosophy.* Ed. Jane Wood. Lampeter, UK: Edwin Mellen, 2010: 237-260. Print.

Laurence, Patricia. "The Facts and Fugue of War: From *Three Guineas* to *Between the Acts*." *Virginia Woolf and War: Fiction, Reality, and Myth.* Ed. Mark Hussey. Syracuse: Syracuse UP, 1991. 225-45. Print.

Lewis, Alison. "Caroline Emelia Stephen (1834-1909) and Virginia Woolf (1882-1941): A Quaker Influence on Modern English Literature." *Quaker Theology* 3 (2000). Web. 30 Sept. 2015.

MacKay, Marina. "Virginia Woolf and the pastoral patria." *Modernism and World War II.* Cambridge and New York: Cambridge UP, 2007: 22-24. Print.

Maggio, Paula. "Taking Up Her Pen for World Peace: Virginia Woolf, Feminist Pacifist. Or Not?" *Virginia Woolf Writing the World: Selected Papers from the Twenty-Fourth International Virginia Woolf Conference.* Ed. Pamela L. Caughie and Diana Swanson. Clemson: Clemson UP, 2015: 37-42. Print.

Mendlesohn, Farah. *Quaker Relief Work in the Spanish Civil War.* Lampeter, UK: Edwin Mellen, 2002. Print.

Mills, Jean. *Virginia Woolf, Jane Ellen Harrison, and the Spirit of Modernist Classicism.* Columbus: Ohio State UP, 2014. Print.

Marcus, Jane. "The Niece of a Nun: Virginia Woolf, Caroline Stephen, and the Cloistered Imagination." *Virginia Woolf and the Languages of Patriarchy.* Bloomington: Indiana UP, 1987. Print.

——. "No More Horses." *Women's Studies* 4 (1977): 265-290. Print.

——. "Some Sources for *Between the Acts*." *Virginia Woolf Miscellany* 6 (Winter 1997): 1-3. Print.

——. "Thinking Back through Our Mothers." *Art and Anger: Reading Like a Woman.* Columbus: Ohio State UP, 1988: 73-100. Print.

Parker, S. Emily. *From the Devotional Diary of a Relief Worker in Spain.* Richmond: S. Emily Parker. n.d. Print.

Pollard, Francis E. *War and Human Values.* Merttens Lectures on War & Peace No 2. London: Hogarth Press, 1928. Print.

Ratcliffe, S. K. *The Roots of Violence.* Merttens Lecture. London: Hogarth Press, 1934. Print.

Rogers, Gayle. *Modernism and the New Spain*. Oxford and New York: Oxford UP, 2012. Ebook.

Ryan, Derek. *Virginia Woolf and the Materiality of Theory: Sex, Animal, Life*. Edinburgh: Edinburgh UP, 2013. Print.

Salter, Sir Arthur. *Economic Policies and Peace*. Merttens Lecture. London: Hogarth Press, 1936. Print.

Silver, Brenda. "Are You a Quaker?" *Virginia Woolf Miscellany* 72 (Fall/Winter 2007): 12-13. Print.

——. "'Anon' and 'The Reader': Virginia Woolf's Last Essays." *Twentieth Century Literature* 25.3/4 (Autumn-Winter 1979): 356-441. Print.

Sim, Lorraine. *Virginia Woolf: The Patterns of Ordinary Experience*. Surrey and Burlington: Ashgate, 2010. Print.

Smith, Amy C. and Isabel Ma Andrés Cuevas. "To the Readers: Virginia Woolf and Spirituality." *Virginia Woolf Miscellany* 80 (Fall 2011): 1-2. Print.

Southworth, Helen. Introduction. *Leonard & Virginia Woolf, The Hogarth Press, and the Networks of Modernism*. Ed. Helen Southworth. Edinburgh: Edinburgh UP, 2010: 1-26. Print.

Spalding, Frances. *Virginia Woolf: Art, Life and Vision*. London: National Portrait Gallery, 2014. Print.

Steere, Douglas V. "Introduction." *Quaker Spirituality*. New York: Paulist Press, 1984. 1-53. Print.

Stephen, Caroline Emelia. *Quaker Strongholds*. Philadelphia: Henry Longstreth, 1891. Print.

——. *Light Arising: Thoughts on the Central Radiance*. Cambridge: W. Heffer & Sons and London: Headley Bros, 1908. Print.

——. *The Vision of Faith and Other Essays*. Cambridge: W. Heffer & Sons Ltd. and London: Headley Bros, 1911. Print.

Stephens, John S. *Danger Zones of Europe: A Study of National Minorities*. Merttens Lecture on War and Peace No. 3. London: Hogarth Press, 1929. Print.

Tseng, Jui-hua. "Walter Pater, the Stephens and Virginia Woolf's Mysticism." *Concentric: Literary and Cultural Studies* 30.1 (2004): 203-26. Print.

Wood, Alice. *Virginia Woolf's Later Cultural Criticism: The Genesis of The Years, Three Guineas, and Between the Acts*. London and New York: Bloomsbury, 2013. Print.

Woolf, Virginia. *A Room of One's Own*. Annotated and introduced by Susan Gubar. New York and London: Harcourt, 2005. Print.

——. *Moments of Being*. Ed. Jeanne Schulkind. New York and London: Harcourt, 1985. Print.

——. "Modern Fiction." *Selected Essays*. Ed. David Bradshaw. Oxford: Oxford UP, 2008. 6-12. Print.

——. *Three Guineas*. Annotated and Introduced by Jane Marcus. Orlando: Harcourt, 2006. Print.

——. "Thoughts on Peace in an Air Raid." *Selected Essays*. Ed. David Bradshaw. Oxford and New York: Oxford UP, 2008: 216-219. Print.

——. *Between the Acts*. Ed. Mark Hussey. Cambridge and New York: Cambridge UP, 2011. Print.

——. *The Diary of Virginia Woolf: Volume III 1925-1930*. Ed. Anne Olivier Bell. New York and London: Harcourt Brace Jovanovich, 1980. Print.

Zwerdling, Alex. *Virginia Woolf and the Real World*. Berkeley and London: U of California P, 1986. Print.

Virginia Woolf and "The Villa Jones" (1931)
Clara Jones

As she struggled with revisions to *The Waves* during the summer of 1931, Virginia Woolf sought solace in the Sussex countryside. In a July diary entry, she records celebrating Leonard's enthusiastic reception of the novel with a solitary walk around the downs:

> what a relief! I stumped off in the rain to make a little round to Rat Farm in jubilation, & am almost resigned to the fact that a Goat farm, with a house to be built, is now in process on the slope near Northease. (*D*4 36)

Woolf's account of this summer of soothing walks on the downs is marked by her concern about changes to the landscape. Such anxiety is clear in her closing reference to the "Goat farm, with a house" being built locally. Woolf's claims to being "almost resigned" to the goat farm are reiterated in her account of a walk later in August: "today over to Northease & back by the marsh; almost forgiving the pink slate abortion on the Telscombe horizon. Goat Farm isn't so much of an eyesore as might have been" (*D*4 37). These local building developments are "almost" forgivable, that is ignorable, but Woolf's attempt at casualness in her reference to the farm here is undermined by her visceral description of it as a "pink slate abortion." The antipathy towards these buildings that Woolf struggles to manage in these diary entries explodes in "The Villa Jones,"[1] a curious unpublished letter that I found in Woolf's 1931 notebook in the Morgan Library in New York.

The red-brick villa becomes an increasingly visible and freighted figure in Woolf's writing from the late 1920s onwards. In her 1927 celebration of the city, "Street Haunting: A London Adventure," Woolf imagines a commuter returning to "a prim little villa in Barnes or Surbiton" (26) where the demands of the everyday "puncture" (27) the daydreams London inspires. In a 1932 (unsent) letter to the *New Statesman*, "Middlebrow," Woolf's artfully constructed highbrow speaks her contempt for middlebrow culture most pointedly through an account of their homes: "red brick villas that have been built by middlebrows so that middlebrows may look at the view" (119). In the "Present Day" chapter of Woolf's 1937 novel, *The Years*, elderly Eleanor Pargiter regrets the "little red villas all along the road"

---

[1] Letter to a Young Poet: Autograph Manuscript, 1931 Sept. 24, The Morgan Library and Museum, MA3333, ff. 3-5. All the quotations that follow from "The Villa Jones" will come from the transcription that accompanies this article. My thanks to the Society of Authors as the literary representative of the Estate of Virginia Woolf for permission to include this transcription.

that she observed on a recent trip to Dorsetshire and her agitated nephew North complains to his family, "how you've spoilt England while I've been away" (*TY* 275). References to villas and bungalows are numerous in Woolf's final novel *Between the Acts*—the Haines's "red villa in the cornfields" (6), the "hideous new house at Pyes Corner" (47) and "Mr. M.'s bungalow" (111).

The manuscript of Woolf's unpublished letter draws on the class symbolism we find in these texts' treatment of the villa and rehearses similar accusations of aesthetic compromise. "The Villa Jones" rails against building in the countryside and creates in Jones, the villa-owner, a figure who appears to stand for a threateningly mobile middle class, bent on invading the countryside. The letter's anxiety about preserving views anticipates the political significance they assume in *Between the Acts* years later. In that novel we are told that the Olivers' "fine view of the surrounding country" (34) from Pointz Hall has remained unchanged since it was described in "Figgis's Guide Book" in 1833. The pleasure the family take in their unspoilt view and their confidence that "It'll be there [...] when we're not" (*BTA* 34) become bound up with the questions the novel asks about complacency, conservatism and progress.

Here I suggest that such questions also concern "The Villa Jones" and argue that it has much to tell us about the social and cultural politics of the interwar English countryside. I build on recent scholarship, which has drawn attention to Woolf's relationship to the rural and its place in her writing.[2] Mark Hussey, in particular, has made a strong case for the influence of the preservation movement on the politics of Woolf's final novel, *Between the Acts*, while Elisa Kay Sparks and Leena Kore-Schröder have foregrounded Woolf's passion for rural Sussex, but also her ambivalence about her status as a "cockney" (*L6* 459) in the countryside. As well as reading its tirade against "voluntary view spoilers" in the context of Woolf's relationship to the countryside surrounding her home in Rodmell, I also emphasize the significant ironic and performative qualities of this piece. The preoccupation

---

[2] Much of this work focuses on Woolf's final novel, *Between the Acts*, the only one of her works to be set entirely in the countryside, including: Jed Esty, *A Shrinking Island: Modernism and National Culture in England* (Princeton: Princeton UP, 2004), 85-107, and Maroula Joannou, *Women's Writing, Englishness and National and Cultural Identity: The Mobile Woman and the Migrant Voice, 1938–62* (Basingstoke: Palgrave, 2012). Also see Christina Alt, *Virginia Woolf and the Study of Nature* (Cambridge: Cambridge UP, 2010), Bonnie Kime Scott, *In the Hollow of the Wave: Virginia Woolf and Modernist Uses of Nature* (Charlottesville: U of Virginia P, 2012) and Alexandra Harris, *Romantic Moderns: English Writers, Artists and the Imagination from Virginia Woolf to John Piper* (London: Thames & Hudson, 2010). Some of this work is representative of a wider effort in modernist studies to consider different sites of modernism, questioning the regular acceptance of literary modernism's symbiotic relationship with urban modernity. See David James and Philip Tew's edited collection *New Versions of Pastoral: Post-Romantic, Modern, and Contemporary Responses to the Tradition* (Madison, NJ: Farleigh Dickinson UP, 2009).

with voice we encounter in "The Villa Jones" signals its imaginative overlap with the other unpublished sketch located in Woolf's 1931 Morgan Library notebook—a three-page sketch written entirely in the voice of a domestic cook.[3] Woolf plays with voice in "The Villa Jones," as she does in much of her creative non-fiction, so it is risky to identify her with the letter-writer she constructs in any straightforward way.

I

"The Villa Jones" can be found three pages into a fifty-two-page notebook devoted to Woolf's draft of her 1932 essay "A Letter to a Young Poet," held at the Morgan Library in New York. The first page of the notebook is dated "1931 Sept. 24th," so we can reasonably assume that "The Villa Jones" was written at around this time. We can also be sure that it was written between this date and October 14th when, fifty or so pages later, she "dash[ed] off" (*D4* 48) the other sketch that shares the space of this notebook. In my 2014 article on this later unfinished sketch, I suggested it be known as the "Cook Sketch," as Woolf had left it without a title. Such an imposition is not necessary in the case of "The Villa Jones" as it is titled and appears to be finished, concluding with the sign-off "Yours," distinguishing it as a letter.

Although it is not addressed to anyone in particular, "The Villa Jones" certainly has the formal ring of a letter to a newspaper. Take its opening:

> The holidays are over; {& what is the most frequent thing we the brown, the sunburnt, &, if you want to} people, in London are talking, not only about money; but about green fields. It rained; it was hot in Shetland; very wet in the Isle of Wight. [Primrose] – did someone say – are to be picked in devonshire. But the refrain we catch, {at} from all over England is the same. Its spoilt now. There's building there.

The voice here is assured and authoritative, but also public. The letter-writer's efforts to speak for people "from all over England" reads as an attempt at inclusivity but her use of a rhetorical "we" undermines rather than reinforces this, sounding more like a royal "we" than the voice of a collective. These opening lines, which attempt to gather and synthesize voices and opinions from all corners of the country, announce this letter's interest in voice. Hints of pretentiousness in its writer also gesture to a parallel preoccupation with the performative. These lines also point to the increasing imaginative hold of what Simon Miller describes as an "English

---

[3] This sketch can be found on pages forty-four to forty-six of the Morgan Library notebook. My article considering Woolf's ventriloquism of a working woman in this piece and a transcription of the untitled ms. was published as "Virginia Woolf's 1931 'Cook Sketch,'" *Woolf Studies Annual* 20 (2014): 1-25.

ideology of ruralism" (90) during the interwar period. The political and economic uncertainty of this moment inspired a nostalgic turn to the rural as a site of authentic Englishness and sound national values. The writer's insistence that people are talking "not only about money; but about green fields" accurately reflects a moment of growing public enthusiasm for the rural, while her bathetic conclusion, "Its spoilt now. There's building there," articulates the anxiety that always edged such ruralism—the feeling that "old England" was always also under threat.

Having sounded this uneasy note, the letter moves onto its main concern—the building of unsympathetic new housing across the countryside. The writer is judicious, cautioning against unfairly blaming builders who, she reports, have frequently "built wisely, usefully with as little damage to the country as possible." Her composure is, however, shaken when she considers the changes to the rural landscape around the capital:

> But the amount of wanton damage that is being inflicted {on by people} for want of knowledge, for want of information, is appalling: {Mount} climb any hill within 60 miles of London & one sees a landscape pricked with red roofs, & white walls.

Here the writer speaks with the voice of an expert. She recommends that "a board of architects" be appointed to "discover what colours" would best suit new buildings. She reflects on the possible cost implications of "dun coloured walls" and an alternative to the popular red roofs, concluding, briskly, that they are "presumably no greater than the cost of red & white." She is confident that such expert advice will be adopted by "thousands" and anticipates no objections from the builders who, she insists, are only really interested in "sanitation & comfort" and have no wish "to do more harm than they must do by building on land which was once a field."

"The Villa Jones" then takes a sinister turn as it introduces the Joneses of its title: "But there is a second class, which is far more destructive, difficult to deal with. These are the voluntary view spoilers." The tone of the sketch becomes almost feverish as we get our first view of the Joneses' home: "In every part of the country one is going for a walk to see a view, & finding instead the Villa Jones." The Joneses, with their ostentatious villa and accompanying trappings of wealth and modernity, their "motor car," which the writer cannot help but spy, epitomize the (literally) upwardly mobile middle class. The writer assumes to speak for the entire community in her condemnation of such interlopers: "we consider Jones who has spoilt ten miles of the view for us no better than a robber, a murderer."

The letter closes with some practical suggestions for dealing with Jones: as he is insensible to the feelings of others, why not get him where it hurts: "In his pocket?" The writer first proposes introducing a tax on "the view values of all new houses." This tax would be made accessible to "the villagers," who will suffer most as a result of Jones's villa, as its ugliness will drive the rich away from the countryside. (How the rich presently contribute to the economy of the countryside or "the villagers" is not made clear.) The writer also suggests a plan involving the coming general election. She recommends that when approaching your candidate ask "not only what are your views upon the dole, the gold standard no: but where do you live? Have you spoilt a view?" Ending in this way, with a provocative unanswered question, highlights the rhetorical qualities of the letter. Bringing this discussion of "eyesores" into the context of the current financial crisis and the coming general election, Woolf politicizes the letter's argument in explicit ways. She suggests that the villa Jones is an "issue" worthy of debate like the economy or unemployment.

The writer's pragmatic take on the general election in "The Villa Jones" implies an absorption in the contemporary political moment that is not matched in Woolf's private writing. The equivocal tone of this August 1931 diary entry casts light on the assertive closing questions of "The Villa Jones":

> Meanwhile the country is in the throes of a crisis. Great events are brewing. Maynard visits Downing Street & spreads sensational rumours. Are we living then through a crisis; & am I fiddling? & will future ages, as they say, behold our predicament (financial) with horror? Sometimes I feel the world desperate; then walk among the downs. (*D*4 39)

The self-criticism discernible in Woolf's reflection "Are we living then through a crisis; & am I fiddling?" encourages us to consider whether the dogmatic voice of "The Villa Jones" might manifest some of this self-reproach. I want to keep the possibility open that this letter presented Woolf with an opportunity to parody her own extreme responses to building in Sussex in the voice of a supercilious letter-writer.

"The Villa Jones" also has much to tell us about the vagaries of Woolf's thinking about social class. Although this letter might appear at the outset to be simply an expression of Woolf's social and aesthetic distaste for the middle classes, the mobility of the voice in this sketch means it is not clear from what position their critique is necessarily levelled or what position the writer occupies in the countryside. She is not one of the working-class "villagers," who she hopes will benefit from her scheme of view taxation, but nor is she identified with the rich who will be put off by the new building. This instability is a product of Woolf's own complicated position in the countryside and her awareness, as a newcomer to Sussex, of her own complicity in the "invasion" of the countryside she laments. The following section will consider how Woolf's experiences as a resident of Rodmell and her exposure to the increasingly prominent discourses of rural preservation in the 1920s and 1930s influenced "The Villa Jones."

II

The villa Jones had a real-world correlative in Rodmell. In a letter to Vita Sackville-West dated September 16th 1931, Woolf complains about this local building just a matter of days before she started work on the draft of "A Letter to a Young Poet" in the Morgan notebook:

> O I'm in such a rage – a serious rage that caught me by the throat and constricted my heart – They've sold the Down above the village, and its all to go in plots, and two bungalows are already being run up, and its all ruined for ever and ever. What are we to do? I would sell instantly: but dont tell L. this. I dont see any point in living here in a suburb of Brighton. I dont suppose there is any pleasure in my life like walking alone in the country: no, I'm not exaggerating. And then to see the downs spoilt – by an infernal Labour candidate – his blasted villa will be there for all time - My God, Vita, I wish one hadn't picked this age to live in: I hate my kind. (*L4* 380)

Mark Hussey has pointed out that "bungalows and villas were a persistent thorn in Virginia Woolf's side, representing to her all that was least desirable about suburban life" and that their "encroachment on the Sussex Downs was a source of particular misery" (10). It is clear that "The Villa Jones" was written in response to this news about Labour candidate Frank Hancock's new home. Both letters mine a common language to express their fury: both refer to landscapes being "spoilt" in perpetuity—"for ever." The situation of Hancock's villa on "the Down above the village" is directly recalled in Jones's decision to plant "himself on the very top of the down." Hancock's status as Labour candidate also casts light on the conclusion of "The Villa Jones." This piece's abrupt turn to the general election and the writer's recommendation that it be used as an opportunity to question candidates about their housing—"where do you live? Have you spoilt a view?"—is clearly wishful thinking on Woolf's part. She envisions an alternate reality in which Hancock might be publicly upbraided for his "voluntary view" spoiling.

In spite of the clear parallels between this letter and "The Villa Jones," I am wary of reading the latter only as a therapeutic writing exercise that allowed Woolf to vent her spleen against Hancock through the figure of Jones. The ambiguous final line of this letter to Sackville-West—"I hate my kind"—draws further attention to the self-critical dimensions of "The Villa Jones." While it can be read as an expression of conservative nostalgia, the syntax and telling word choice of this apparently uncompromising line suggest another reading. In saying "my" rather than "that" Woolf identifies with and even claims kinship with Hancock. Although "kind" might refer to the human race here, it might also operate more specifically and mean Woolf's own sort, her type, or even, interestingly, her class. The OED entry for the name "Jones" lends weight to this reading: "used esp. in the plural to designate one's neighbours or social equals."[4] Woolf's choice of the name Jones for the villain of her piece is a nod to the by then popular phrase "keeping up with the Joneses"—shorthand for the social pressure not to "be outdone by one's neighbours."[5] Frank Hancock's status as a "Labour candidate" (one who it should be noted would from December 1931 be a regular attendee at the Rodmell Labour Party meetings held at Monk's House [Light 239]) makes this sideways claim of kinship all the more rich and strange. Woolf appears to be at once displaying and disparaging her political loyalties in this letter to Sackville-West.

Read in this light "The Villa Jones" becomes not just about the Joneses or Hancocks, but also about the Woolfs and their position in the countryside. Leena Kore-Schröder has observed, the Woolfs' "adoption of Sussex as a second home" (145) meant they were implicated in the very incursion into the countryside bemoaned in "The Villa Jones." Hussey also suggests that Woolf's complaints about building developments in Sussex are "typical of the resistance to change of those who feel their own presence in a rural setting has done nothing to spoil it" (10-11). It is striking then that Woolf's uncompromising claim in her letter, "I hate my kind," emerges in "The Villa Jones," re-worked as the writer's bitterest accusation: "we consider Jones [...] a hater of his kind."

The Woolfs' purchase of Monk's House in 1919 and their increasing identification with rural England coincided with a period of rapid change in the countryside in which it was "more obviously affected by urban influences than ever before" (Burchardt 89). Woolf's fear that the East Sussex countryside around her home might be turned into "a suburb of Brighton" does not express simply a private grievance. The 1920s and 1930s witnessed building on a grand scale and the majority of this was housing. Jeremy Burchardt describes this "intense phase of suburban growth" (89) focusing on the emergence of the ribbon development—"housing extending out for miles into the countryside along the line of a major road" (90-1). (Woolf nods to the popularity of ribbon building in "The Villa Jones" when the writer wonders why Jones did not buy a "site on the road.") Burchardt states that the "interwar years probably witnessed the highest annual loss of rural land to development of any period of British history" (110).[6]

---

[4] Jones, n., *OED* Online. September 3 2015
[5] Keep, v., *OED* Online. September 3 2015.
[6] As John Lowerson has noted, East Sussex was the site of particularly striking growth: "the archetypal example was Peacehaven on the Sussex Downs, whose population had increased from 400 to over 3,000 in the first four years of the 1920s" (260). In her discussion of Woolf's essay "Evening Over Sussex: Reflections in a Motor Car," Kore-Schröder suggests it is significant that Woolf takes her bearings "from the very chain of towns—Eastbourne, Bexhill, St Leonards—where the speculative building and ribbon development that was to disfigure the south coast between the wars had already started" (145).

The rapid building undertaken during the interwar period gave both Woolfs cause for concern. In January 1930 Leonard Woolf went as far as writing to Prime Minister Ramsay MacDonald on the subject of the "building menace":

> Would there be any possibility of the Government talking about the problem of protecting the countryside from the building menace? [...] Living as I do part of the year in the Sussex downs, I am appalled by the inroads already made and still more threatened by builders and building syndicates. I was talking to J. M. Keynes, who also rents a house in the same neighbourhood, about it this week and he thought it would be possible to work out a scheme under which special areas would be scheduled and protected at no great cost to the country [...] I feel that the Government would have an immense amount of sympathy and support for action in the matter. (LWP SxMs-13/2/1/4/A)

While Leonard Woolf seems less anxious than his wife about his position as only a semi-permanent resident in the countryside, "living [...] part of the year in the Sussex downs," his letter to MacDonald goes some way to showing that rural building projects were a political issue up for discussion at this time. In "The Villa Jones" Woolf responds not only to a local issue, but to a wider public debate about the future of the countryside and the relationship between the urban and the rural. She was obviously as clued into the discourses of rural preservation as her husband. If anything, the recommendations she makes in "The Villa Jones" are rather more progressive and imaginative than her husband and John Maynard Keynes's "scheme" for scheduling certain rural areas. They identify her strongly with key representatives of the Council for the Preservation of Rural England (CPRE), whose mode of expression and style of argument she apes in this letter.

The CPRE was established in 1926 in order to unite a number of subsidiary groups with an interest in maintaining the amenity of the countryside while taking a proactive approach towards town and country planning. Architects and town planners were well represented in the CPRE executive and the organization was responsible for publishing a number of well-received books on the subject of rural preservation around the time Woolf wrote "The Villa Jones." These include pamphlets and books by CPRE co-founder and honorary secretary, Patrick Abercrombie,[7] flamboyant architect and CPRE advocate Clough Williams-Ellis and geographer, Vaughan Cornish.

---

[7] Hussey suggests that Woolf may have been referring to Patrick Abercrombie when she wrote to Ottoline Morrell in February 1930 asking for the address of the man she had encountered at her house over the summer "who was connected with preserving downs" (11).

The emphasis on planning and expertise we find in "The Villa Jones" is consistent with the values of the CPRE. David Matless explains that "[p]reservationists offered a scene of leadership and action, with the expert rather than the ordinary person the key shaper of the land" (30). In his 1933 work *Town and Country Planning*, Patrick Abercrombie recommends a proactive approach to planning that recognizes the interdependence of urban and rural areas (18-19). Vaughan Cornish advocates a similar approach in his 1932 *The Scenery of England*: "The fundamental fact is that England needs planning for amenity as a whole, town not less than country" (11). In "The Villa Jones" the writer's confidence in the experts—"Let our experts decide"—and her proposal that a "board of architects" be appointed to stipulate codes and rules for new rural housing is in keeping with the CPRE's agenda. A 1930 CPRE pamphlet concerning "small houses and bungalows suitable for the peak district" does exactly what "The Villa Jones" recommends, that is "print, publish & post" a "proposed portfolio of designs" (*Small Houses* 1) produced by an advisory panel made up of architects. The pamphlet's description of the advisory panel's role exactly mirrors the one imagined in "The Villa Jones": "ADVISORY PANELS were set up […] for the purpose of assisting builders, local authorities and the general public, chiefly by means of free advice on the appearance of houses in country districts" (*Small Houses* 1).

The colour and grouping of new buildings, which preoccupy "The Villa Jones," also concern Abercrombie and Nash. "The colour question," Abercrombie writes, "is not an easy one; it is by no means always the case that a retiring colour is the best, as witness the gleaming white Welsh cottage. But there is such a thing as good colour and bad colour, appropriate and inappropriate" (197). Cornish recommends "the maintenance of quiet tone and colour in rural architecture so that the new building shall take its place unobtrusively amidst natural features" (13). Woolf's letter writer agrees, suggesting that "[o]f all colours, red & white are the most antipathetic to the <natural colour> greens & browns & greys of the fields."

These parallels with Abercrombie's and Nash's recommendations and its alignment with CPRE principles encourage us to reflect on the politics of "The Villa Jones." Contrary to what we might expect, the political allegiances of the CPRE tended to be left of center. As Matless has argued, they self-identified as both a progressive and modern organization. For the CPRE, "preservation entailed not a conservative protection of the old against the new but an attempt to plan a landscape simultaneously modern and traditional under the guidance of an expert public authority" (Matless 25). It is easy to see how such an agenda would bring the CPRE into conflict with conservative *laissez faire* principles and Matless has pointed out that its emphasis on planning and the productive interaction of urban and rural contrasted starkly with Stanley Baldwin's conservative ruralism (30). Woolf's letter, with its investment in expert panels and state intervention, aligns itself with this progressive arm of the preservation movement. The writer's view-taxation scheme is remarkably close to a recommendation made by Abercrombie and does not sound like one that would have gone down at all well with the landed interests. Woolf writes in 1931: "Taxes are {everywhere}: Why not tax the view values of all new houses; & {tax those} who build & let the villagers [access/assess] the tax." Abercrombie would suggest later in 1933: "when land is ripe for development and is to be sold by the owner for building it must pay a betterment tax" (210).

The play on CPRE rhetoric we find in "The Villa Jones" allows Woolf to experiment with voice and move between registers. This is evident in the way her letter-writer veers between the rational, even-handed tone of Abercrombie and Nash and the extravagant style of preservationists such as Clough Williams-Ellis. The judicious voice that recommends an expert panel of architects and who cautions against any nostalgic, anti-modern sentiments—"{Now} it is [futile] to sit down in London & lament the spread of {a} population, cheap motorcars, the growth of a week end clan. These things have to be"—rehearses the proactive arguments of Abercrombie in his own reasonable voice. By contrast, the voice that emerges as the sketch moves on to discuss Jones and other "voluntary view spoilers" relies on the same bombastic language found in Williams-Ellis's 1928 diatribe *England and the Octopus*.

Williams-Ellis was among a number of CPRE members who were also identified with the Labour Party, and in *England and the Octopus* his left-wing politics are reflected in his stance on rural preservation. In this book Williams-Ellis reiterates the standard CPRE line on the need for planning to prevent the further "disfigurement" of the countryside. But he reserves a special animus for exploitative speculators and declares his political and aesthetic preference for council rather than private housing projects (121-2). Williams-Ellis's condemnation of speculators is made in language that reminds us of "The Villa Jones": "Pure and whole-hearted diabolists are as rare in aesthetics as in morals, but that there are those who will still defy their consciences for the sake of personal gain—in any place and at any time—is incontestable" (19). The grand intertwining of moral and aesthetic crimes here is striking, as is the prominent place "conscience" occupies. The writer of "The Villa Jones" riffs on a similar theme when she suggests "the Jones' are impervious—it goes without saying—to other people's feelings. {W} Could we not therefore hurt Jones where {also} he is vulnerable. In his pocket?"

Woolf's shorthand of "voluntary view spoilers" and her comparison of Jones to a "robber" and a "murderer" recall the "pure and wholehearted diabolists" of Williams-Ellis's book. However, *England and the Octopus* suggests itself as an intertext for "The Villa Jones" most strikingly because it also includes a character called Jones. Like Woolf, Williams-Ellis uses the Joneses as an archetype:

> As the Joneses fly from the town, so does the country fly from the pink bungalow they have perched so hopefully on its eligible site. The true countryman will know that the area is infected – the Joneses have brought the blight of their town or suburb with them – and in all probability they and their home will be followed by an incursion of like-minded people similarly housed, and the country will be found to have further withdrawn itself beyond the skyline in its losing retreat towards the sea. (40)

The Joneses of *England and the Octopus* cut rather more pathetic figures than their relatives in "The Villa Jones," who have more in common with the diabolical speculators of Williams-Ellis's imagination. Their suburban roots and their hopeful "pink bungalow" code these Joneses as aspirational lower-middle class. Woolf's Joneses, with their motorcar, are more well-to-do. Consequently, Williams-Ellis's recommendations for dealing with his Joneses are less extreme than Woolf's; an effort must be made to "make town life not merely tolerable but attractive – and also to show how one may in very truth genuinely escape to and live in real country without offence and without thereby trampling underfoot and annihilating the very things that are so justly desired and so valiantly sought" (40).

"The Villa Jones" is steeped in the discourses of rural preservation; this is clear not only in the specific recommendations it makes but also the language Woolf uses to make them. On first reading, its account of a countryside "spoilt" by "weekenders" and "motor-cars" appears characterized by anti-modern nostalgia. "The Villa Jones" certainly reproduces familiar snobbish assumptions—witness the feckless builders and brash middle classes. However, the writer's contempt for Jones and her concern for "the villagers" also registers CPRE suspicion of speculators and the private housing boom. Ross McKibbin has suggested that this housing model was widely identified at the time as a way of undermining support for left-wing politics: "private housing of the villa-garden type was thought to turn people away from 'socialism'" (77). "The Villa Jones" is marked by an awareness of this too. The writer's horror at Jones's imperviousness to community feeling and his disregard for his neighbors and her persistent references to "selfishness" reveal an anxiety about the relationship between the individual and the community. In the last few lines of "The Villa Jones" there is stark evidence of the ambivalence that characterized Woolf's attitudes to practical politics. A deleted passage recommends that at the general election "let {all} lovers of his {kind refuse to vote}." It is interesting that this first instinct toward non-participation is suppressed. The writer's presentation of the general election as an opportunity for people to ask their candidates "not only" for their views on the economy but to lobby for greater awareness of irresponsible building in rural areas shows instead a readiness to engage with the political system.

This gesture to the value of representational politics at the close of the letter serves as an imaginative link with the so-called "Cook Sketch." In that sketch Woolf's cook muses on Ramsay MacDonald's betrayal of labor and asks: "What the government is for if it isn't to protect us working classes I don't know." These Morgan Library drafts show Woolf thinking hard about political representation and in both it is difficult to separate these political concerns from Woolf's aesthetic decisions. Woolf's allegiance to CPRE principles allowed her to test her ear and try out new voices. The epistolary form of "The Villa Jones" is also significant, although it remained an unsent letter. It is both a performative and participatory form—the heightened sense of being addressed we experience when reading the letter-essay make it an ideal form for polemic writing and, as such, it was a politically apposite form for Woolf. It was for practical as well as aesthetic reasons she turned to it throughout the 1930s, in the "Introductory Letter" to *Life As We Have Known It*, "The Villa Jones," "Middlebrow" and, most famously, *Three Guineas*, in order to probe the questions about class, culture, community and political action that are so integral to Woolf's thinking in this period.

My thanks to the Society of Authors as the Literary Representative of the Estates of Virginia Woolf and Leonard Woolf for permission to include a transcription of "The Villa Jones" and a facsimile of the manuscript, and to quote from Leonard Woolf's unpublished letter to Ramsay MacDonald.
I am grateful to Michèle Barrett for her feedback on drafts of this article, and I am indebted to both Anna Snaith and Mark Hussey for their advice on the transcription of the letter.

Works Cited

Abercrombie, Patrick. *Town and Country Planning*. 1933. London: Oxford UP, 1959. Print.
Burchardt, Jeremy. *Paradise Lost: Rural Idyll and Social Change Since 1800*. London: I. B. Tauris, 2002. Print.
Cornish, Vaughan. *The Scenery of England: A Study of Harmonious Grouping in Town and Country*. London: Council for the Preservation of Rural England, 1932. Print.
Leonard Woolf Papers, LW to Ramsay MacDonald 3 January 1930, Neighbours Property, SxMs-13/2/1/4/A. The Keep, Sussex.
Hussey, Mark. "*I'd Make it Penal*." The Rural Preservation Movement in Virginia Woolf's Between the Acts. London: Cecil Woolf, 2011. Print.
Jones, Clara. "Virginia Woolf's 1931 'Cook Sketch'." *Woolf Studies Annual* 20 (2014): 1-25.
Kore-Schröder, Leena. "'Reflections in a Motor Car': Virginia Woolf's Phenomenological Relations of Time and Space." *Locating Woolf: The Politics of Space and Place*. Ed. Anna Snaith and Michael H. Whitworth. Basingstoke: Palgrave, 2007. 131-47. Print.
Light, Alison. *Mrs Woolf and the Servants*. London: Penguin, 2007. Print.
Lowerson, John. "Battles for the Countryside." *Class, Culture and Social Change: A New View of the 1930s*. Ed. Frank Gloversmith. Brighton: Harvester, 1980. Print.
McKibbin, Ross. *Classes and Cultures: England, 1918-1951*. Oxford: Oxford UP, 1998. Print.
Matless, David. *Landscape and Englishness*. London: Reaktion, 1998. Print.
Miller, Simon. "Urban Dreams and Rural Reality: Land and Landscape in English Culture, 1920-1945." *Rural History* 6.1(1995): 89-102. Print.
Small Houses and Bungalows Suitable for the Peak District. Sheffield: Council for the Preservation of Rural England, Sheffield and Peak District Branch, 1930? Print.
Sparks, Elisa Kay. "Woolf on the Downs." *Virginia Woolf Miscellany* 81 (2012): 20-22.
Williams-Ellis, Clough. *England and the Octopus*. 1928. Portmeirion: Golden Dragon, 1975. Print.
Woolf, Virginia. *Between the Acts*. With introduction and notes by Gillian Beer. London: Penguin, 2000.
——. *The Diary of Virginia Woolf*. Ed. Anne Olivier Bell. Volume Four, 1931-1935. New York: Harcourt Brace Jovanovich, 1982. Print.

——. *The Essays of Virginia Woolf.* Volume Five. 1929-1932. Ed. Stuart N. Clarke. London: Hogarth, 2009. Print.

——.*The Diary of Virginia Woolf.* Ed. Anne Olivier Bell. Volume Five, 1936-1941. New York: Harcourt Brace Jovanovich, 1984. Print.

——. "Middlebrow." *The Death of the Moth and Other Essays*. London: Hogarth, 1942. Print.

——. "Street Haunting: A London Adventure." *The Death of the Moth and Other Essays*. London: Hogarth, 1942. Print.

——. *The Years*. With an introduction and notes by Jeri Johnson. London: Penguin, 1992. Print.

"THE VILLA JONES"

Transcription: "The Villa Jones"

Letter to a Young Poet: Autograph Manuscript, 1931 Sept. 24, Morgan Library and Museum (MA3333) ff. 3-5

Symbols used in transcription:

{word} cancelled word or phrase
<word> interlinear or marginal insertion
 [word] uncertain transcription
? illegible

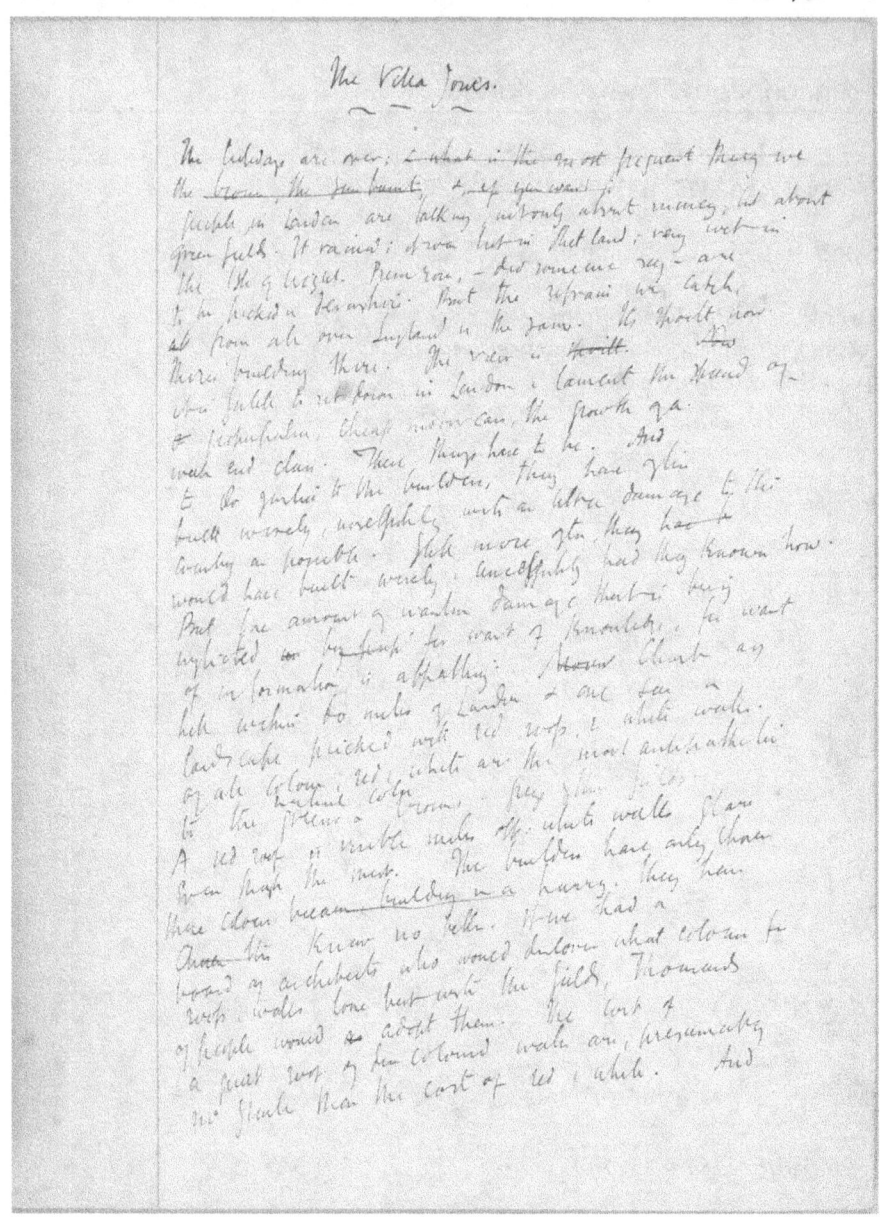

Letter to a young poet: Autograph manuscript, 1931 Sept. 24. p. 3.
The Pierpont Morgan Library, New York. MA 3333. Purchased on the Fellows Fund with the special assistance of Miss Anne S. Dayton, Mrs. Enid A. Haupt, Mrs. James H. Ripley, Mr. and Mrs. August H. Schilling, and Mr. John S. Thacher, 1979. Photographic credit: The Pierpont Morgan Library, New York.

f. 3
The Villa Jones.

The holidays are over; {& what is the most frequent thing we the brown, the sunburnt, &, if you want to} people, in London are talking, not only about money; but about green fields. It rained; it was hot in Shetland; very wet in the Isle of Wight. [Primrose] – did someone say – are to be picked in devonshire. But the refrain we catch, {at} from all over England is the same. Its spoilt now. There's building there. The view is {spoilt}. {Now} it is [futile] to sit down in London & lament the spread of {a} population,[8] cheap motorcars,[9] the growth of a week end clan.[10] These things have to be. And to do justice to the builders, they have [often] built wisely, usefully with as little damage to [the] country as possible. Still more often, they {have to} would have built wisely & usefully had they known how. But the amount of wanton damage that is being inflicted {on by people} for want of knowledge, for want of information, is appalling: {Mount} Climb any hill within 60 miles of London & one sees a landscape pricked with red roofs, & white walls. Of all colours, red & white are the most antipathetic to the <natural colour> greens & browns & greys of the fields. A red roof is visible miles off: white walls glare even through the mist. The builders have only chosen these colours because {, building in a} hurry, they have {chosen this} know no better. If we had a board of architects who would discover what colours for roofs,

---

[8] The period between the wars saw marked demographic shifts with many urban dwellers moving into newly created suburbs. Jeremy Burchardt notes that "the most intense phase of suburban growth was during the interwar years" (89).
[9] This is something of an exaggeration. Although car ownership among the middle class increased steadily during the interwar period, it was by no means "cheap" to own and run a car. See Sue Bowden, "The New Consumerism," in *Twentieth-Century Britain: Economic, Social and Cultural Change*, ed. Paul Johnson (Harlow: Longman, 1994), 244-45. The Woolfs purchased their first car, a second-hand Singer, in 1927 (Lee 508-09).
[10] Private motor-cars and communal charabancs made the countryside newly accessible to the urban middle and working class and weekend excursions became increasingly popular in the interwar period (Matless 63). Woolf might also be referring to those who, like she and Leonard, rented or owned two properties, one in the town and the other in the country, and weekended in the countryside.

Letter to a young poet: Autograph manuscript, 1931 Sept. 24. p. 4.
The Pierpont Morgan Library, New York. MA 3333. Purchased on the Fellows Fund with the special assistance of Miss Anne S. Dayton, Mrs. Enid A. Haupt, Mrs. James H. Ripley, Mr. and Mrs. August H. Schilling, and Mr. John S. Thacher, 1979. Photographic credit: The Pierpont Morgan Library, New York.

f. 4

most of the new builders {are} are concerned with sanitation & comfort[11] & have no wish to do more harm than they must do by building on land which was once a field. Let our experts decide: & let their decision be printed, published & posted in all places where building is in progress. The unselfish builders will surely take the hint. But there is a second class, which is far more destructive, difficult to deal with. These are the voluntary view spoilers. {There are ? now, all round London} All round London {there are} hills & downs {which} are being sold: {for building for building: A class of} without [restriction]. In every part of the country {if you are selfish} enough you can secure a splendid view for your own home if you are so selfish as to spoil for ever the views of your neighbours. And {One goes to climb a hill} {One} In every part of the country one is going for a walk to see a view, & finding instead the Villa Jones. Jones – he may be ? or [Plantagenet] for anything I know – could have bought a {h} site on the road, in the valley, with other [careful] builders. But no – Jones has planted himself on the very top of the Down. Where one once saw ? , plough land one now [sees ? sham],[12] Jones at dinner, Jones' [pig ?], Jones's motor car: if the [corner/women] of the countryside [could] [appeal] ? [let us] ? Jones that he [says] then. Let us inform him that we never pass his villa without [heaping maledictions] on him & all his progeny: that {what we do} that we consider Jones who has spoilt ten miles of the view for us no better than a robber, a murderer,[13] & a hater of his kind. But the Jones' are impervious – it goes without saying – to other people's feelings. {W} Could

---

[11] In 1931 the Woolfs improved the "sanitation & comfort" of Monk's House by having it electrified and fitted with "electric fires in the bedrooms and a Frigidaire in the kitchen." Victoria Rosner, "Virginia Woolf and Monk's House," in *The Edinburgh Companion to Virginia Woolf and the Arts*, ed. Maggie Humm (Edinburgh: Edinburgh University Press, 2010), p. 184.

[12] Although I am uncertain that "sham" is correct here there are a number of things that suggest this transcription. "Shamness," Matless notes, "was the final term of abuse" (49) for new buildings that aspired to an old world authenticity in their design. Mock-Tudor and imitation Georgian houses were particularly distressing to the CPRE. Woolf also makes conspicuous and repeated use of this word in "Middlebrow." Her middlebrow's taste for expensive "sham antiques" (118) is a symptom of their aesthetic illiteracy equivalent to their preference for "red brick villas."

[13] In Woolf's final novel *Between the Acts*, the "megaphonic, anonymous" voice that scolds the audience of Miss La Trobe's pageant during its final act, imitates local objections to new buildings as part of its reproach: "*Consider the gun slayers, bomb droppers here or there. They do openly what we do slyly. Take for example* (here the megaphone adopted a colloquial, conversational tone) *Mr. M's bungalow. A view spoilt for ever. That's murder . . .*" (111).

Letter to a young poet: Autograph manuscript, 1931 Sept. 24. p. 5.
The Pierpont Morgan Library, New York. MA 3333. Purchased on the Fellows Fund with the special assistance of Miss Anne S. Dayton, Mrs. Enid A. Haupt, Mrs. James H. Ripley, Mr. and Mrs. August H. Schilling, and Mr. John S. Thacher, 1979. Photographic credit: The Pierpont Morgan Library, New York.

f. 5

we not therefore hurt Jones where [also] he is vulnerable. In his pocket? Taxes are {everywhere}: Why not tax the view values of all new houses; & {tax those} who build & let the villagers [access/assess] the tax. For [assuredly] the villagers are going to suffer. The rich are not going to come to the country in order to see the Villa Jones. {The week enders, the} where they used to see [gulls] {& the sea} <?>. Before the {elec} And at the general election let {all} lovers of his {kind refuse to vote} ask their candidate where he {whether he is} not only what are your views upon the dole, the gold standard[14] no: but where do you live? Have you spoilt a view?

yours

---

[14] Woolf is referring to the general election held on 27 October 1931 which resulted in a landslide victory for the majority Conservative National Government, formed by Ramsay MacDonald in August after his Labour cabinet failed to support his proposed budget cuts to deal with the depression. A cut to unemployment benefits was the proposal that MacDonald's Labour cabinet found most difficult to stomach and the "dole" remained a significant political issue. In its early weeks in September 1931 the new National Government went off the gold standard, much to the upset of the City. *A Short History of the Labour Party*, ed. Alastair J. Reid and Henry Pelling (Basingstoke: Palgrave, 2005), 58-63.

Guide to Library Special Collections

This list includes updates or changes received in 2015.

Name of Collection: The Beinecke Rare Book and Manuscript Library

Contact: Kevin Repp, Curator of Modern Books and Manuscripts
Nancy Kuhl, Curator of American Literature

Address: Yale University Library
P.O. Box 208240
New Haven, CT 06520-8240

URL: http://beinecke.library.yale.edu/

Access Requirements: Registration required at first visit

Holdings Relevant To Woolf: General Collection includes autograph manuscript of "Notes on Oliver Goldsmith." Comments on Edward Gibbon, William Beckford Collection. Letters from Virginia Woolf in the Bryher Papers, the Louise Morgan and Otto Theis Papers, and the Rebecca West Papers. Related material: 41 letters from Vita Sackville-West to Violet Trefusis; files relating to Robert Manson Myers's From Beowulf to Virginia Woolf in the Edmond Pauker Papers.

Yale Collection of American Literature includes typewritten manuscripts of "The Art of Walter Sickert," "Augustine Birrell," "Aurora Leigh," "How Should One Read a Book?" "Letter to a Young Poet," "The Novels of Turgenev," "Street Haunting." Dial/Scofield Thayer Papers: manuscripts of "The Lives of the Obscure," "Miss Ormerod," and "Mrs. Dalloway in Bond Street." Letters from Virginia Woolf in the William Rose Benet Papers, the Benet Family Correspondence, Henry Seidel Canby Papers, the Seward Collins Papers, the Dial/Scofield Thayer Papers, and the Yale Review archive. Material relating to translations of Woolf in the Thornton Wilder papers. Related material: Clive Bell, "Virginia Woolf" (Dial/Scofield Thayer Papers); 43 letters from Leonard Woolf to Helen McAfee (Yale Review); 11 letters from Leonard Woolf to Gertrude Stein.

Name of Collection: The Henry W. and Albert A. Berg Collection of English and American Literature

Contact: berg@nypl.org for access procedures
Isaac Gewirtz, Curator
isaacgewirtz@nypl.org

Address: New York Public Library, Room 320
Fifth Avenue & 42nd Street
New York, NY 10018

Telephone: 212-930-0802
Fax: 212-930-0079
Email: isaacgewirtz@nypl.org

Hours: Tue.–Wed.: 11 am–6:45 pm
Thu.–Sat.: 10 am–5:45 pm
Closed Sun., Mon., and Legal Holidays

Access Requirements: After acquiring Library card in room 315, check outerwear and all containers (briefcases, computer cases, handbags, folders, etc.) in Ground Floor cloakroom, and proceed to the Berg Collection. Traceable and photo identification required. Undergraduates working on honors theses need letter from faculty advisor to be sent to the Berg's Curator and to receive an affirmative response prior to scheduling an appointment with the Berg librarians. No books may be brought to the reading tables, including notebooks.

Restrictions: Virginia Woolf's bound MSS, because of their fragile condition, are made available on microfilm and CD. URL for Berg finding aid:

GUIDE TO LIBRARY SPECIAL COLLECTIONS 99

http://www.nypl.org/research/manuscripts/berg/brgwoolf.xml. N.B. All the Berg's Woolf MSS are on microfilm and 90 percent of them on CD published by Research Publications and available at many research libraries.

Holdings Relevant To Woolf: Manuscripts/typescripts of all of the novels except *Orlando*, including: *Between the Acts, Flush, Jacob's Room, Mrs. Dalloway* (notes and fragments), *Night and Day, To the Lighthouse, The Voyage Out, The Waves, The Years*; 12 notebooks of articles, essays, fiction and reviews, 1924–1940; 36 volumes of diaries; 26 volumes of reading notes; correspondence with Vanessa Bell, Ethel Smyth, Vita Sackville-West and others. Su Hua Ling Chen's Bloomsbury correspondence.

Recent Acquisitions: Proof copy of *A Room of One's Own* (July 1929); ALS Vanessa Bell to Vita Sackville-West, April 29, 1941 [in Marler, *Selected Letters* 478-80]; Frank Dean, *Strike While the Iron's Hot: Frank Dean's Life as a Blacksmith and Farrier in Rodmell*, ed. Susan Rowland (S. Rowland, 1994) [includes map, accounts of search for VW's body and of her funeral]; Vita Sackville-West, *Marian Stranways*, autograph manuscript, [1913].

Name of Collection: The British Library Manuscript Collections

Contact: Manuscripts and Maps Reference Team

Address: 96 Euston Road
London NW1 2DB
England

Telephone: 0207-412-7513
Fax: 0207-412-7745
Email: mss@bl.uk

Hours: Mon.: 10 am–5 pm; Tues.–Sat.: 9:30 am–5 pm

Access Requirements: British Library Reader Pass (signed I.D. required and usually proof of post-graduate academic status, or other demonstrable need to use the collections—see www.bl.uk). In addition, access to most literary autograph material only available with letter of recommendation.

Restrictions: Paper Copies, Microfilms, and Photography of selected items available upon receipt of written authorization for photo duplication from the copyright holder.

Holdings Relevant To Woolf: *Diaries* 1930–1931 (microfilm); *Mrs. Dalloway* and other writings (1923–1925) three volumes (Add MS 51044-51046); letter from Leonard Woolf to H. G. Wells (1941) (Add MS 52553); two letters from Virginia Woolf and three letters from Leonard Woolf to John Lehmann (1941) (Add MS 56234); letters from Virginia Woolf (1923-1927) and one written on behalf of Leonard Woolf to S. S. Koteliansky (1946) (Add MS 48974); notebook of Virginia Stephen (1906–1909) (Add MS 61837); Stephen family papers (Add MS 88954); travel and literary notebook of Virginia Woolf (Add MS 61837); A sketch of the past revised ts (1940) (Add MS 61973); letters from Virginia Woolf in the correspondence files of Lytton and James Strachey (Add MS 60655-60734); letter from Virginia Woolf to Mildred Massingberd (Add MS 61891); letter from Virginia Woolf to Harriet Shaw Weaver(1917) (Add MS 57353); (in the same volume as the letter on behalf of Leonard); letter from Virginia Woolf to Frances Cornford (1929) (Add MS 58422); letter from Virginia Woolf to Ernest Rhys (1930) (Egerton MS 3248); correspondence of Virginia Woolf in the Society of Authors archive (1934–1937) (Add MS 63206-63463); letter and postcard from Virginia Woolf to Bernard Shaw (1940) (Add MS 50522); three letters (suicide notes) from Virginia Woolf (1941)

GUIDE TO LIBRARY SPECIAL COLLECTIONS 101

(Add MS 57947). "Hyde Park Gate News" 1891–1892, 1895 (Add. MSS 70725, 70726). Letters of Virginia and Leonard Woolf to Lady Aberconway, 1927–1941 (Add MS 70775). Letters from Virginia Woolf to Macmillan Co. 1903, 1908 (Add MS 54786-56035). Collection of RPs ("reserved photocopies"– copies of manuscripts exported, some subject to restrictions).

Name of Collection: Harry Ransom Center

Contact: Head, Research Services

Address: Harry Ransom Center
The University of Texas at Austin
P.O. Box 7219
Austin, TX 78713-7219

Telephone: 512-471-9119
Fax: 512-471-2899
Email: reference@hrc.utexas.edu

Hours: See web site for most current information: www.hrc.utexas.edu

Access Requirements: Completed online research application; current photo identification

Holdings Relevant To Woolf: The manuscript collection includes the typed manuscript with autograph revisions of *Kew Gardens*, and the typed manuscript and autograph revisions of "Thoughts on Peace in an Air Raid." The Center holds 571 of Woolf's letters, including correspondence to Elizabeth Bowen, Lady Ottoline Morrell, Mary Hutchinson, William Plomer, Hugh Walpole and others. Further mss. relating to Virginia Woolf include letters to her from T. S. Eliot and reviews of her work. A substantial collection of the first British and American editions of Woolf's published works, as well as 130 volumes from

Leonard and Virginia Woolf's library and a collection of books published by the Hogarth Press, is also housed.

An art collection holds a landscape painting of Virginia's garden and a series of Cockney cartoons in a sketch book, signed "V.W." The center also has extensive holdings of materials related to Leonard Woolf, Ottoline Morrell, Mary Hutchinson, Lytton Strachey, Dora Carrington, E. M. Forster, Clive Bell, Roger Fry, Vanessa Bell, Bertrand Russell, Elizabeth Bowen, William Plomer, Stephen Spender and Hugh Walpole.

Name of Collection: Monks House Papers/Leonard Woolf Papers/Charleston Papers/Nicolson Papers

Contact: University of Sussex, Special Collections

Address: The Keep
Woollards Way
Brighton & Hove
BN1 9PB

Telephone: 01273 482349
Email: library.specialcoll@sussex.ac.uk
URL: http://www.thekeep.info

Access Requirements: By appointment. Identification to be presented on arrival. Registration and material requests should be made through our website.

Restrictions: Photocopying strictly controlled

Holdings Relevant To Woolf: The University of Sussex holds two large archives relating to Leonard and Virginia Woolf: The Monks House Papers, primarily correspondence and MSS of Virginia Woolf, including the three scrapbooks relating to *Three Guineas*, and Virginia Woolf's engagement diaries from 1930 to her death in 1941;

and The Leonard Woolf Papers, primarily correspondence and other papers of Leonard Woolf. (Monks House Papers are available on microfilm in many research libraries.) The Charleston Papers consist in the main of letters written to or by Clive and Vanessa Bell and Duncan Grant which had accumulated in their home; the library houses Quentin Bell's photocopied set; letters from Roger Fry, Maynard Keynes, Lytton Strachey, Virginia Woolf, Vita Sackville-West, E. M. Forster, T. S. Eliot, Frances Partridge and others. The Maria Jackson letters comprise some 900 letters from Maria Jackson to Julia and Leslie Stephen. The Nicolson Papers complement these three Sussex archives relating to the Bloomsbury Group, and consist of Nigel Nicolson's correspondence relating to his editorial work as principal editor of the six-volume *Letters of Virginia Woolf*, published between 1975 and 1980.

The Bell Papers. A. O. Bell's correspondence relating to her editorial work on Virginia Woolf's diaries, a parallel collection to the Nicolson Papers. Collection level description may be accessed at www.archiveshub.ac.uk

Name of Collection: The Lilly Library

Contact: Joel Silver, Director
Cherry Williams, Curator of Manuscripts

Address: The Lilly Library, Indiana University
1200 East Seventh Street
Bloomington, IN 47405-5500

Telephone: 812-855-2452
Fax: 812-855-3143
Email: liblilly@indiana.edu, silverj@indiana.edu, chedwill@indiana.edu

Hours:	Mon.–Fri. 9 am–6 pm; Sat. 9 am–1 pm; *Closed Sundays and Major Holidays*
Access Requirements:	Valid photo-identification; brief registration procedure
Restrictions:	Closed stacks; material use confined to reading room; wheelchair-accessible reading room and exhibitions (but no wheelchair-accessible restroom)
Holdings Relevant To Woolf:	Corrected page proofs for the American edition of *Mrs. Dalloway*; letters to Woolf from Desmond and Mary (Molly) MacCarthy; 77 letters (published in *Letters*) from Woolf to correspondents including Donald Clifford Brace, Robert Gathorne-Hardy, Barbara (Strachey) Halpern, Richard Arthur Warren Hughes, Desmond MacCarthy and Molly MacCarthy; "Preliminary Scheme for the formation of a Partnership between Mr Leonard Sidney Woolf and Mr John Lehmann to take over The Hogarth Press" (includes contract signed by Lehmann, Leonard Woolf, and Virginia Woolf and receipt for Lehmann's payment to Virginia Woolf to purchase Virginia Woolf's share in the Hogarth Press); photographs of Virginia Woolf, Leonard Woolf, Lytton Strachey, Strachey family, Roger Fry, and Vanessa Bell (Hannah Whitall Smith mss.); (Richard) Kennedy mss. (four hand-colored lithographs of Virginia Woolf: artist's proofs for RK's portfolio, VIRGINIA WOOLF: "AS I KNEW HER"; Sackville-West, V. mss. (10,529 items: includes the correspondence of Vita Sackville-West, and Harold Nicolson); MacCarthy mss. (ca. 10,000 items: papers of Desmond and Molly MacCarthy); correspondence between LW and Mary Gaither regarding publication of *A Checklist of the Hogarth Press* (1976, repr. 1986); Todd Avery, *Close and Affectionate Friends: Desmond and Molly MacCarthy and the Bloomsbury Group* (The Lilly Library/Indiana University Libraries, 1999).

GUIDE TO LIBRARY SPECIAL COLLECTIONS 105

Name of Collection: The Morgan Library & Museum

Contact: Reading Room

Address: 225 Madison Avenue
New York, NY 10016

Telephone: 212-590-0315
Email: readingroom@themorgan.org
URL: www.themorgan.org

Access Requirements: Admission to the Reading Room is by application and by appointment. See www.themorgan.org/research/reading.asp for application form.

Holdings Relevant To Woolf: Virginia Woolf. Autograph manuscript notebook, 1931 Sept. 24. 1 item (52 p.); 265 x 208 mm. Contains drafts of "A Letter to a Young Poet," a brief letter to the press entitled "The Villa Jones" [ff. 3–5] and a monologue by a working-class woman [ff. 44–46]. MA 3333. Purchased on the Fellows Fund with the special assistance of Anne S. Dayton, Enid A. Haupt, Mrs. James H. Ripley, Mr. and Mrs. August H. Schilling, and John S. Thacher, 1979.

Virginia Woolf. Autograph letters signed (2) and typed letter signed, dated London [etc.], to E. McKnight Kauffer, 1931 Apr. 4–23, and undated. 3 items (4 p.). Concerning a drawing of her and a bibliography of her works. MA 1679. Purchased in 1959.

Vanessa Bell. 84 autograph letters, 3 typed letters, 7 postcards, and 3 telegrams. Most, but not all, are written by Vanessa Bell to John Maynard Keynes. Concerning Duncan Grant, Roger Fry, Clive Bell, the Bell children, Leonard and Virginia Woolf, Lytton Strachey, John Maynard and Lydia Lopokova Keynes, David Garnett, Ottoline

Morrell, and others. MA 3448. Items in this collection are described in 97 individual records (MA 3448.1-97). Purchased on the Fellows Fund, special gift of the Gramercy Park Foundation (Mrs. Michael Tucker), 1980.

Name of Collection: 1. Katherine Mansfield Papers
2. Arts Club of Chicago Papers

Contact: Martha Briggs, Lloyd Lewis Curator of Modern Manuscripts

Liesl Olson, Director, Scholl Center for American History and Culture

Address: The Newberry Library, 60 West Walton Street, Chicago, IL, 60610

Telephone: 312-255-3554 (Briggs)
312-255-3665 (Olson)

Email: briggsm@newberry.org
olsonl@newberry.org

Hours: Tues.-Fri.: 9am–5pm; Sat.: 9am–1pm

Access Requirements: The Newberry's reading rooms are open to researchers who are at least 16 years old or juniors in high school. Before using the collections, all researchers must apply for and receive a reader's card. Issued in the Reference Center on the third floor, cards require a valid photo ID, proof of current home address, and a research interest that is supported by the Newberry's collections.

Holdings Relevant To Woolf: The papers of the Arts Club of Chicago—since 1916, a private club and preeminent exhibitor of international art—contain material related to Bloomsbury artists and how they were received in Chicago. The papers of Katherine Mansfield contain manu-

GUIDE TO LIBRARY SPECIAL COLLECTIONS 107

script copies of some of Mansfield's important work, and outgoing correspondence—the bulk to artist Dorothy Brett and Lady Ottoline Morrell. There are a few incoming miscellaneous letters, printed works, photographs and memorabilia.

Name of Collection: University of Reading Special Collections

Contact: Special Collections Service

Address: Special Collections Service
University of Reading
Redlands Road
Reading RG1 5EX

Telephone: 0118-378-8660
Fax: 0118-378-5632
Email: specialcollections@reading.ac.uk
URL: http://www.reading.ac.uk/special-collections/

Access Requirements: Prior appointment suggested to consult material; Permission required to consult or copy material in the Hogarth Press, Jonathan Cape, and Chatto & Windus collections from Random House:

Random House Group Archive & Library
1 Cole Street
Crown Park
Rushden
Northants. NN10 6RZ

rushdenqueries@randomhouse.co.uk

Holdings Relevant To Woolf: Hogarth Press (MS 2750): editorial and production correspondence relating to publications of the Press including Woolf's own titles. Production ledgers 1920s–1950s. Correspondence between Leonard Woolf and Stanley Unwin about progress with his collected edition of the works of Freud. Order books – e.g. lists of booksellers, book clubs and how many books they have ordered for a particular title. Newscuttings—press clippings of advertisements for Hogarth Press books including Virginia Woolf publications.

Chatto & Windus (CW): small number of letters 1915–1925; 1929–1931.Various letters and notes by Leonard Woolf; outgoing letters to Leonard Woolf: 22 November 1927 (CW A/119); outgoing letters to Virginia Woolf: 29 January 1936 (CW A/172), 22 December 1931 (CW A/135), 31 December 1931 (CW A/135), 15 December 1920 (CW A/100), 20 December 1920 (CW A/100).

George Bell & Sons (MS 1640): 5 letters from Leonard Woolf 1930–1966.

Routledge (RKP): Reader's report by Leonard Woolf on George Padmore's "Britannia rules the blacks" (1935); "How Britain rules Africa." 1 letter from Leonard Woolf (June 1941) from Miscellaneous publishing correspondence 1941-1942 Wi-Wy RKP 174/15. Draft introduction by Leonard Woolf to *Letters on India* by Mulk Raj Anand (1942) and 1 letter to Leonard Woolf from Mulk Raj Anand 1942-1943 RKP 178/3. Correspondence concerning the publication of *The War for Peace* by Leonard Woolf, 1939-1940 RKP 160/5. 1 letter from Virginia Woolf declining an invitation from Routledge to write a biography of Margaret Bondfield, 25 May 1940 RKP 160/5.

Megroz (MS 1979/68): 2 letters from Leonard Woolf, 1926.

Allen & Unwin (MS 3282): Correspondence with Leonard Woolf c.1914-1918 (re. his book *International Government*), 1923-1924; 1939-1940; 1943; 1946; 1950-1951; 1953; 1965 (concerning ill-founded rumors about the Hogarth

Press); 1967 (concerning a reprint of *Empire and Commerce in Africa*).

Jonathan Cape (MS 2446): All correspondence from file JC A43. Correspondence between Jonathan Cape and Virginia Woolf and Cape and A. C. Gissing concerning Virginia Woolf's introduction to George Gissing's *Ionian Sea* to which A. C. Gissing objects. 1 postcard (1935), 1 letter (1933), 2 letters (1932) from Virginia Woolf. 1 letter (1932) from Virginia Woolf declining to write an introduction to Jane Austen's *Northanger Abbey*. 4 letters (1931) from Virginia Woolf declining to write an introduction to one of Miss Thackeray's books.

Letters from Vanessa Bell: 1 letter from Bell CW 152/2; 1 letter from Bell CW 171/10; 2 letters from Bell CW 578/1; 1 letter from Bell CW 59/9; 1 letter from Bell (1936) CW 61/10. Artwork by Vanessa Bell for various Virginia Woolf titles.

Artwork by Angelica Garnett, Philippa Bramson and others for various books in the Chatto & Windus archive.

Name of Collection: Frances Hooper Collection of Virginia Woolf Books and Manuscripts.
Elizabeth Power Richardson Bloomsbury Iconography Collection.

Contact: Karen V. Kukil, Associate Curator of Special Collections.

Address: Mortimer Rare Book Room
William Allan Neilson Library
Smith College
7 Neilson Drive
Northampton, MA 01063

Telephone: 413-585-2908
Fax: 413-585-2904
Email: kkukil@smith.edu
URL: www.smith.edu/libraries/libs/rarebook

Hours: Mon.–Fri.: 9 am–5 pm

Access Requirements: Appointment to be made with the Curator

Holdings Relevant To Woolf: The Hooper Collection emphasizes Woolf as an essayist but also includes many Hogarth Press first editions, limited editions of Woolf's works, and translations. The collection includes page proofs of *Orlando*, *To the Lighthouse*, and *The Common Reader*, corrected by Woolf for the first American editions, a proof copy of *The Waves* that Woolf inscribed to Hugh Walpole, and the proof copies of *The Years* and of *Flush*. The Collection also has one of the deluxe editions of *Orlando* that was printed on green paper. Other items include twenty-two pages of reading notes from 1926, three pages of notes on D. H. Lawrence's *Sons and Lovers*, thirty-three pages of notes for *Roger Fry*, a six-page ms. "As to criticism," a five-page ms. of "The Searchlight," and a fourteen-page ms. of "The Patron and The Crocus." The Hooper Collection also owns 140 letters between Woolf and Lytton Strachey as well as other correspondence, including a 13 February [1921] letter to Katherine Mansfield and ten letters to Mela and Robert Spira.

The Richardson Collection is a working collection of books and materials used by Richardson in preparing her *Bloomsbury Iconography*. It includes Leslie Stephen's photograph album, ninety-eight original exhibition catalogs dating back to 1929, clippings and photocopies of such items as reviews of early Woolf works, and Bloomsbury material from British *Vogue* of the 1920s. The Collection also has three preliminary pencil drawings by Vanessa Bell for *Flush*.

GUIDE TO LIBRARY SPECIAL COLLECTIONS 111

The Mortimer Rare Book Room also owns Woolf's 1916 Italian ms. notebook and her corrected typescripts of "Reviewing" and "The Searchlight." In addition, there is a 1923 photograph of Woolf at Garsington. Original cover designs for Hogarth Press publications include *The Common Reader*, *On Being Ill*, and Duncan Grant. The Mortimer Rare Book Room also has a Sylvia Plath collection that includes eight of Woolf's books from Plath's library, several of which are underlined and annotated, as well as Plath's notes from her undergraduate English 211 class at Smith (1951–1952) in which she studied *To the Lighthouse*. The collection also includes Woolf's 26 February 1939 letter to Vita Sackville-West, a 1931 bronze bust of Virginia Woolf by Stephen Tomlin, a 1923 Hogarth Press edition of T. S. Eliot's *The Waste Land*, a 1919 Hogarth Press edition of *Paris* by Hope Mirrlees and first editions of Vita Sackville-West and Katherine Mansfield publications. Additional Bloomsbury items include *Original Woodcuts* (Omega Workshops, 1918), Vanessa Bell's original woodcut for the cover of *Monday or Tuesday* (1921), and exhibition catalogs for *Manet and the Post-Impressionists* (Grafton Galleries, 1911), Friday Club Members (Mansard Gallery, 1921) Paintings and Drawings by Vanessa Bell (Independent Gallery, 1922). Additional photographs include the Mary L. S. Bennett (née Fisher) Family Photographs. Online exhibitions are available on the Mortimer Rare Book Room's website.

Name of Collection: Literature & Rare Books, Special Collections, University of Maryland Libraries

Contact: Doug McElrath, Acting Head of Special Collections and University Archives (SCUA)

Address: University of Maryland
2208 Hornbake Library
College Park, MD 20742

Telephone: 301-405-9212
Fax: 301-314-2709
Email: askhornbake@umd.edu

Hours: Dates and hours of operation subject to change. Regular hours are Mon.-Fri.: 10 am to 5 pm. Extended hours are available on select days during the academic school year.

Email askhornbake@umd.edu before planning a research visit.

Access Requirements: Photo ID

Holdings Relevant To Woolf: Papers of Hope Mirrlees contain five autograph letters and postcards (1919–1928) from Virginia Woolf to Mirrlees. Also in the collection are 113 letters from T. S. Eliot to Mirrlees, and three letters from Lady Ottoline Morrell to Mirrlees. A finding aid is available at http://hdl.handle.net/1903.1/1536.

Name of Collection: Woolf/Hogarth Press/Bloomsbury

Contact: Lisa J. Sherlock

Address: Victoria University Library
71 Queens Park Crescent E.
Toronto M5S 1K7
Ontario Canada

Email: victoria.library@utoronto.ca
URL: http://library.vicu.utoronto.ca/special/bloomsbury.htm

Hours: Mon.–Fri. 9 am–5 pm

Access Requirements: Prior notification; identification

Restrictions: Limited photocopying

Holdings Relevant To Woolf: This collection, the most comprehensive of its kind with nearly 5,700 items, contains all the work of Virginia and Leonard Woolf in various editions, issues, variants and translations; all the books hand-printed by Leonard and Virginia Woolf at the Hogarth Press, including many variant issues and bindings, association copies and page proofs; a nearly comprehensive collection of Hogarth Press machine printed books to 1946 (the year Leonard Woolf and the Press joined Chatto & Windus) including presentation copies, signed limited editions, page proofs, variants as well as substantial amounts of ephemera, such as the *Catalogue of Publications to 1939* with annotations by Leonard Woolf. The collection is also very strong in Bloomsbury Art and Artists, especially the decorative arts, including important examples of Omega Workshops publications and exhibition catalogues. Materials include the catalogue of the second post-impressionist exhibition, 1912; catalogues relating to Vanessa Bell and Duncan Grant exhibitions; bronze medal of Virginia Woolf by Marta Firlet; oil on canvas portrait of Amaryllis Garnett by Vanessa Bell (c.1958); Portrait sketch of Leonard Woolf by Vanessa Bell; Duncan Grant and Vanessa Bell designed Clarice Cliff dinner plates; original Vanessa Bell and Duncan Grant sketches and designs for dust jackets, novels, and other special projects; Duncan Grant charcoal portrait of Virginia Woolf (1968); Quentin Bell set of five pottery plates based on the novels of Virginia Woolf (ca. 1979); Quentin Bell pottery figurine in aid of Charleston (ca. 1980); bronze busts of Lytton Strachey and Virginia Woolf by Stephen Tomlin (1901–1937); as well as the Marcel Gimond bust of Vanessa Bell and the Tomlin bust of Henrietta Bingham. Book hand bound by Virginia Woolf. Wooden plaque from the Hogarth Press at 24 Tavistock. Examples of programmes, posters, and handbills relating to productions of plays, movies, and dance productions with content relating to Bloomsbury group members. Original correspondence and mss. material includes that by Vanessa Bell; Leonard Woolf; Ritchie family re: Anne Thackeray Ritchie/ Stephen family; Duncan Grant; Quentin Bell; S. P. Rosenbaum mss. Letters from E. M. Forster, Bertrand Russell, James Strachey, Raymond Mortimer, David Garnett, Nigel Nicolson and others in the Bloomsbury Circle; as well as biographers, scholars and bibliographers such as Joanne Trautmann, Carolyn Heilbrun, J. Howard Woolmer, Leon Edel, Leila Luedeking, P. N. Furbank, Noel Annan and others. Large Ephemera Collection includes items revealing Virginia Woolf's effect on popular culture.

Name of Collection: Library of Leonard and Virginia Woolf (Washington S U)

Contact: Trevor James Bond, Head, Manuscripts, Archives, and Special Collections

Address: Washington State University Libraries
Pullman, WA 99164-5610

Email: tjbond@wsu.edu
URL: www.wsulibs.wsu.edu/holland/masc/masc.htm

Hours: Mon.–Fri.: 8:30 am–4:30 pm

Access Requirements: Letter stating nature of research preferred; student or other identification.

Restrictions: Materials must be used in the MASC area under supervision. Photocopying or photographing is permitted only when it will not harm the materials and is permitted by copyright.

Recent Acquisitions: Correspondence to Clive and Vanessa Bell (approximately 30 items), with most items addressed to Clive. Correspondents include Stephen Tallant, Eric MacLagan, John Pollock, H. J. Norton, Lyn Irvine (including one letter mentioning Mrs. Raven Hill), Sir George Grahame, Karen Costelloe, John Alford, Ivor Churchill, the Earl of Sandwich, George Lansbury, Clifford Sharp, F. H. S. Shepherd, Gilbert Seldes, Lord Evan Tredegar, C. E. Stuart, Max Eastman, E. Hilton Young, Col. Heward Bell.

Holdings Relevant To Woolf: WSU has the Woolfs' basic working library including many works which belonged to Woolf's father, Sir Leslie Stephen, and other family members. Over 800 titles came from their Sussex home, Monks House, including some works bought at auction soon after Leonard Woolf died in 1969. Later additions include: 1,875 titles from his house in Victoria Square, London; 400 titles from his nephew Cecil Woolf; and over 60 titles from Quentin and Anne Olivier Bell. WSU has been actively collecting: all works in all editions by Virginia Woolf; all titles by Leonard Woolf; dust jackets; works published by the Woolfs at the Hogarth Press through 1946; books by their friends and associates, especially those by Bloomsbury authors and about Bloomsbury artists; relevant correspondence and original works of art. Original artwork by Vanessa Bell; scattered letters by Vanessa Bell, E. M. Forster, Roger Fry, Leslie Stephen, Lytton Strachey, and Leonard Woolf. Original artwork by Richard Kennedy for illustrations in his book *A Boy at the Hogarth Press*; scattered letters by Roger Fry, Leslie Stephen, Ethel Smyth, and Leonard Woolf. Virginia Woolf's initialed copy of *Cornishiana*; Leonard Woolf's annotated copy of *An Anatomy of Poetry* by A. Williams-Ellis; Leslie Stephen's copy of *Lapsus Calami and Other Verses*, inscribed by James Kenneth Stephen. Several letters from

Virginia Woolf, including two written in 1939 to Ronald Heffer, and a letter to Edward McKnight Kauffer. New in the Hogarth Press Collection are a copy of E. M. Forster's *Anonymity, an Enquiry*, bound in cream paper boards, and what Woolmer calls the third label state of Forster's *The Story of the Siren*. The Library of Leonard and Virginia Woolf is once again shelved separately so that scholars visiting Pullman may see the collection apart from the other rare book collections.

Name of Collection: Yale Center for British Art

Contact: Elisabeth Fairman, Senior Curator of Rare Books and Manuscripts

Address: 1080 Chapel Street
P.O. Box 208280
New Haven, CT 06520-8280

Telephone: 203-432-2814
Fax: 203-432-9613
E-mail: elisabeth.fairman@yale.edu

Hours: Tue.-Fri.: 10 am–4:30 pm

Access Requirements: Permission needed in order to reproduce

Holdings Relevant To Woolf: Rare Books & Mss Department: 94 letters from Vanessa Bell and Duncan Grant to Sir Kenneth Clark; Prints & Drawings Department: 4 drawings by Vanessa Bell; 4 drawings by Duncan Grant; 6 drawings by Wyndham Lewis; 1 drawing by Frederick Etchells; Paintings Department: 1 painting by Vanessa Bell, 4 paintings by Duncan Grant (including portrait of Vanessa Bell); 3 paintings by Roger Fry. 6 letters from Lytton Strachey (to Clive Bell, Siegfried Sassoon, et al.).

Reviews

Mrs. Dalloway. Virginia Woolf. Ed. Anne E. Fernald.
(Cambridge: Cambridge UP, 2015) ciii + 378pp.

Explaining the brevity of her preface for the 1928 Modern Library edition of *Mrs. Dalloway*, included in this edition, Woolf notes that while "Books are the flowers or fruit stuck here and there on a tree which has its roots deep down in the earth of our earliest life," a full explication of the relationship between "fiction" and "life" would "need not a page or two of preface but a volume or two of autobiography" (356-7). If Woolf was famously reticent about such connections in her introduction, her editors have more than filled in the gap: since Woolf's works began coming out of copyright in the United Kingdom, six scholars have tackled *Mrs. Dalloway*: G. Patton Wright (Hogarth Press, 1990), Stella McNichol (Penguin, 1992), David Bradshaw (Oxford, 1992), Morris Beja (Shakespeare Head, 1996), and Bonnie Kime Scott (Harcourt, 2005), not to mention various other reprints. Readers and scholars might well think there is little need for yet another *Mrs. Dalloway*, but, as Fernald's new edition demonstrates, they would be wrong. Each previous edition has its particular strengths, and Fernald's surely lies in the capaciousness of her annotations, the section of the edition many readers will turn to most frequently, after the main text of the novel itself. What it would have meant to encounter a novel in the moment of its historical production is something that is inherently unknowable, as Peter Shillingsburg argues in "The Faces of Victorian Fiction," but Fernald's notes take us a long way toward that impossible dream, while also working from a clear understanding of the contemporary reasons for continuing to read Woolf generally and *Mrs. Dalloway* in particular.

With an introduction stretching over 57 pages, and another 126 pages of explanatory notes, Fernald tracks down a truly impressive range of references, from intertextual allusions, to historical circumstances, to detailed connections with people and events in Woolf's life, to the etymology of every character's name, and much else besides. To cite but a few of hundreds of examples: we learn that Clarissa's "silver-green mermaid's dress" (155) contains allusions to T. S. Eliot's "The Love Song of J. Alfred Prufrock," John Donne's "Song," Homer's *Odyssey*, and even the *Diary of Lady Anne Clifford*, which Woolf read in 1923 or '24 (liii). Or there is the traffic accident in April 1924 when Woolf's five-year-old niece Angelica was run over by a car and was initially thought to require life-saving surgery, which leads Woolf in her diary to associations with learning Greek (lessons in that language having served "as a kind of consolation after her mother's death" [lxvii]) and thus to the essay "On Not Knowing Greek," written for *The Common*

Reader alongside *Mrs. Dalloway*, with this incident surfacing again in the novel through Richard's feeling that "it did make his blood boil to see little creatures of five or six crossing Piccadilly alone" (104). As Fernald notes, traffic signals were sporadic in London at the time, and did not become electric until 1929 (lxviii). We even discover that Scrope Purvis (my own personal favorite name of any character in any novel) takes his surname from an Anglo-French word meaning "dweller at a 'parvis' or porch," though it may also be a Northumbrian variant of the Middle English *purveys*, a name for the person responsible for supplying a monastery or manor house, and that Arthur Blaikie Purvis (1890-1941) purchased $25 million of acetone during the Great War on behalf of the Novel Explosives Company Ltd. (183). In the Purvis case, Fernald does not establish that Woolf necessarily had any of this information at her own fingertips, but her annotative method on the whole is to provide the curious reader with as many connections as possible, and to let the edition serve as a starting point for interpretation.

Fernald's introduction and notes will be of particular interest for readers and scholars focused on Woolf's composition, revision, and publication practices. As Fernald explains through several detailed examples, Woolf was deliberately moving back and forth between *Mrs. Dalloway* and *The Common Reader*, with a broad range of intertextual moments in the novel apparently arising from their simultaneous consideration in the *Reader* drafts. While Woolf calls revision "the dullest part of the whole business of writing; the most depressing & exacting" (*D* 3, 4) while in the midst of reworking early drafts of *To the Lighthouse*, Fernald demonstrates the extent to which Woolf was engaged with the process for *Mrs. Dalloway* (as indeed was the case for almost all her works, diary complaints notwithstanding). As late as her receipt of the first set of proofs from the Edinburgh printers R. & R. Clark, Fernald points out, Woolf was still rewriting the details of Septimus's suicide (lxxv-lxxvii). Such comparatively late stage revision is nothing compared to Joyce's famous expansion of several chapters in *Ulysses* from their proofs, but as Fernald observes (and as Julia Briggs has discussed as well), Woolf's first hand knowledge of the publishing process makes her willingness to revise here more pronounced than a case like Joyce's, who was of course working with a novice publisher in Sylvia Beach. This is one of many instances when readers and scholars already familiar with *Mrs. Dalloway* will find much to reward their attention to Fernald's meticulous explanations of how the published novel came to occupy that state. While Fernald attends to the novel's production and reception, though, she offers comparatively little history of its marketing and distribution by the Hogarth Press, or of its later incorporation into the Uniform Edition in 1929.

In addition to the extensive introduction and annotations, this edition includes two chronologies, one for Woolf's life and career and another detailing the composition of *Mrs. Dalloway*, from its possible origins in 1920 when

Vanessa Bell's servant, Mary Wilson, was taken to St. Pancras Hospital suffering from "hysteria"; as well as a textual apparatus, textual notes, Woolf's 1928 introduction, and a bibliography. Fernald explains that her choice of copy-text, the first British edition, is constrained by the Cambridge University Press's "general editorial policy" in the Woolf edition (lxxxiv), but she makes a persuasive case for this edition as the optimal copy-text in any case, especially for its handling of the typographical spacing used to indicate the breaks between the novel's twelve sections. This careful division, presumably corresponding to both the hours of the book's manuscript title and perhaps to the months of the year as well, has been lost in almost all editions after the 1925 British, including even the original American edition from Harcourt, Brace. As Briggs points out, the lack of chapter divisions subtly emphasizes the "unifying impulse" spread across the novel's disparate characters, who may not interact directly but still "share the novel's time continuum" (117). Such readings will be much more readily apparent in Fernald's edition.

While Fernald cites the work of a few major editorial theorists (George Bornstein, Hans Walter Gabler, Jerome McGann, Shillingsburg) she does not engage conceptually with the questions they have raised about what textuality entails and what an edition should be, as they might have pertained to this edition (especially absent the Cambridge policy). Fernald's edition can only gesture toward Woolf's drafts and manuscripts, as well as the proofs circulated among her printer R. R. Clark, Harcourt, and her dying friend Jacques Raverat, and the editions produced during Woolf's lifetime, but the ability to navigate freely among these various textual states lies outside the scope of this or any print edition (in contrast to the wealth of materials available for *To the Lighthouse* in the Woolf Online project, for instance). Despite that structural absence, for those common readers and scholars interested in situating *Mrs. Dalloway* in the full history of its time, Fernald's edition is without doubt the best option available—if you have $150.

—John K. Young, *Marshall University*

Works Cited

Briggs, Julia. *Reading Virginia Woolf*. Edinburgh: Edinburgh UP, 2006. Print.
Shillingsburg, Peter. "The Faces of Victorian Fiction." In *The Iconic Page in Manuscript, Print, and Digital Culture*. Eds. George Bornstein and Theresa Tinkle. Ann Arbor: U of Michigan P, 1998. Print.
Woolf Online. http://www.woolfonline.com/. Web. Accessed 2 October, 2015.

Vanessa and Her Sister. Priya Parmar
(New York: Ballantine Books, 2014) xi + 368pp.

Adeline. Norah Vincent
(New York: Houghton Mifflin Harcourt, 2015) 288pp.

Virginia Woolf in Manhattan. Maggie Gee
(London: Telegram Books, 2015) 480pp.

Over the years, beginning with Quentin Bell's 1972 biography of his aunt, Virginia Woolf's literary work has become inseparable from her life. As the volumes of letters, diaries and essays rolled out, lovingly edited and compiled by those who knew her best, the novels began to be read against a background of deeply personal and often private writings. It is difficult to think of another writer whose inner life and artistic production have become so intertwined that it is nearly impossible to consider them entirely separately. Readers of Woolf look for interpretive literary clues in the autobiographical, and apply the gleanings of the essays and diaries to the analysis of the novels.

If Bell's book appeared at an important moment of feminism and social change, making Woolf into a cultural icon and an object of self-making desire (a hairdresser in Cambridge, Massachusetts once commented that young women brought the book into his salon and asked for their hair to be styled in the loose knot that she wore on the cover of the biography), Hermione Lee's magisterial biography should have been the full stop to the stream of Woolf biographies that had included an important one by Lyndall Gordon. Yet others, by Julia Briggs and Nigel Nicolson, followed Lee's. With so much compelling evidence of the internal and personal life of Woolf, one wonders what is left to say about her? Every stone, it would seem, has been turned, every letter read, every servant considered.

Yet Woolf herself wrote in "Not One of Us" that "there are some stories which have to be retold by each generation" (*DM* 119). Judging by a recent crop of books, the answer to how to imagine Woolf's life and even afterlife now seems to lie in fiction. In the past year, three different novelists have offered three different attempts to get at the "truth" of a life and to go beyond the verifiable facts. Woolf herself acknowledged the "problem" of biography lay in its supposed reliance upon facts. If the biographer "invents facts as an artist invents them," she wrote in "The Art of Biography," "they destroy each other" (*DM* 192, 193). Richard Holmes went even further, giving the subtitle "Inventing the Truth" to an essay he wrote on biography.

As both a biographer and a novelist, Woolf was clear about which of the two forms was superior. Where the biographer is tied to evidence, the artist's imagination allows her to play fast and loose with facts, and authenticity lay in the freedom of the artist's vision in a world that is "rarer, intenser, and more wholly of a piece than the world that is largely made of authentic information supplied by other people" (*DM* 193). These three novelists create worlds informed, but not restricted by, documented language and events. Perhaps in doing so they come closer to the truth of the lives they portray.

One need only look at novels like Colm Toibín's *The Master*, which breathes new life into the elusive Henry James, to think about ways that novelists can re-envision the lives of earlier novelists, and immerse themselves in the bodies, hearts, and minds of their literary forebears. As Woolf concluded, "the novelist is free; the biographer is tied" (*DM* 188). But free to do exactly what? What assumptions does each novelist make about her reader? Would these novels— each strong and compelling as fiction—be as effective to a reader unfamiliar with the biographies? When an interviewer remarked to Lee that "novelists traffic in a different kind of truth from biography," Lee succinctly remarked, "Well, they make things up. I don't make things up" (Interview). As novelists, these writers definitely make things up.

Unlike biography, each of these new novels concentrates on a segment of Woolf's life. Priya Parmar's *Vanessa and Her Sister*, which tackles the years 1905-12, is told through diaries and letters and is only obliquely—even in its title—about Woolf herself. However, by burrowing into the early maturity, loves, and marriage of Vanessa, Parmar gives us a Virginia who is troublesome, clinging, and untrustworthy, while Vanessa slowly and necessarily frees herself from her husband and her sister as she matures. Borrowing from the style, but not the actual words, of its writers, Vanessa's fictional introspection lets us inside her creation of family and friendships, as she slowly comes into her own.

Norah Vincent's *Adeline*, another oblique title that refers to Woolf's actual first name, pits the adult Virginia nearing the end of her life against her child self, whose experiences made her what she became. Written in alternating internal monologues told in the third person, and in long conversations with Leonard Woolf, Lytton Strachey, Dora Carrington and others, the novel is grounded by a deep analytical intelligence.

Finally, Maggie Gee's flight of fancy into Woolf's afterlife when she magically reappears in twenty-first century Manhattan in the company of a self-absorbed modern popular English novelist, is a thoughtful and comic foray into the differences between a protected and self-published Woolf and a modern woman writer in thrall to the demands of agents, conferences, and a publicity machine. Taken together, all three novels, each with a distinctive narrative style and tone, say what biography cannot through their invented truths.

Parmar's novel is an act of bravery. Because Bell, unlike Woolf, left descendants, it takes enormous courage for an American-raised novelist who did not learn to read until she was nearly ten and is not a Woolf scholar to decide to write in the voices of some of the most studied and discussed figures of the early twentieth century. Yet perhaps it is just this courage and academic distance that allows her to absorb and replicate the voices of Vanessa Bell, a young and troubled Virginia Woolf, a tentative and lonely Leonard Woolf in Ceylon, and a pre-*Eminent Victorians* Lytton Strachey. These exhaustively analyzed figures come to life in this young novelist's ear, despite occasional word issues (Virginia Nicholson, Vanessa's granddaughter, appreciated the novel but let Parmar know that her grandmother would have said "napkin" and not "serviette"; to which I would add that I expect Virginia would have said "porridge" and not "oatmeal").

But these aside, even the skeptical reader finds herself falling into the cadence and emotions of a young Vanessa who experiences courtship, marriage, motherhood and adultery again a backdrop of family tragedies. "I still collect funny things all day long to tell Thoby," Vanessa writes of their recently lost beloved brother (142). "I know Virginia and Adrian and Clive and Lytton do it as well, but grieving has become a private business. The wound seeps, but we no longer speak of it. Instead, it rests like an iron anchor on a thick chain dropped under the water. To speak of it, everyone, all together, would drown us" (142). Vanessa's painterly awareness vibrates under her private words, and a woman who appears largely silent in social settings pierces the loquaciousness of others who fail to realize how well she sees and hears. Similarly, a flighty Lytton Strachey is slowly revealed to be aching with unrequited love for his cousin Duncan Grant, while gently nudging Leonard to return to England and marry a Virginia he barely knows. The letters and journal entries are invented, but uncannily capture the cadence and speech of these familiar characters. However it is Vanessa, in her diary revelations, who is the revelation.

But this Virginia herself is also unlike the Virginia we've known before. In Parmar's hands, and through Vanessa's voice, we see her as a problem, a burden, an already unsettled young woman unable to care for herself and so deeply in love with her sister and so jealous of her sister's marriage that she tries to unmake it and creates untruths. When Thoby dies, she sends a friend letters describing his slow recovery. Like the death of her brother, the babies Julian and Quentin cannot be unmade, however. As Vanessa moves gently and determinedly into her own, Virginia is pushed out into a new direction necessary to both women's survival.

Unlike Parmar's novel, Norah Vincent's *Adeline* no less bravely concentrates on a slice of Woolf's life. The late part of Woolf's life and her tragic end are so well known that to revisit them is an undeniably bold move. At times it seems that Vincent's aim is to write a scholarly book on Woolf; the internal monologues are so deeply analytical and self-aware that it is as if the ideas she has on Woolf can only be presented as the thoughts that Woolf herself would have had: "A book is a fold of paper and thread, in itself inert, yet in the right hands, it transmits. In the mind of the reader, the hearer, the writing lives. The transference occurs, leaping from one mind to another over time and space and even death. Hence the anonymity of the authorial feat" (86). Vincent's "authorial feat" is to channel, and indeed inhabit, her subject.

However, it is through the alternating conversational chapters that we see crucial other aspects of Woolf's personality. In the garden, smoking cigarettes while Leonard gardens or Lytton visits, the back and forth of conversation, the pauses and lulls, the arrogance or contriteness, give another dimension entirely. This interweaving of the internal and the external sheds light on Virginia's relationships with others. An excruciating visit from T. S. Eliot and his wife Vivien in which the couple become rapidly and inappropriately drunk turns into such a fiasco that "Tom is frozen with his eyes fixed firmly on the ground, terrified, mortified or both" (167). Yet later, when she discovers that Eliot has at last reluctantly committed his mad wife to an asylum, she falls apart and takes her terror to Vanessa, who uncharacteristically turns on her sister, accusing her of thinking she is "a wreck who only narrowly escaped being carted off like Vivian, like [their insane sister] Laura, and like this Lucia [James Joyce's daughter]" (221).

Vincent's Woolf, so brilliant in the monologue chapters, exposes her flaws in the company of others, as she spirals into conversational games of one-upmanship and self-centeredness that she often later regrets. Her meeting with the poet Yeats, whom she had earlier disparaged, turns into an inspiration when he deliberately leads her to a poem that changes her own writing. But it is chillingly on display when she reluctantly goes to visit a suicidal Carrington, devastated by Lytton Strachey's death, at the house they shared.

Those readers who know the details of Woolf's life know that the homosexual Lytton once proposed marriage to Virginia—a mistake quickly corrected—and earlier chapters in the novel saw their even deeper friendship. To this fictionalized Virginia, Carrington was no match for Lytton's intellect or wit. Even so, her behavior to the shattered woman across from her is appalling. "Deluded fool, Virginia thinks. As she tries stroking Carrington's hand, the putrid thoughts go on inside her head" (141). When Virginia finally escapes this house of death, we know that Carrington will soon end her own life, just as Virginia eventually will.

The trick to pulling off these two Virginias is to show how she became this way, and to create great sympathy and admiration for her despite her sometimes unpleasant behavior. Vincent accomplishes this by the introduction of the young Virginia, Adeline, with whom she still, in her madness, converses. This disturbing bifurcation shows a woman both shaped by the past, in love and in struggle with her younger self, and in deep need of comfort and protection. The question becomes how to produce an ending which is so familiar to us, and with which biographers also struggle. By turning to the introspection of her lonely end, Vincent produces a moving conclusion, albeit one that biographers often fall back upon, of having earlier friends or characters process through the writer's final thoughts.

Maggie Gee's *Virginia Woolf in Manhattan*, a madcap romp through Woolf's afterlife could not be more different than the two other novels. Despite being much longer than the others, it also is a faster read. Once the willing suspension of disbelief occurs, the reader accepts that Woolf is somehow pulled back into the physical world by means of a book that Angela Lamb is carrying on a rocky flight from London to New York. Ultimately on her way to a Woolf conference in Istanbul, Lamb is quickly revealed to be completely self-absorbed, a terrible wife and mother who ignores her daughter, and overly concentrates on her career as a popular novelist. Once she finds she has the real Woolf in tow, she drags her through the modern world, exposing her to the Internet, and the only-as-good-as the last book whirlwind of a twenty-first century woman writer's life. The charm of Woolf's reincarnated naivety rubs against Angela's brusqueness; the coolly patrician Woolf charms doormen and even manages to carry off the expensive wardrobe Angela buys for her, despite Virginia's initial unwillingness to bathe. (Interestingly, in Parmar's novel, Vanessa seems to constantly take baths.) Obsessed with money, Angela resents her absent husband's request to help fund his Arctic explorations and turns deafly away from their daughter Gerda's deepening troubles. Berating Virginia, Angela exclaims, "It's all right for you. I'm sure Leonard never asked you for money," and Virginia replies, "But it isn't, as you say, 'all right for me.' I'd give anything for Leonard to telephone one morning. And I would give him whatever he asked for" (339). So *au fond*, it is a love story.

This is a clear reference to the Woolfs' celibate marriage, and in true modern fashion the resolution will have to lie in two things: Angela's conference speech and familial reconciliation, and Virginia's sexual satisfaction with a man. We know that Angela will have to somehow become the wife and mother she has failed to be, and that Virginia must find in the physical world something she lacked in her actual life, before moving back into the spiritual realm. The question that keeps the reader turning pages is how Gee will accomplish this. While this could seem in some ways very pat, she does do something we do not always see in more tragic nonfiction portrayals: a kinder, gentler Woolf who enjoys the world. Whether this represents the "real" Virginia is not the issue here. The real story is about the Angelas of the modern world, the driven women who have achieved success and need to regain lost their bearings.

Unlike Parmar and Vincent, Gee has no pretension to be rewriting a life. Rather, Woolf's afterlife does make us think about the way we approach Bloomsbury, and Woolf in particular, as a subject. What is the link between fiction

and biography, and what is the best way to rethink a life we thought we knew? Or, as Virginia says to Lytton in Vincent's novel, "I have taken refuge in fiction when telling the stories of real people's lives. Fiction is all there is, and all of my fiction has been, more or less, the stories of real people's lives" (106).
—Gretchen Holbrook Gerzina, *University of Massachusetts, Amherst*

Works Cited

Holmes, Richard. "Biography: Inventing the Truth." *The Art of Literary Biography*. Ed. John Batchelor. Oxford: Clarendon Press, 1995: 15-25. Print.
Lee, Hermione. *Virginia Woolf*. New York: Alfred A. Knopf, 1999. Print.
——. Interview with Louisa Thomas. "Hermione Lee, The Art of Biography, No. 4." *Paris Review*, 205 (Summer 2013). Web.
Woolf, Virginia. "The Art of Biography." *The Death of The Moth, and other essays*. New York: Harcourt, 1947: 187-97. Print.
——. "Not One of Us." *The Death of The Moth, and other essays*. New York: Harcourt, 1947: 119-28. Print.

Contemporary Woolf/Woolf contemporaine.
Claire Davison-Pegon and Anne-Marie Smith-Di Biasio.
(Montpellier: Presses universitaires de la Méditerranée, 2014) 261pp.

This new bilingual essay collection was edited by two British scholars long resident in France, where a number of important contributions to Woolf studies have been made in recent years.[1] The contemporary is an apt subject for a transnational approach, suggesting a horizontal leveling of Woolf studies: we are all here, now, at the same time, studying Woolf; but what does it mean for us to coincide temporally, if not spatially?

But the essays here depart from a notion of the contemporary as simultaneity, reading it against the grain, as non-coincidence. Many take up the term in the sense Giorgio Agamben gave it in a 2008 essay, that to be contemporary is to keep "a singular relationship with one's own time, which adheres to it and, at the same time, keeps a distance from it. More precisely, it is that relationship with time that adheres to it, through a disjunction and an anachronism" (11). There is a lovely

---

[1] Several of the essays are in French; the translations that follow are mine.

resonance across the contributions, as they treat similar motifs and images and mine them for their implications.

One theoretical node centers on questions of perception and Woolf's notion of the present as a "platform" from which the critic surveys the literary landscape, past, present, and to come. In the first essay in the collection, Laura Marcus considers Woolf's approach to the writing of literary history, a problem which Woolf considered at several moments in her career, and wrote about in at least two essays: "Reading" and "Phases of Fiction." Marcus analyzes the tension Woolf experienced between respecting and disrupting chronology: early on she considered a chronological approach, but later adopted transhistorical categories like "the Truth-teller" and "the Romantics," as organizing heuristics (30). Woolf's critical contemporaries—Viktor Shklovsky, Percy Lubbock, Edwin Muir, E. M. Forster—were also grappling with establishing a poetics of the novel form, but their transhistorical approaches could not accommodate the "questions of the contemporary" that Woolf found so pressing (26). The complexities Woolf perceived, as she scanned the horizon, would inform her writing both as a critic and novelist.

In theorizing Woolf's image of the platform, Nathalie Pavec turns to Nietzsche's idea of the *inactuel*, the not current, which works "against the times [contre le temps] [...] in favor of a time to come" (76). The present tense, in this schema, reads as a semiotic fracture—the platform is built on shaky foundations. This fracturing or fissuring is an image that Angeliki Spiropoulou considers as well. Woolf was fascinated by what defined her era, precisely, as modern, and tried many times to articulate this. But the "gesture itself," Spiropoulou writes, "of addressing how (modern) contemporaneity already involves a temporal fissure, in that she addresses the present both as contemporary to it and simultaneously from outside it" (155). We find shades of Agamben here as well. Walter Benjamin noted that it is one of modernity's central myths about itself that it represents a radical break with tradition, and yet (as we see throughout Woolf's work, as the contributors here are well aware) Woolf regarded this "break" as both destructive and enabling. Spiropoulou reminds us that Woolf's "discontinuous narratives, moving in jolts, fissures, and breaks, replete with thought and dialogue fragments, repetitions, intercepted memories, and scenes that arrest time, introduce different temporalities at once" (159). Woolf's work opens up caesurae that function as interruptions of linear temporality, and "make space for the past to appear in the present" (162). This is a key idea driving all the contributions to this collection: finding these moments in Woolf's work, where the present is at an angle to itself, and analyzing its textual effects. The fact that Agamben edited the Italian version of Benjamin's collected works in the 1980s and 90s most certainly accounts for the resonance of Agamben's theory of the contemporary with Benjamin's dialectical materialism.

The question of historicity animates Michael F. Davis's narratological analysis as well as Claire Rosé's reading of the motif of conversation through the poetic line; she considers the "aporetic" definition of poetry Woolf gives when she terms it "what is timeless *and* contemporary" (italics mine). This splitting in the moment of the poem—casting it as at once eternal and forever breaking with its previous moment—is aligned with the extensive domain Woolf allowed poetry, both the thing itself, contained in a poem, and the work of the writer: "The writer is poetic, and his meaning inseparable from his language" (54). These aporetic moments appear as hauntings of the spectre of virginity and the impossibility of childbirth in Anne-Marie Smith-Di Biasio's excellent readings of *A Room of One's Own* and *To the Lighthouse*. And for Adèle Cassigneul, they take the form of the "contre-discours" of the invisible photographs in *Three Guineas* (145).

Questions of contemporaneity are given a wider context in essays by Adriana Varga and Derek Ryan, who take up, respectively, the musical structure and the rhizomatic becomings of Woolf's work to find productive forms of thinking past the binaries to which some of the other essays fall prey. Noriko Kubota's contribution is also particularly compelling, detailing how Woolf's encounter with Japonisme against the backdrop of the Japan-British Exposition in 1910 (which on one day attracted 460,200 people) enabled her to consider new ways of perceiving, and to consider the more impactful power of illusion over realism (37). Christine Froula traces adaptations of *Orlando* the world over, from Taiwan to Estonia.

There is a desire in these essays to consider Woolf *our* contemporary, as in Monica Latham's reading of Woolf together with Ian McEwan and Rachel Cusk, in addition to Anne-Laure Rigeade's critical pairing of Woolf with Nathalie Sarraute. In Kathryn Simpson's essay, "'Shop Windows Blazing; and women gazing': Woolf, Commodity Culture, and the Gift Economy," we are given the chance to consider the ways in which Woolf's awareness of the tension between the desires and "dangers" of commodity culture may put her more in step with our own time than with hers (44). Simpson reads Woolf's "emphasis on perception and the spectacular in her representations of contemporary culture" as an essential element of the "subversive politics" of her work (44).

And yet the paradox at the heart of Agamben's definition of the contemporary leads many of the critics included here to take Woolf's love of contradiction perhaps a bit over-zealously (or maybe it is the combined effect of reading these essays one after the other). While the theoretical conceit of the paradox permits us to think through the contradictions at the heart of Woolf's work, we must be on our guard that we are not forever asserting that a work simultaneously does one thing and the precise opposite. We may find the richest implications of paradox in Woolf's confrontations with power, and adopt syncretic, supple critical practices that take

their lead from Woolf's own way of looking at the world, as Chantal Delourme writes of Woolf's diary, "'reading' its discourses and inscribing ever-renewed sites of enunciative dissonance" (193). In her adoption of Lyotard's "affect-phrase," Delourme locates the political resonance of Woolf's paradoxical contemporaneity, which is what made Woolf necessary to her own time, and invaluable in our own.
—Lauren Elkin, *American University of Paris*

Works Cited

Agamben, Giorgio. "What is the Contemporary?" *What is an Apparatus? and Other Essays*. Trans. David Kishik and Stefan Pedatella. Stanford: Stanford UP, 2009. Print.

Virginia Woolf: Twenty-First-Century Approaches.
Jeanne Dubino, Gill Lowe, Vara Neverow, and Kathryn Simpson, eds.
(Edinburgh: Edinburgh UP, 2015) ix + 230pp.

But, you may say, what would characterize a new collection of essays on Virginia Woolf as specifically "twenty-first-century"? What new approaches and critical innovations might we find reading Woolf in and through our own post-millennial moment? Edited by noted and prolific Woolf scholars Jeanne Dubino, Gill Lowe, Vara Neverow, and Kathryn Simpson, this collection draws much of its inspiration from the Twenty-First Annual Conference on Virginia Woolf, held at the University of Glasgow in 2011. That gathering, entitled "Contradictory Woolf," featured a plenary panel showcasing papers by the editors, versions of which appear here, and many of the essays in the collection emerged from other presentations at that event as well. Taken together, they generate a robust conversation about the current state and the future of Woolf studies, as well as offering numerous avenues for further scholarship.

Woolf herself famously wrote in *To the Lighthouse*, "For nothing is simply one thing," and the theme of contradictions that inspired the collection under review does justice to Woolf's own multiplicity. As the editors offer in their introduction, they hoped to provide a collection that "examines patterns in Woolf's life and work that are unstable, multilateral, or evolving; fractured but also fused; contradictory yet connected . . . examin[ing] unresolved dissonances, binaries and doubles; ruptured meanings, and oppositional factors, and focus[ing] on ambivalence, antithesis, and paradox" (1). As the introduction seeks to chart out new territory, it also gives a sense of the existing landscape by noting significant contemporary publications in Woolf studies over the last decade. This review of the literature, along with substantial bibliographies at the conclusion of each essay in the volume, serves as an invaluable and thoroughly learned resource for readers.

The essays themselves are organized into five thematic sections. The first, "Self and Identity," features Gill Lowe's "'I am fast locked up,' Janus and Miss Jan: Virginia Woolf's 1897 Journal as Threshold Text" and Nuala Hancock's "Elusive Encounters: Seeking out Virginia Woolf in Her Commemorative House Museum." These two essays make new claims for perennially significant themes in Woolf's oeuvre: self, subjectivity, identity. For Woolf, the self and identity can be refracted through multiple lenses, and here Lowe demonstrates how the author versions herself through journal writing as an adolescent woman. Hancock, by using space and place-making as a lens, shows how we as Woolfians come to different versions of the author by experiencing multiple iterations of her personal life and personal space in the context of material culture, namely, through the creation of the museum at Monk's House. Hancock's essay is of particular interest, as it traces in fine detail the processes of recreation needed to make Monk's House into the monument to Bloomsbury and Woolf it has become, as well as our own processes of place-making as we move through a space meant to be both creative and commemorative. In these two essays, the motif of contradictions is made clear: past and present, inexperience and maturity, self-presentation and self-concealment, authenticity and performance.

The second section of the volume is called "Language and Translation," and contains "'*Can I Help You?*': Virginia Woolf, Viola Tree, and the Hogarth Press," by Diane F. Gillespie; and "Bilinguals and Bioptics: Virginia Woolf and the Outlandishness of Translation," by Claire Davison. Anchoring this section is Woolf's work for the Hogarth Press, and the essays by Gillespie and Davison illuminate Woolf's contributions to modernist publishing as well as the truly multifaceted nature of the Hogarth Press agenda and catalog. These essays make a major contribution to our understanding of Woolf's publishing endeavor. Davison, in particular, draws on her own groundbreaking research into Woolf's relationship with S. S. Koteliansky and her interest in Russian literature. Gillespie's essay is a significant intervention into our sense of Woolf's engagement with the middlebrow and with politics. She reads Tree's self-help book on etiquette and decorum through Woolf's own "Am I Snob?," and then makes a persuasive claim via *Three Guineas* that both Woolf and Tree seek to "translate" social rules into civilizing impulses in the face of fascism and militarism. In this way, Woolf's choices as a publisher become a kind of feminist, pacifist translation.

Commodity culture and politics continue to make themselves felt as important themes in the third section of *Virginia Woolf: Twenty-First-Century Approaches*, entitled "Culture and Commodification." Ann Martin's essay, "'*Unity--Dispersity*': Virginia Woolf and the Contradictory Motif of the Motor-Car," reads Woolf as fully participating in modernity through her status as a motor-car owner. In fact, not only was Woolf, by the 1930s, the owner of a luxury car (a Lanchester), but she was also an enthusiastic motorist and road-tripping aficionado. Martin's well-researched and entertaining essay gives us new insight into Woolf as a consumer and as an embracer of speed and machines. In "'Am I a Jew?': Woolf's 1930s Political and Economic Peregrinations," Kathryn Simpson looks at a different side of Woolf: her antisemitism. Simpson reads Woolf's writing about Jews and Jewishness, especially in *The Years*, as a working through of anxieties around outsiderhood. Perceiving herself as an outsider—more so in the increasingly militarized England of the 1930s—Woolf took the figure of the Jew as a trope for alienation, and used it to negotiate a shifting comprehension of otherness.

The theme of otherness further characterizes the fourth section, "Human, Animal, and Nonhuman." This part of the volume feels the most cohesive, mainly because both essays focus on readings informed by animal studies and ecocriticism. Both essays take as touchstones the writings of Charles Darwin as well as the German biologist Jakob von Uexküll (1864-1944), especially his concept of *umwelt*, or the ways in which animals make meaning out of their environment. Woolf was familiar with the work of both men, and the reading of her fiction through their ideas, theorized by way of current trends in ecocriticism, strike this reviewer as especially innovative, timely, and necessary. Jeanne Dubino's essay, "The Bispecies Environment, Coevolution, and *Flush*," reads *Flush* (to this reader's mind one of Woolf's most underappreciated texts) according to the intersections of four coevolutionary environments essential to *umwelt*, and to understanding human-animal relationships in all their fluidity and contradictions: predator-prey, competitors, host and guest, and mutual beneficiaries. Dubino concludes with a compelling statement on why reading Woolf, and other literary works, through this lens is so urgent: "A coevolutionary approach to literary studies, one that analyzes four forms of bispecies relationships, shows how Woolf, ever attuned to the fluidities, volatilities, and disruptions that are a part of human relationships, was also sensitive to the ebbs and flows of the patterns of interactions among nonhuman and human animals" (144). Dubino's words gesture towards the wider applicability and relevance of the trends at work in this volume, and position the readings in *Virginia Woolf: Twenty-First-Century Approaches* on the cutting edge. Likewise, Derek Ryan, in "Posthumanist Interludes: Ecology and Ethology in *The Waves*," offers a luminous reading of Woolf's most poetic novel, and gives new insight into the elusive interludes woven throughout that fiction. In Ryan's reading, we are called upon to resist the anthropomorphizing of the natural world, to serious ethical effect.

Finally, the fifth section of *Virginia Woolf: Twenty-First-Century Approaches* offers new readings of themes we see throughout Woolf's work, those of gender and sexuality. In a profoundly sympathetic and well-written essay, "Indecency: *Jacob's Room*, Modernist Homosexuality, and the Culture of War," Eileen Barrett considers Woolf's novel by way of scandals surrounding homosexuality in the late 19th and early 20th centuries, those which also influenced her gay male friends such as Lytton Strachey and E. M. Forster. Barrett shows that Woolf's friendships with these figures influenced her depiction of Jacob, including his covert homosexuality, and that their pacifism, existing in intersection with their queerness, helped formulate her fictional response to the Great War. Vara Neverow looks back to another influence, Henry Fielding, in her discussion of that author's pamphlet *The Female Husband* and the ways it shaped Woolf's *Orlando*; and Kristin Czarnecki considers how we might read Woolf herself as influencing and intersecting with Native American fiction, in particular the novels of Louise Erdrich. These final two essays, "Multiple Anonymities: Resonances of Fielding's *The Female Husband* in *Orlando* and *A Room of One's Own*" and "Two-Spirits and Gender Variance in Virginia Woolf's *Orlando* and Louise Erdrich's *The Last Report on the Miracles at Little No Horse*," both show that new discoveries are always being made in our readings of Woolf, and that new connections and conversations continue to reveal themselves. *Virginia Woolf: Twenty-First-Century Approaches* brings together a lively variety of original readings that call upon us to reimagine once again a writer, reader, and feminist who only becomes more relevant and necessary as time goes on.

—Janine Utell, *Widener University*

Modern Manuscripts: The Extended Mind and Creative Undoing from Darwin to Beckett and Beyond.
Dirk Van Hulle (New York: Bloomsbury, 2014) xviii + 271pp.

One of the challenges of working with a writer's library is interpreting the marginalia. In *Modern Manuscripts*, Dirk Van Hulle addresses marginalia as one of several genres that record writers' thoughts. Because modernist writers often represent the workings of their characters' minds, Van Hulle argues that remnants of writers' composition strategies and responses to their reading provide a potential source of inspiration for their characters' thoughts. Beginning with

Charles Darwin, Van Hulle turns to different facets of nineteenth and twentieth century writers' archives in order to theorize the relationship between thoughts and modern writers' representations of them.

As a reader and researcher, Darwin recorded copious records of his observations and reading, providing an antecedent for modernist records of mental life. For Van Hulle, Darwin represents a time in which "both scientific and literary authors became increasingly aware of the intellectual value of manuscripts as material traces of thought processes. In this respect, Charles Darwin's marginalia, notes and manuscripts serve as a representative corpus" (12). Van Hulle assesses materials recording Darwin's ideas, including his "reading notes (from marginalia in Darwin's library to extracted notes in separate copybooks) in order to chart the interplay of writing and/as thinking" (14).

Van Hulle focuses on Darwin in Part One of *Modern Manuscripts*, "The Preservation of Unfavoured Traces," attending to the particularities of reading present. In contrast to Virginia Woolf, Darwin filled many of his texts with marginal inscriptions. These "paper fossils" remain as fragile shells of ideas in Darwin's library (14). Theorizing the functions of marginalia, Van Hulle observes that they do not necessarily mirror thoughts, but, drawing on Edgar Allan Poe's essay titled "Marginalia," they represent "not so much a copy of the mind but rather . . . a *part of* the mind" (153). With regard to Darwin, Van Hulle insists that "it is necessary to try and retrace all the paths and dead ends in the maze of Darwin's reading traces. Again, mapping the labyrinth gives the false impression of a chaotic mind at work, but it is clear that the creation of this mess was an integral part of, perhaps even a precondition for, the written invention which resulted in *On the Origin of Species*" (54). Scholars who have worked with Woolf's letters, diaries, or reading notebooks may be familiar with the often fragmentary nature of these materials, and the experience of encountering facets of ideas that may have informed her fiction.

Van Hulle begins Part Two of *Modern Manuscripts*, "Combining 'Source'-oriented and 'Discourse'-oriented Research" with a "Prologue: Beyond the 'Inward Turn.'" Woolf provides an anchor for Van Hulle's consideration of modernism, because he takes her "look within" in "Modern Fiction" (1919) as one way that critics have imagined modernist composition. At one point, Van Hulle takes Woolf to represent writers of her time: "it seems strange that a generation of writers who were so interested in evoking the workings of the mind would insist that this involved *intro*spection, according to Virginia Woolf's phrase 'Look within'" (142). We do not know how many writers listened to Woolf and only some modernist writers demonstrate stream-of-consciousness. In the next sentence he adds, "it is even more remarkable that for such a long time, literary criticism has propagated this introspective or 'internalist' view" (142). That may be true, but a wealth of criticism in past decade has also proposed more expansive considerations of modernism. Van Hulle's point, however, is that Woolf's model continues to serve as a dominant one for modernists' rendering of thought when "cognitive science has developed the theory of enactivism, which nuances this metaphorical representation of the mind as an interior space" (142).

Van Hulle demonstrates that Woolf's "The Mark on the Wall" (1917) runs counter to her advice, examining the way that the protagonist's thoughts respond to her surroundings (142). Assessing Woolf's earlier story in light of her later essay might appear problematic, but her instruction to "Look within" and "Examine for a moment an ordinary mind on an ordinary day" does not necessarily mean that she was advising people to consider their own minds; it might suggest that they imagine others' minds. For Van Hulle, "The Mark on the Wall" documents a process altogether different from contemplation of one's mind alone, which may have been the case in Woolf's composition process. And, while Van Hulle does not address her later fiction, her depiction of thoughts may also resemble the tendency he noticed at work in "The Mark on the Wall."

Van Hulle finds the perspective of Woolf's protagonist in "The Mark on the Wall" to be in concert with cognitive scientists' understanding of thought processes. In order to shift between mental life and the representation of it, Van Hulle works from "David Herman's survey of cognitive narratology," concluding that "If the writer's experience of her own process of writing . . . can serve as a model for re-creating the mind of others, this 'mind' is not an interior space, but an enactive complex" (144). "The Mark on the Wall" depicts a process in which "the mind 'swarms' the wall, and a new hypothesis about what the mark might be sets off a new string of thoughts. The structure of the text mimics this interactive way in which an intelligent mind negotiates opportunities for action and interaction within an environment" (148). For a writer, Van Hulle adds, the context "can simply be a notebook" (148).

Van Hulle begins his chapter on "Exogenesis: Writers' Libraries and the Extended Mind" with Kajsa Dahlberg's *A Room of One's Own/A Thousand Libraries* (2006) project depicting readers' inscriptions of library copies of Woolf's essay in Sweden (151).[1] Dahlberg created "a copy of the text with – in the margins and between the lines – numerous layers of comments, exclamation marks and other reactions of various readers" (152). Woolf's essay provides a model case study for the ways that readers engage with texts. As a result, "Dahlberg's work of art shows how a plurality of 'ones' 'own' the text – how they appropriate it, mark it, personalize it – how much energy they are willing to invest in it, and consequently how intense the impact can be" (152).

---

[1] See Kajsa Dahlberg, *A Room of One's Own /A Thousand Libraries*. http://kajsadahlberg.com/work/a-room-of-ones-own--a-thousand-libraries/.

Following Woolf, Van Hulle turns to the reading and reception of her contemporaries.

With regard to Irish writers, Van Hulle focuses first on James Joyce's reading and composition strategies alongside his fiction and then considers Flann O'Brien and Samuel Beckett. Considering all three writers, Van Hulle aspires "to map, first of all, these authors' processes of cognitive transformation and, second, the way they employ the experience of this cognitive enaction to give a literary shape to the process of cognition in their fiction" (154-155). He revisits to Woolf, drawing comparisons ranging from his consideration of the cloud that Stephen Dedalus and Leopold Bloom observe in *Ulysses* as a focal point akin to Woolf's "mark on the wall" to the ways that both writers' work differs from the theories critics have gleaned from and applied to their writing (156). With regard to Joyce's epiphanies in *Stephen Hero*, Van Hulle finds that "there seems to be a discrepancy between Stephen's abstract definition of the epiphany and his concrete example. In the definition, the epiphany is reduced to the sudden spiritual manifestation" (157). In order to consider Joyce's influence, Van Hulle then interprets O'Brien's marginalia in his copy of *Ulysses*, presenting a parallel to Dahlberg's assemblage of responses to *A Room of One's Own*. Woolf remains a touchstone as Van Hulle addresses Beckett, whose composition strategies and translations provide a subject for the remaining chapters.

Van Hulle leaves his readers with a sense of the potential for digital projects to enable future scholarship in his "Conclusion: Manuscript Research and Enactive Cognition." He cites the "Time Passes" manuscripts that are now part of *Woolf Online* as a project that can "make the genesis of texts more accessible and present the written work not only as a single published text, but as a complex interplay between completion and incompletion" (246). This kind of resource can "change the way a new generation of readers looks at literature" (246). Both digital resources and monographs like *Modern Manuscripts* can inspire scholars to examine writers' archives and the development of their ideas.

While Van Hulle opens *Modern Manuscripts* with a segment titled, "Reassessing the so-called 'inward turn' in literary modernism," perhaps he could have acknowledged throughout the volume the limitations he is placing on his treatment of modernism and the ways the field has changed. He observes that "To many students of literature, modernism is still seen as a deliberately 'difficult' or 'elitist' literary movement, notably because of its insistence on a seemingly self-absorbed, 'introspective' preoccupation with 'interior' mental spaces" (6). Many critics have addressed Woolf's responses to social, cultural, and political concerns and Van Hulle might have analyzed further the ways that these interests shaped her composition strategies. On the whole, however, *Modern Manuscripts* is an exemplary contribution to genetic criticism and textual studies.

—Amanda Golden, *New York Institute of Technology*

Roomscape: Women Writers in the British Museum from George Eliot to Virginia Woolf. Susan David Bernstein (Edinburgh: Edinburgh UP, 2013) xii + 231pp

In her essays and fiction, Virginia Woolf depicts the British Museum Reading Room as uninviting to women. She implies that there women will find themselves excluded from the cultural record the library houses, anxious about the outcomes of their research activities, while their male peers completely feel at home consulting texts beneath the "band of famous names" (*AROO* 26)—almost all of them men's—that circle its dome. In *Roomscape*, Susan David Bernstein challenges that view, arguing that in the late Victorian and early Modernist periods the Reading Room gave women access to materials and networking opportunities that sustained careers outside the domestic sphere. It is thus important to Bernstein that the space is seen as productive and empowering because it is public, even egalitarian in its accessibility. She claims that "Woolf's thesis that 'a woman must have money and a room of her own if she is to write fiction' has been taken too literally" (156), and her account of how women writers used the library at the British Museum succeeds in questioning the easy agreement Woolf's conclusion may have promoted. The insightful archival research and close readings of essays and fiction in *Roomscape* make a convincing case for reexamining the British Museum Reading Room as a working environment for writers.

Roomscape is notable for a profile of Woolf that pays special attention to her early career when libraries were important to her as a reviewer for periodicals and a lecturer at Morley College. During that time, she regularly visited the British Museum as well as the London Library (her father Leslie Stephen was president of that institution from 1892 until his death in 1904). Bernstein also concentrates on *Jacob's Room* and *A Room of One's Own*, the two "Room books" in which Woolf discusses the British Museum directly. This focus allows her to consider how "a desire to recognize and acknowledge women writers moves back and forth between imaginative writing and research" (85), for Woolf as well as the other authors Bernstein studies. Indeed, a major strength of *Roomscape* is Bernstein's willingness to see literary work in an expansive way, valuing not only original poetry and fiction but also the production of translations, anthologies, and biographies. These activities, she believes, allowed women writers to increase the visibility of female authorship and better understand their gender's contributions to literature and scholarship. Bernstein examines rich examples, such as Eleanor Marx-Aveling's translation of *Madame Bovary* and *The Doll House*, anthologies of women's poetry edited by Elizabeth Amelia Sharp, and the "Eminent Women" biography series, to which Mathilde Blind contributed a study of George Eliot. Bernstein even recognizes women copyists and researchers who worked for hire, though she does not actually put a face to this anonymous contingent. Bernstein's British Museum appears progressive in its liberal admissions policies, and it facilitated professional encounters in ways a local library could not. Her focus on access aligns her with Woolf in *Three Guineas*, an essay that stresses that women need avenues for self-education and aims to enlarge what is perceived as women's labor. Woolf's indictment of the British Museum Reading Room, then, reflects a distaste for the nationalist self-congratulation inherent in one particular facility and reveals some of her own classist assumptions. Woolf ridicules the mixed company of the Reading Room—its unserious and ignorant readers who do not critically examine the canonical collections—just as Victorian critics did in order to claim that women were undeserving of a space under the dome.

Woolf's Reading Room—the dome like a bald man's forehead (*AROO* 26)—is a tongue-in-cheek caricature. Bernstein dismantles this exaggeration by way of penetrating historical observations. The names around the dome probably receive undue attention in *Jacob's Room* and *A Room of One's Own*, she argues, because Woolf was present in the British Museum right after this decoration was completed in 1907 as part of a major renovation. Woolf's recollections of the library informed her writing at this stage of her career because she was no longer a regular patron, skewing her portrayal of the Reading Room. Bernstein discusses books in the British Museum's collection written by women that indeed would have contributed to the narrator's research on "Women and Poverty" in *A Room of One's Own*. Finally, Woolf's parodic list of subject headings from the Reading Room catalog (*AROO* 28-29), like the fixation on the number of women's names listed on the dome, is evidence of what Bernstein calls a "catalogical" reading of gender—the frequency of references taken for a measure of the recognition of women. Throughout the book Bernstein rightly disputes the overreliance on indexical data, typically compiled in such a way to leave out women and their concerns in the first place, which Woolf intended to illustrate through the fictitious subject headings. Not content to say Woolf replicates the very bias she mocks, Bernstein contends that the narrator of *A Room of One's Own* doodling cartwheels on call slips (*AROO* 27, 32) symbolizes her fluid, inclusive approach to research and that of her female peers—the opposite of mechanical notetaking performed with false assuredness. She ties this insightful analysis to a passage in *Jacob's Room* where the layout of the round Reading Room library is in fact compared to a cartwheel (*JR* 105).

Throughout *Roomscape*, Bernstein is mindful of the British Museum Reading Room as an actual physical space with an effect on researchers' outward behaviors and interior states. Its cartwheel layout could facilitate collaboration or make readers feel exposed, which she shows was the case with George Eliot who preferred to work in private. Although one of Bernstein's goals is to show the "overdetermined value of privacy and autonomy" (1) when discussing working spaces for women writers, it is difficult for her to downplay how privilege prompts inclinations to solitude. Investigating class further would transform the book into a different study, however—one that would need to extend far beyond the British Museum. Nonetheless, Bernstein excels in illustrating how working in the Reading Room caused women writers to reflect on their place in history and in culture. In *Jacob's Room*, Woolf envisions its dome as a skull enveloping a great brain where the past comes alive in the present (*JR* 105). She is far from alone in writing fiction that imbues the Reading Room with a sense of the uncanny, which Bernstein emphasizes through her fascinating reading of Amy Levy's ghost story, "The Recent Telepathic Occurrence at the British Museum" (1888). *Roomscape* draws upon basic theories of spaces and archives when considering the architecture of the library, yet these references are not nearly as compelling as Bernstein's historical research on the British Museum. She looks to Foucault, Benjamin, and Derrida to affirm that the Reading Room is best seen as a space of possibility, rather than of disciplined behaviors, but does so in a manner of blunt application that unfortunately gives the impression that covering theory is for her a necessary inconvenience.

Woolf is the point of departure for *Roomscape* and the subject of the book's final chapter, whereas the intervening chapters are focused on late Victorian writers, including Clementina Black and Constance Black Garnett, among the others mentioned previously in this review. The women writers Bernstein follows aside from Woolf and Eliot involve themselves much more in networking opportunities afforded by working in the Reading Room. Bernstein knowingly reveals a divide between women reliant on access to the British Museum for their work and those who have access to books outside its walls and can visit the Reading Room when most appropriate for their purposes. She admits, too, that some of the associations and mentorships the women had with male patrons and employees were helpful but not ideal, because they were still freighted with dismissive attitudes towards women (e.g., Richard Garrett's backhanded compliments for women writers he befriended in entries written for the *Dictionary of National Biography*). Relationships like these make it difficult to accept Bernstein's suggestion that the Reading Room functioned as a *de facto* salon. To be sure, *Roomscape* is not a study of direct collaborations among writers; it instead reveals common concerns underlying individual projects performed in and around a library designed for solitary study. One cannot deny that the Reading Room environment promoted a *feeling* of community among patrons. Woolf herself recognized that readers in the British Museum, under the influence of the library's "most official discreet impersonal mood," devoted themselves to making new books out of old ones (*D3* 80). This particular kind of work, when carried out in earnest in the Reading

Room, always implied a shared sense of purpose. The British Museum Reading Room is for Susan David Bernstein a place where women could come to locate themselves within artistic and scholarly traditions "that extended backwards into the past, and forwards, with revolutionary possibility, into the future" (76). Woolf's "room of one's own" is only one vision of that future, Bernstein affirms, and, as another option, she encourages us to consider the library a communal workshop.
—Matthew James Vechinski, *Virginia Commonwealth University*

Modernism and Autobiography. Maria DiBattista and Emily O. Wittman, eds. (New York: Cambridge UP, 2014) xix + 228pp.

Robert Scholes once waggled a finger at me during his office hours and said, "The author is not dead, just sleeping." Indeed, while years of post-structuralism and new criticism once made literary scholars leery of comprehending the author, these modes eventually led them to re-conceive of authorship, and repurpose it to suitable ends. Two decades-ish ago, modernist studies rediscovered the author through greater attention to modernism's public faces and institutions—newfound scrutiny of the publication processes, publicity, celebrity, legal wrangles, and general involvement of modernist writers with the culture of the market. This model of scholarship treated the author not as (if I may set up a bit of a strawman) a reified *a priori* psychological origin of text but as an aspect of modernist textuality. In other words, modernist studies has used the text of authorship to theorize its authors in ways that produce fresh readings of culture.

This development opens the door for new readings of modernists' personal chronicles, the autobiographies, memoirs, and diaries that have often been relegated to secondary status in the field, for new analyses of how writers of the period made use of these genres, and what is more, for new understandings of the role such works play in the culture of the (long) early Twentieth Century. Maria DiBattista and Emily O. Wittman's edited collection *Modernism and Autobiography* expertly addresses this critical aperture through its sixteen excellent essays and its argument, announced at the start, that "modernist writers transformed the conventions and expanded the scope of autobiographical writings" (xi). DiBattista and Wittman's introduction gracefully yet forcefully lists narrative characteristics untraditional but nonetheless shared by the autobiographies addressed in the volume: depictions of brief transformative periods at the expense of greater trajectories (Virginia Woolf), upending of chronology (Jean Rhys), ellipses and evasions (Henry Adams), subversion, grammatical and plural, with the notion of self (Gertrude Stein, Alice Toklas, W. B. Yeats, Ernest Hemingway), or interrogations of the journey to self-awareness that govern much traditional autobiographical writing (Katherine Mansfield). In this way, the editors argue, modernist autobiography "troubles both the 'bios' ... and the 'auto'" (xii).

The chapters that follow, penetrating case studies by a stellar cast of scholars perfectly suited to their subjects, deliver on the high standard of nuance promised by DiBattista and Wittman. The first section, "Ancestries," addresses some of the early modernists—Edmund Gosse (Francis O'Gorman), Yeats (Rónán McDonald), Joseph Conrad (Michael Levenson), and Henrys James and Adams (Lee Mitchell)—its thematic highlighting the essays' shared concern with the status of memory. The segment concludes with Elizabeth Abel's "Spaces of Time: Virginia Woolf's Life-Writing," which chronicles Woolf's sustained investment in "life-writing" (Woolf's coinage), and reads her diaries and "A Sketch of the Past" for the way they theorize autobiographical writing. Abel cites Woolf's note to self that an individual life "must lack centre" (qtd. 56) as a key to the impersonal character of Woolf's life-writing, marked by "gaps that had always existed in the original atmosphere" (61). Woolf's depiction of the traumatic childhood event when her stepbrother Gerald sexually molested her is, Abel says, readable in this context, a fragmented, visual anecdote that in turn fragments the earlier passages. Woolf's treatment of autobiography, to Abel, provides the key to grasping Woolf's oeuvre overall, her ongoing search for a form that would depict "the force of life" (qtd. 65).

Abel's essay, despite its foray into Woolf's fiction, trains itself on autobiographical writings. Indeed, one of the strengths of *Modernism and Autobiography* is its consistent focus on under-analyzed nonfictional writings. Section Two, "Emerging," maintains this approach while showing modernist life-writing negotiating issues of identity. It begins with Jonathan Greenberg's treatment of Waugh's first travel volume, *Labels*, as demonstrating a carefully conceived "writing personality" (71); moves to Barbara Will casting Toklas's *Cook Book* as part of a pattern of "queer autobiographical masquerade" (85) that Stein had established; Allen Hepburn on Elizabeth Bowen's autobiographical works in relation to her vexed but carefully managed public persona; and Marc C. Conner reading Ralph Ellison's autobiographical essay about his Oklahoma roots, "Leaving the Territory," as an acknowledgment of the omnipresence of the past.

Section Three, "Surviving," starts with the volume's sole excursion into non-Anglo culture, Santanu Das's look at the lives of working-class Indian soldiers and civilians during World War I, and includes Jay Dickson on Mansfield, Max Saunders on T. S. Eliot, and DiBattista on Hemingway. The section considers the mediation of autobiographical writings, exemplified by the fragmentary archive scrutinized by Das, by Saunders's portrayal of Eliot as anxious about how employing a typist will alter the meaning of his letters, and by DiBattista's considering Mary Hemingway's editorial hand in *A Moveable Feast*, contributing to a text self-consciously replete with wish-fulfilling historical revisionism, legible in the text's vacillations between first- and second-person narration.

Modernism and Autobiography finishes strong. The final section, "Disappearing," starts with Wittman's essay about Rhys, highlighted by her reading of the posthumously edited and published *Smile, Please* as darkly subverting the idea of a coherent autobiographical persona. Robert Caserio's essay, "Abstraction, Impersonality, Dissolution," treats a variety of writers, among them W. E. B. DuBois, H. G. Wells, Stein, F. Scott Fitzgerald, and Henry Miller. It is a bravura piece, ranging quickly but never seeming restless or impatient; the editors are canny to break the pattern that dominates the volume. The last essay, Michael Wood on—who else?—Samuel Beckett, also departs from the established mold, reading Beckett's fictions for their depictions of characters' own life-writing, and the attendant theorizations of autobiography.

Modernism and Autobiography thus covers a wide terrain while reading mostly as a taut and coherent collection. Modernist scholars will find the volume essential for its readings of individual writers, for the theoretical gauntlet thrown down by DiBattista and Wittman, and, most of all, for being the most sustained and thorough treatment of its pairing of modernism and life-writing. The volume shows modernist studies' participation in a wider re-examination of such texts: "Narrating Lives" was the theme of the annual MLA meeting's Presidential Forum in 2011. The book's tight focus on Anglo-American writers invites scholars of international modernism to theorize autobiography in modernist culture of other geographies. Similarly, devotees of modernist life-writings unrepresented here but thematically comparable (Anaïs Nin, James Joyce, Vera Brittain, Rebecca West, Woody Guthrie, etc.), can use the volume as a springboard, to rationalize writing and publishing treatments of modernism and autobiography that support, skew, or expand the picture painted here.

—Jonathan Goldman, *New York Institute of Technology, Manhattan*

A Poetics of Postmodernism and Neomodernism: Rewriting Mrs. Dalloway. Monica Latham (New York: Palgrave Macmillan, 2015) vii + 272pp.

Fiction following Woolf, that is, in some way featuring Woolf as a character or a muse, has a lively recent history in a variety of genres. Some examples: literary intrigue (Morgan, *A Book for All or None*); suspense (Barron, *The White*

Garden); espionage (Hawkes and Manso, *The Shadow of the Moth*); sci-fi (Scott, *I, Vampire*); lesbian pulp (Pass, *Zoe's Book*); biofiction, (Nunez, *Mitz: The Marmoset of Bloomsbury*; Freeman, *But* Nobody Lives in Bloomsbury; Sellers, *Vanessa and Virginia*). Perhaps the best-known of these recastings, Michael Cunningham's *The Hours* is the first of several contemporary novels discussed in Monica Latham's *A Poetics of Postmodernism and Neomodernism: Rewriting* Mrs. Dalloway. By limiting her readings to literary fiction following a single Woolf novel, she is able to elaborate on the style and structure both of what she calls (after Genette) Woolf's hypotext and the contemporary hypertexts which play off it. To organize her discussions, she groups the novels under the critical rubrics of her title. The book might have benefitted from reversing the title and subtitle. The readings of post-Woolf novels provide a fine commentary on the style of *Mrs. Dalloway* and the book brings attention to several novels not usually considered closely in their Woolfian contexts. It is, however, less successful in formulating a poetics of post- and neo-modernism because, while it uses these terms to differentiate various *Dalloway* successors, it does not offer new formulations of them.

The "rewriting" of the subtitle refers both to Woolf's own writing of the novel in its several versions, and to the hypertexts produced by later writers in a Woolfian afterlife. Latham's first chapter, in which she lays out the genetic dimension of *Mrs. Dalloway* by carefully recording the genesis and progress of its composition, is especially useful. Using Woolf's relevant notebooks, stories, and manuscript versions, referring as well to passages in her letters and diaries, Latham establishes what she calls somewhat infelicitously "Dallowayisms" (a term borrowed from Seymour Chatman) to pave the way for her later examinations of contemporary fictions. She argues that in order to best appreciate the impact *Mrs. Dalloway* has had on some subsequent writers, one must first identify the origins and developments of some key features of Woolf's style and structure. In the process of tracing these elements, Latham argues for a kind of narrative of progress, in which Woolf increasingly refines and makes more striking her own most identifiable prose markers. Though this argument and the chronological account of the composition of Woolf's novel is not the main focus of the book as a whole, it makes a particularly valuable contribution to Woolf studies in its clarity and succinctness. Latham draws with much care and appreciation on Helen Wussow's manuscript work, on the earlier genetic accounts of scholars, such as Charles Hoffman, more recent accounts of the evolution of *Mrs. Dalloway* and of Clarissa from the related short stories and earlier novel versions.

Of the many stylistic features that she might have discussed as typical, Latham wisely focuses on just two extended examples in *Mrs. Dalloway* to demonstrate the conflation of Dallowayisms that appear in the published novel after being worked through in the short stories and manuscript versions. She argues that the first of these, Septimus's hallucinations at home, grow increasingly irrational with each iteration as Woolf rewrites scenes in the British Museum Notebooks, sometimes adding autobiographical details and reworking earlier motifs (e.g. fire, water, light). Latham quotes materials from the notebooks as they are rewritten and as they finally appear in *Mrs. Dalloway*. Similarly, in her second example, she interprets rewritings of significant "moments of being" like Clarissa's and Sally's kiss, and Clarissa's meditations on the old lady across the way. In doing so, Latham traces how stylistic and structural patterns of repetition create "more accomplished poetic distillations" to provide a distinct rhythm and structural unity to her novel that are not present in the earlier versions.

Latham's sustained attention to Woolf's own rewriting is a valuable contribution to scholarship, but is only one kind of rewriting discussed in the book. The other refers to writers following Woolf who have reworked or referenced *Mrs. Dalloway*'s themes, motifs, and stylistic markers. She distinguishes between two groups of writers by categorizing them as postmodern or neomodern and argues first that the number and quality of these writers sustain, enhance and "ultimately enshrine" *Mrs. Dalloway* as a crucial modernist text ever open to new generations of readers. Her cogent discussions of hypertexts make this first argument quite convincingly. Her second aim is "to assess the state of current literary fiction and look into postmodernist and neomodernist approaches to fiction" (209) by tracing the ways some (mostly) recent (mostly) British writers have "remembered and updated modernism's innovations," or have "dismembered and reassembled them" (210). This claim is less successful than the first because, while she provides careful readings of a number of novels, she does not significantly advance discussions of what the terms postmodern and neomodern indicate. As she notes, there are many such extant commentaries, especially of postmodernism, and while she calls on some of them in her readings, she spends most of her discussions on how the post-Woolf hypertexts draw on, reconfigure, and play with *Mrs. Dalloway*.

The pomo/neo distinction does provide a useful heuristic for ordering her discussion, however. The "postmodernist" "Dalloway-esque" novels she takes up are Michael Cunningham's *The Hours* and Robin Lippincott's *Mr. Dalloway*. She names these writers "ventriloquists" in detailing both how they rely on Woolf's hypotext and also how they transform it with their own innovations. Drawing especially on discussions of postmodern parody and pastiche by Jameson and others and on the use of self-referentiality, she traces the ways in which Cunningham and Lippincott "replicated, prolonged and amplified" the source text using much-discussed tenets of postmodern style (93). In so doing, she argues, they brought attention from contemporary readers to Woolf's novel by popularizing it. Unlike some other Woolf scholars, Latham applauds Cunningham's novel for creating "an enjoyable text," one that is easier to read than *Mrs. Dalloway* and that provides its own stand-alone attractions. At the same time, both novels provide the knowledgeable Woolf reader the satisfaction of following the carefully-wrought revised uses of Dallowayisms (97).

Latham's next chapter, on postmodernist followers, focuses not on novels, but on two shorter parodic pieces and one novel excerpt. The most entertaining of these inclusions is a twitter version of *Mrs. Dalloway* put together by Alexander Aciman and Emmett Rensin in *Twitterature*. Who knew that the intensity of Septimus's hallucinations might be tweeted as "On a side note, has anybody noticed that @Septimus's posts have become a little erratic since the war ended?" (Aciman and Rensin 121). Another parodic text she discusses, John Crace's caricature of *Mrs. Dalloway* in *Brideshead Abbreviated: The Digested Read of the Twentieth Century*, is much less fun. Though Latham describes it as a respectful hypertext, it also seems a little mean-spirited, especially in its closing: "'One of my patients committed suicide today,' Bradshaw announced. 'Delayed shell-shock is a terrible condition.' Clarissa's eyes glazed over. Just like yours" (Crace 93). Latham closes the chapter on these "parodic games" with a brief discussion of an excerpt from David Lodge's *The British Museum is Falling Down*, a series of "complex patchwork[s]" of various authorial styles, including that of *Mrs. Dalloway* (119). As she does with the other parodies discussed in this chapter and the novels of Cunningham and Lippincott, Latham underlines Lodge's effort both to entertain and to challenge his readers through his use of parody and pastiche.

The postmodernist heirs of Woolf's legacy have recognizable correspondences to *Mrs. Dalloway*. The neomodernists often do not. Instead, they carry over the modernist "aura" of the novel; rather than parodying Woolf's hypotext, they reanimate and reinvent "Dalloway-esque" strategies in their rewritings (129). Latham selects some of the novels she does (Isherwood's *A Single Man*; McEwan's *Saturday*; James Hynes's *Next*; John Lanchester's *Mr. Phillips*) because they use the single-day format and because they are especially interested in writing interiority and/or pursuing Woolfian topics—time and war particularly. Isherwood, McEwan, and Hynes have specifically noted their interest in Woolf's work in general and *Mrs. Dalloway* in particular. Latham again does an excellent job of following their stylistic and structural choices in arguing for them as "neomodernist heirs." The second group of heirs she discusses (Rachel Cusk, Jon McGregor, and Ali Smith) are even further removed from direct references to *Mrs. Dalloway*, although, as she notes, the opening of Smith's *Hotel World* in which a character's fall in a broken dumbwaiter becomes "what a fall what a soar what a plummet what a dash into dark into light what a plunge what a glide thud crash" will be instantly recognizable to *Dalloway* readers (196). Instead, these writers rewrite *Mrs. Dalloway* by extending modernist sensibilities and stylistic choices. Wisely, her final discussion of Smith's *Hotel World* remarks on its postmodern as well as neomodern character. In loosening these two organizing rubrics, she allows them the fluidity necessary for her discussion of *Mrs. Dalloway*'s very different successors. Although her contributions to further understandings of "postmodern" and "neomodern" are necessarily limited by her fuller focus on the details of Woolf's novel, her book gives Woolf scholars a chance once again to appreciate the achievement and staying power of *Mrs. Dalloway*.

—Carolyn Allen, *University of Washington*

Works Cited

Aciman, Alexander and Emmett Resin. "Mrs Dalloway." *Twitterature*. New York: Penguin 2009.121-22.

Crace, John. "Mrs. Dalloway." *Brideshead Abbreviated: The Digested Read of the Twentieth Century*. London: Arrow Books, 2011.91-3.

The Cambridge Companion to Modernist Culture. Ed. Celia Marshik (New York: Cambridge UP, 2015) vii + 257pp.

The Cambridge Companion to The Bloomsbury Group. Ed. Victoria Rosner (New York: Cambridge UP, 2014) vii + 245pp.

With the turn in modernist literary studies toward a more interdisciplinary and expansive exploration of the crossings, networks, and confluences that produced culture between 1890 and 1940, both *Modernist Culture* and *The Bloomsbury Group*, new additions to the Cambridge Companion series, will come as sweet relief to students and scholars feeling overwhelmed by the amount of material one must master in order to call oneself a modernist. Celia Marshik notes in her introduction to *Modernist Culture* that such a turn presents a "high barrier to students and scholars, who are now expected not only to familiarize themselves with texts like *Ulysses* and *The Great Gatsby* and with movements such as Futurism, Symbolism, and the Harlem Renaissance but also to understand the significance of the Charleston, the gramophone, little magazines, 'talkies,' the bias cut" (2)—a list that can go on and on and does within the pages of this valuable, and rather fun, collection of essays.

True to the intent of the Cambridge series, *Modernist Culture* is meant to be a resource for beginning research on topics like sports, religion and spirituality, fashion, film, dance, and travel; while each essay can stand alone as an excellent starting point for students new to the topic, the book is also highly engaging as a cover to cover read as it combines sharp, incisive essays with thoughtful organization. The essays as a group explore the ways in which cultural, material, political, social, and technological innovations both inspired and were inspired by modernism (3), and clear connections between essays evolve across the book. For example, Ulrike Maude's smart piece, "Science, Technology, and the Body," sets up modern attitudes about innovations like the X-ray, telephone, automobile, airplane, and cinema and their effects on the human body. Maude's inclusion of the "seemingly innocuous" cinema which "offered vicarious thrills" and "posed risks to the nervous constitution of the spectator" (37) is later historicized in Susan McCabe's expansive piece "Modernist Film and Cinema Culture," and emerges again in Carrie Preston's "Dance," which beautifully articulates the desire to capture the most fleeting kind of human movement on film. Thus, a topic like "cinema" is articulated through several modes of its influence on modern culture, enriching our comprehension of it. Another strong combination exists between Elizabeth Outka's "Consumer Culture," which imagines a shopping trip for a middle-class white woman, from the newspaper ads that would greet her while she drank her morning tea to the way that the department store would aid in helping her invent a fluid sense of identity, despite her class, and Ilya Parkins's essay, "Fashion," which explores how consumers of fashion might play with "self-invention, reinvention, imitation, masquerade" (103). It becomes clear, when reading the two essays together, that high fashion and everyday consumption are imbricated, challenging categories of high, middle, and low and offering a more nuanced discussion of sartorial expression and modern life. One of the chief successes of the collection is to present the modern and modernity (and by implication the terms "modernism" and "modernist") as fluid, malleable, unfixed to any particular moment, movement, or group; "What we have understood as modernism continues to change. We see facts differently; the subjectivity of objectivity is what modernism shows us again and again," writes Jessica Burstein in her chapter, "Visual Art" (156).

The geographic mobility of the individual (the ex-pat, the tourist) has long been a centerpiece of how we theorize the period, but by balancing her introductory argument on the term "cultural translation," Marshik deepens the impact of such movement to establish that modes of cultural production cannot be understood without acknowledging their movement across not only color and class lines, but national borders and around the world (5). The impact of cultural translation and its implications should offer a welcome perspective to scholars who through transnationalism and "new modernist studies" are interrogating the hierarchy and institutionalized patriarchy embedded in more traditional approaches to modernism; however, the particular essays largely reinforce the expected "centers" of modernism, Paris, London, New York, Berlin, and Hollywood. This should not be read as a shortcoming of the collection, but rather a call to recognize that a turn toward interdisciplinarity and cultural translation necessitates considering geographic locations apart from those expected as this branch of the field continues to develop.

One expected "center" of modernist culture that continues to grip us is, of course, the Bloomsbury Group. The energetic and agitated discussion over the Woolf listserv during the summer of 2015 about BBC Two's three-part miniseries, *Life in Squares*, in which many list-members lamented the program's focus on the gossip and sex lives of the Bloomsberries while also to some degree enjoying it as a "guilty pleasure" revealed the tensions that inevitably crop up when historical situations are fictionalized for a mass audience. Once again, literary and cultural history is overtly sexualized to keep it interesting for the masses, or all of us who watched the program. Thus, *The Bloomsbury Group* comes as a timely and necessary source to which we can direct those who might have questions about the dynamic relationships, cultural production, political leanings, and public engagements of the members of the group.

Victoria Rosner writes in her introduction that the collection serves to present a "group portrait, with the focus on the ideas, philosophies, predilections, and affinities members of the group often shared" and while the book does not rely on anecdotes, it also does not skirt the importance of the relations between members as they impacted the productivity and cultural output of its members (12). With such a focus on how the friendships among members of the group aided in developing strong yet highly nuanced political, artistic, and social critiques, the essays resist categorization and blanket terminology and tackle some of the more difficult complexities these thinking, living, working individuals deliver through the copious written archive they left behind. A strong example of this can be seen in "Bloomsbury and Empire," in which Gretchen Holbrook Gerzina notes the difficulty that scholars often make for themselves in wanting to "explain away" (113) prejudices held by Virginia Woolf and others and uses her essay to face the complexity of attitudes about empire developed in childhood that "clashed, often quite deliberately, with the ways that they now constructed their lives and work" (114), especially when it came to the added disillusioning effects of the Great War. Gerzina's contribution serves as a solid companion piece to Christine Froula's "War, Peace, and Internationalism," which, through its analysis of Bloomsbury's conscientious objectors and pacifists, brings into relief that the "voluminous archive of private life and public discourse slices myriad cross sections through this violent era" (97) and places the members within a "history of peace movements" to reveal their significant effect on public discourse (108).

The book's section titled "Arts" presents three smart essays that can and should be read together. Mary Ann Caws's "Pens and Paintbrushes" sets up the relationship between the writing of Virginia Woolf, Leonard Woolf, Lytton Strachey, Clive Bell, and Vita Sackville-West and the painting of Roger Fry, Dora Carrington, Vanessa Bell, and Duncan Grant as intertwined and dependent upon each other for full expression. While the intersections of all these figures are too numerous for Caws to treat in this essay, she provides a wonderful sketch of the networks among them that are necessary for digging deeper into these artistic relationships. Helen Southworth's essay, "The Bloomsbury Group and Book Arts," follows naturally after Caws to offer a history and impact of the aforementioned artists' contributions to the book covers for the Hogarth Press. Southworth draws the relationship between writing and painting/illustrating into the marketplace, a valuable way of showing how modernists not only made but also sold culture, thereby shaping and translating their aesthetics to a broader audience. In particular, Laura Marcus's "Bloomsbury Aesthetics" traces Roger Fry's development from an art critic to an art theorist and how his contributions to an aesthetic particular to Bloomsbury culture would influence Clive and Virginia in their reception of visual art.

The book's final section's three essays ruminate on the impact of Bloomsbury. Vesna Goldsworthy's "The Bloomsbury Narcissus" explores the massive archive of life writing left behind by members of the group and their far-flung networks and thoughtfully considers the implications of the resurfacing of unknown documents. Brenda Silver's fascinating essay documents the group's reception (both positive and negative) in the decades immediately following World War II when pre-war conceptions of class, elitism, and intelligentsia were being challenged in Britain and the United States ("Intellectual Crossings and Reception"). The collection closes with "Bloomsbury's Afterlife," in which Regina Marler reaffirms Rosner's hope that a study of the group as a whole, their complex relationships with each other, their development of aesthetics and intellectual rigor, as well as an examination of Bloomsbury revivalism in contemporary popular culture, offers a heretofore needed perspective about the complicated impact of Bloomsbury on notions of culture, class, gender, sexuality, and the arts, not only in their time, but in ours. There is no sign of an ebb in popular culture's attention to the figures, innovations, fashions, and practices of the interwar period, and both *Modernist Culture* and *The Bloomsbury Group* serve as essential, reliable, well researched sources for scholars, students, and common readers whose interests might be initially piqued by what they see on their television screens.

—Sarah E. Cornish, *University of Northern Colorado*

The Cambridge Companion to To the Lighthouse. Allison Pease, ed.
(New York: Cambridge UP, 2015) xix + 182pp.

For many Woolf scholars, the great appeal of her writing—and the factor that draws us back to her writings time and again—is the way in which they remain open to new critical interpretations. If proof were needed, there is no text better than *To the Lighthouse*, which continues to attract new lines of research. It is also a popular choice of text for teaching Woolf, for it provides opportunities to analyze Woolf's modernist style, to relate her writing practices to contemporary developments in the visual arts, to consider familial and biographical influences, and to discuss her engagement with social issues such as gender and class. The *Cambridge Companion* series aims to cater to both these markets by introducing students to key critical issues, while keeping lecturers interested by presenting new interventions by respected scholars. There is a delicate balance to be struck here of course, and this collection contains many noteworthy pieces without quite giving the student a sound introduction to the range of critical enquiry on this novel. It is symptomatic of the uneven structure of the collection that the summary of contents that follows does not match the order of the chapters—neither does it match the editor's overview of contents in the introduction.

The collection starts on a high note, with Anne Fernald's excellent essay "*To the Lighthouse* in the Context of Virginia Woolf's Diaries and Life." Fernald deftly draws links between the novel and Woolf's family background, her daily life, and national affairs. However, in a careful study of how Woolf's diary entries shed light on her practices as a writer, Fernald invites us to be cautious about how far we should look for her life in her novel. As Fernald wisely comments, "In the end, the asymmetries between art and life have as much to teach us as the correspondences do" (6).

Fernald's piece has an interesting counterpart in the penultimate chapter by Hans Walter Gabler, which applies genetic criticism to examine the novel's evolution through successive drafts. This chapter highlights the process by which life (or, more specifically, memory) is gradually reshaped and changed into fiction: he argues that draft materials provide "significant clues to the construction, transformation, and variation underlying the conversion of memory into fiction" (147).

Chapters Two and Three are both concerned with stylistic analysis of the novel. Michael Levenson presents a brilliant analysis of the effects of Woolf's rapid and often subtle shifts in time and space. Taking apart the idea that there may be a "narrator" in this text, he makes a close reading of the use of indirect discourse while also drawing our attention to key moments of apparent omniscience. Jane Goldman's article, "*To the Lighthouse*'s Use of Language and

Form" takes a wider scope than its title suggests. There is some close investigation of Woolf's linguistic practices, including framing and parentheses (particularly the perennially moving sentence narrating Mrs. Ramsay's death, and the "Yes" of the opening and closing sentences), but Goldman also demonstrates how Woolf's prose follows the artistic practice of "mosaicking," a key concept from Roger Fry that was taken up by Vanessa Bell. This is used to generate alternative readings of Woolf's sketch of "two blocks joined by a corridor" in her "Notes for Writing," making interesting parallels with art, mathematics, and architecture.

The next three chapters explore philosophical perspectives on the novel. Two of these place Woolf within her intellectual heritage. Paul Sheehan, in "Time as Protagonist in *To the Lighthouse*," traces the influence on Woolf of the techniques of Proust and Pater, and the philosophies of Russell, Bergson, Einstein, and most significantly, the Cambridge Apostles. These are brought most powerfully to bear on the treatment of time in the novel, including an analysis of Woolf's use of different tenses to show how experimentation with time was essential to Woolf's aesthetic. Emily Dalgarno, agreeing with Sheehan's suggestion that Woolf's knowledge of philosophy came mainly from her "intellectual milieu" rather than "comprehensive" knowledge (49), points to other influences, including G. E. Moore and Leslie Stephen, particularly in his writings on Hume. Dalgarno makes a convincing case that the novel engages its reader in philosophical considerations (through rhetorical questions such as Lily Briscoe's "what does it mean?") and that these questions remain open rather than being resolved. Chief among these questions is the problem of representation and how this relates to truth.

The intervening philosophical chapter by Melba Cuddy-Keane exemplifies a more recent trend in Woolf studies of analyzing her work through the lens of current concepts: in this case "embodied cognition," or the idea that "the body thinks" because "bodily experience is the shape of thought itself" (58). Cuddy-Keane uses this theory to present some excellent detailed analyses of characters' bodily experience and gestures and how these relate to their thought patterns, such as the cognitive significance of Cam's simple gesture of dipping her hand in the water on the voyage to the lighthouse.

Chapters Seven to Ten explore *To the Lighthouse* in the context of social and political issues. There is a telling contrast between the first and last of the chapters in this group. Gabrielle McIntire's chapter is on "Feminism and Gender," a somewhat vague topic which sets out the now dated account of Woolf as an angry reactionary to patriarchy or, more narrowly, to her father. In contrast to Fernald and Gabler's more sophisticated accounts of how life is transmuted into art, Mr. and Mrs. Ramsay are read as straightforward representatives of Julia and Leslie Stephen. Cam's attempted rebellion is not considered independently of her brother James and there is little on Lily's resistance to traditional roles.

This neglect of generational differences in gender is admirably addressed by Ana Parejo Vadillo's excellent analysis of the tensions between Victorian and modernist attitudes towards women's roles. The chapter is valuable for its detailed readings of the work of John Ruskin and Coventry Patmore as intertexts (rather than as straw men). The chapter includes a nuanced reading of the photograph of Woolf wearing her mother's dress as "a form of loving and a form of mourning both at a biographical and at a symbolic level" (128). Identifying the limitations in Woolf's rejection of the Victorians, Vadillo also draws attention to ways in which she wrote out the New Woman as the draft character of Miss Sophie Briscoe was transmuted into Lily.

It is important for the collection to include discussion of the significant topic of race in Woolf. However, as Urmila Seshagiri's slightly forced chapter demonstrates, *To the Lighthouse* has less to offer than some of the other novels, such as *Orlando* with the battered head of a Moor, or *Mrs. Dalloway* and Peter Walsh's Indian baggage. Some of Seshagiri's claims, such as the suggestion that "Woolf's images of the family's teacups and china remind us that even the most banal signifiers of English civility stem from centuries of racial conflict" (98), needed to be more fully supported by postcolonial theory to be convincing.

Overall, the collection would have benefited from more contributions that take the lead from critics like Anna Snaith and Mark Hussey in recognizing the more radically politicized Woolf and locating her in the real world. This school of thought is ably represented, however, by Kathryn Simpson's chapter on class, which makes insightful links between the novel and class politics of 1909-19, including the General Strike, and also builds on Alison Light's recent work on Woolf and servants for a reading of Mrs. McNab.

Perhaps surprisingly, given the centrality of Lily Briscoe's creative process to the novel, there is only one chapter on art. This is contributed by Suzanne Bellamy, who is well known as a professional artist whose work has inspired many at the Annual Virginia Woolf conferences. Bellamy discusses Woolf's engagement with a range of artists and artistic movements, including her uncomfortable relationship with formalism. She also draws attention to Woolf's dramatic use of visual objects like James's axe or Lily's kitchen table to disrupt the fabric of the text (137), a device that paradoxically questions the efficacy of verbal representation and provides greater freedom than a material canvas could afford (143).

As can be seen, this volume has much to interest Woolf scholars and to challenge stronger undergraduates. It would have been a more coherent collection, and therefore more beneficial to a wider range of students, if there had been a more helpful introduction, leaving out the lengthy plot summary (which could be easily be found online if absolutely needed), and including a clearer map of the contents

and the structure of the collection. Like the round-up of criticism in the final chapter, the introduction would have benefited from an overview of how Woolf studies have responded to changing trends, such as the contrasting influences of Anglo-American feminism and French feminism, as well as the rediscovery of a politically engaged Woolf, and developments in textual scholarship that have accompanied successive waves of editions (most recently the Cambridge editions). But since these new editions are still emerging, it leaves room for a further collection, revisiting *To the Lighthouse* for another generation of students.
—Jane de Gay, *Leeds Trinity University*

Works Cited

Woolf, Virginia. "Notes for writing." *Woolf Online*. Web. October 16, 2015. http://www.woolfonline.com.

Interdisciplinary/Multidisciplinary Woolf: Selected Papers from the Twenty-Second Annual International Conference on Virginia Woolf.
[University of Saskatchewan, Saskatoon, Canada, 7-10 June 2012]
Ann Martin and Kathryn Holland, eds.
(Clemson, SC: Clemson U Digital P, 2013) iii + 298pp.

Virginia Woolf and the Common(wealth) Reader: Selected Papers from the Twenty-Third Annual International Conference on Virginia Woolf.
[Simon Fraser University, Vancouver, Canada, 6-9 June 2013]
Helen Wussow and Mary Ann Gillies, eds.
(Clemson, SC: Clemson U Digital P, 2014) iii + 250pp.

I'm partial to manners. It's an aspect of the scholarship of the late Jane Marcus (intellectual upstart that she was) to credit your sources, acknowledge the work and reputations of the scholars, students, and common readers alike, whose work informs your own. Jane loved the annual Virginia Woolf conference. She recognized it as an inspiration and forum for new ideas and used it as a resource for her own professional and creative output. To acknowledge, to say please and thank you, to help create, foster, and continue a network of conversations, especially those by and about women and marginalized voices, in general, for Jane, as for Virginia Woolf, was a public, purposeful, and political act. The two editions of *Selected Papers* under discussion in this review represent a significant body of work (63 essays in total) by many established and influential Woolf critics writing today. Additionally, the two volumes provide avenues of inquiry begun by emerging Woolf scholars, eager to build on the conversation and investigate its relevance and effect in relation to the urgency of our own contemporary times. Yes, please. And thank you.

Interdisciplinary/Multidisciplinary Woolf, deftly edited and introduced by Ann Martin and Kathryn Holland, notes that the 22nd Annual International Conference held in Saskatoon, Saskatchewan, "on Treaty Six territory," was the first Woolf conference held in Canada, and the conference organizers "recognized the significance of place" as scholars convened from around the globe to discuss issues of "discursive and methodological differences, as well as the point at which disciplines could be integrated and distinctions could be questioned" (vii). The political significance of the conference thematics, suggestive of borders, border-crossings, and border-sharings, became glaringly apparent, when Conor Tomás Reed and J. Ashley Foster, my two co-panelists, (who also happened to be students of Jane Marcus), were refused entry into the country because of Conor's involvement in peaceful protests against tuition hikes at the City University of New York. Conor was sent home on a bus at his own expense; Ashley arrived late, outraged, physically and emotionally exhausted by further interrogation procedures she endured during her second attempt at entering the country to attend the conference; and our panel on the politics of fascism, patriarchy, and oppression as outlined in Woolf's *Three Guineas* was re-scheduled, missing Conor, and read to a small audience of roughly five individuals, as a result of the now necessary reshuffling of time slots. If we were interested in keeping score, it may appear out in the left field bleachers, the street-credentialed "cheap seats," as: Fascists 1; Woolf scholars 0. But pacifists like Woolf understood that "peace is a process," and she often recognized and exposed the faulty reasoning behind outcome assessments and institutionally revered results. And so, to the conference organizers' credit, the entire 22nd Annual International Conference on Virginia Woolf, the faculty and administration of the University of Saskatchewan, and, if I may be permitted my belief that thoughts are things, Woolf herself, as if arriving *dea ex machina*, expressed and provided immediate concern and support in light of the incident itself, which was "out of proportion to the situation" and moving forward raised questions about "the policies and procedures that inform border officials' actions" (n.2, xii). Included in this volume, J. Ashley Foster's essay "Stopped at the Border: Virginia Woolf and the Criminalization of Dissent in Democratic Societies" and Conor Tomás Reed's "'Q. And babies? A. And babies': On Pacifism, Visual Trauma, and the Body Heap," serve as important responses to the consequences of excessive policing and patrolling of borders in a climate of fear, as well as a marker of the relevance and efficacy of critical trends in Woolf Studies today.

Another boon to the gathering together of *Selected Papers* is that if you miss one of the plenaries or were unable to attend the conference, these are in the main assembled here. Maggie Humm's opening essay, "Multidisciplinary Woolf/ Multiple Woolfs?" usefully deploys Agamben and Rancière to examine ways in which multidisciplinarity shapes our approaches to Woolf. The essay is instructive for those interested in visual pedagogies and technologies and the ways in which Woolf both resisted and respected "generic signatures" (10). Brenda Silver's plenary, "Waving to Virginia," a title she borrows from Patti Smith's performance and reading of excerpts from *The Waves* on the anniversary of Woolf's death in 2008, links Woolf to, in addition to Smith, Cuban writer Reinaldo Arenas. Her talk serves somewhat as a follow-up to her groundbreaking study *Virginia Woolf Icon* (1999) as she charts the ways in which Woolf's iconic status has changed over the years, but also remains entrenched in stereotypical representations. Here, her research has led her to "feel more strongly than ever" that Woolf's suicide can be read "not only as considered and principled, but, perhaps, also exemplary: an act of resistance in the face of political and personal circumstances that threatened everything she believed in" (81). In her pairing of Woolf with Arenas, Silver argues that Woolf's emblematic presence, her photo hanging on the wall in Arenas's New York City apartment as he is dying of AIDS, becomes "a nod to what they shared as artists, including the courage to fight against the odds, to write the literature they felt they had to write in order to survive and, when they felt they could no longer write, their decision to die in their own way" (87). Silver's plenary is an eloquently turned analysis, which continues to challenge an iconic version of Woolf as "the tragic woman artist" (92).

Other highlights include Madelyn Detloff's "'The law is on the side of the normal': Virginia Woolf as Crip Theorist," which uses Woolf's "Worshipping proportion" in *Mrs. Dalloway* to investigate "the genesis of radical counterdiscourses that question the primacy of the norm" (102). The essay is an exemplar of scholarship unafraid to test new theoretical frameworks in adjusting our thinking about Woolf. Leslie K. Hankins's rhetorical collage, "Time has Whizzed Back an Inch or Two on Its Reel," provides an exercise in "aesthetic time travel" (146) connecting Woolf to artist Emily Carr via postcards from St. Ives and her considerable research in the archives studying the diaries and letters of members of the St. Ives artist communities. Lively, imaginative, and informed, the essay reminds us of the importance of finding joy in the process of research and of keeping open to the fluctuations and porousness of time and space as we continue to question and raise questions about Woolf and her work. Elisa K. Sparks, in "Sunflower Suture: Disseminating the Garden in *The Years*," explores the metaphorical and "unexpected thematic alignments" of the flowers in Woolf's predominantly urban novel. She calls *The Years* "one of Woolf's most floral fictions" (119) as she charts the trope of flowers throughout the novel, as well as its earlier manuscript versions in *The Pargiters*. Combining a textual study with her analysis of the novel, Sparks concludes that the floral imagery throughout the evolution of the novel gestures towards "their defining centrality as images not only of Eleanor's identity but also the novel's search for some pattern of stability to suture the years together" (124). Sparks's interest in flowers in Woolf's work has since manifested itself online as "Woolf in Bloom: A Floral Almanac," a blog excerpting quotations from Woolf's work linked to flowers "usually inspired by what is in bloom" (woolfbloom.blogspot.com).

Maria Aparecide de Oliviera's "Virginia Woolf and Clarice Lispector: Thinking back through Brazilian Mothers" brings us new work pairing Woolf with the underrepresented, but brilliant, Lispector. The essay examines the ways in which both authors used language to subvert patriarchy and transgress generic boundaries. Michael J. Horacki's essay, "Apollonian Illusion and Dionysian Truth in *Mrs. Dalloway*," explores Nietzsche and Apollonian and Dionysian constructs in Woolf's fiction, but is suggestive of further work to be done on Woolf and the classics. And, finally, the conference also marked the rollout of Susan Brown, Patricia Clements, and Isobel Grundy's *Orlando* project and their goals and strategies for this extensive and comprehensive database are outlined here.

Virginia Woolf and the Common(wealth) Reader, while lacking the in-real-time political drama of having some of its attendees stopped at the border, attests to the fact that "reading and writing about Woolf is certainly an act of communication which takes place on a privileged site, but it is one that embraces critiques and protests as central to that task" (xii). As in the earlier volume, the editors of this one, Helen Wussow and Mary Ann Gillies, emphasize the importance of place, as the conference, hosted by Simon Fraser University, was held "on the traditional territories of the Musqueam, Squamish, and Tsleil-Waututh Nations" (vii). Their introduction articulately addresses the attendant complexities and nuances of writing both inside and against the "common(wealth)" one that "necessarily embodies tensions between the communal and the individual, between traditional cultural forms and emergent ones, between indigenous peoples and colonial powers, and between literary insiders and outsiders" (vii), and the essays included here represent the range and depth of that discussion.

The volume, which begins with four poetic invocations, especially brings into focus Woolf's relationship to race and class. Focusing on the two *Common Readers*, Sonita Sarker's plenary, "Virginia Woolf in the British Commonwealth," argues that "Woolf and the British Commonwealth grew up together and separately; that is, they changed on parallel and intertwined tracks" as Woolf writes both within and against her sense of Englishness. Sarker writes that Woolf's "privilege in some aspects and marginalization in others exists at the same time" which allows Woolf to claim both "a cultural-national belonging even as she opposes a statist-nationalist position that she identifies with jingoist masculinism in the later *Three Guineas*" (66). Recognizing her own positionality "both inside and outside the body of a post-Colonial, British Commonwealth subject," Sarker problematizes Woolf's relationship as subject while "this political/cultural entity called the Commonwealth was still coming in to being" as she raises the question and erasure of Woolf's own connection via, "according to some research," her "matrilineal heritage, to a Bengali woman, Marie Monique" (74). Sarker's essay is especially strong in its analysis of the *Common Readers*, an extensive body of work in and of itself, and instructive in placing both Woolf, and Canada, the site of the conference, within a historical frame based on British imperial power and policies.

Given the geo-political underpinnings of the conference, essays on the Stephen family and on Leonard Woolf point to the ways in which Woolf's work intersects with the political interests and goals of her familial and social circles. Jane de Gay's "James Stephen's Anti-Slavery Politics: A Woolfian Inheritance," while important in bringing forward work on James Stephen, misrepresents Jane Marcus as overlooking him (see, *Hearts of Darkness: White Women Write Race* 24-58, 27,71; and, *Virginia Woolf and the Languages of Patriarchy* 5, 82-84, 99); and Catherine W. Hollis's "Leslie Stephen's Science of (Ecological) Ethics" charts the "homely and domestic" referents in Stephen's discourse on ethics to argue that "the source of all ethical behavior starts at home" (49). Her essay also gestures towards the need for additional work on Woolf's own formulation and understanding of ethics as a figure straddling both late nineteenth century utilitarian conceptions of philosophers, such as Henry Sidgwick, and early twentieth century thinkers in the analytic tradition, such as G. E. Moore, both of whom Virginia Woolf revised. Wayne Chapman's "Synthesizing Civilizations: Leonard Woolf, the League of Nations, and the Inverse of Imperialism, 1928-1933" brings forward Leonard's pivotal role in helping to construct a post-war peace, and Christine Froula's plenary "War, Peace, Internationalism: Bloomsbury Legacies" reads the little known pacifist allegory by "Goldie" Lowes Dickinson *War and Peace: A Dramatic Fantasia*, placing it within the context of Bloomsbury pacifism and the history of the peace movement in general. Both essays indirectly address the complex nature of Woolf's own pacifism in relation to that of her husband and other members of her Bloomsbury circle.

Woolf's interest in and concern for outsider causes are incisively represented in essays by Kristin Czarnecki, Vara Neverow, Ira Nadel, and Patrizia Muscogiuri. Czarnecki pairs Woolf with Leslie Marmon Silko and Neverow examines Woolf's fiction in relation to Margaret Atwood's *The Handmaid's Tale*. Nadel focuses on the representation of trauma in the photographs in *Three Guineas*, and Muscogiuri on gender, imperialism, and race in *The Voyage Out* and *The Waves*. Each of these essays comprise a body of work demonstrating Woolf's advocacy of marginalized groups and a radical critique of patriarchy and empire. In contrast, essays exploring Woolf's contradictions and discomfort with privilege and her own position as British subject round out the contours of the debate surrounding Woolf and issues of race and class. Lisa Coleman's "Woolf's Troubled and Troubling Relationship to Race: The Long Reach of the White Arm of Imperialism" and Martin Winquist's "A 'Bloodless and Pernicious Pest': The Middlebrow's 'Common Man' in the Essays of Virginia Woolf" speak to Woolf's relationship to race and class, respectively. Coleman's excellent essay deploys Gayatri Spivak, Sonita Sarker, and Jane Marcus in a thought-provoking reading of Woolf's *The Voyage Out*, as she both challenges and extends Marcus's reading of *A Room of One's Own* that suggests feminists in the twenty-first century may have to reassess the text taking into account "the changing context within which the treatise is read and the multicultural readership that is assessing it" (167). Coleman's essay is a step in that direction, noting Woolf's position in relation to race as dynamic as she is read by new generations of readers informed by postcolonial critical trends.

The conference also marked the introduction of the Modernist Archives Publishing Project (MAPP), spearheaded by Nicola Wilson, Elizabeth Willson Gordon, Alice Staveley, Helen Southworth, and Claire Battershill, who outlined the challenges and benefits to archival scholarship in launching an international, digital archive. MAPP is using The Hogarth Press as "the ideal pilot study" (223), with obvious advantages for Woolf scholars seeking "to trace the evolution of Woolf's writing practice alongside her work as editor" among other potential uses in Woolf research; their experiences in developing this digital database are outlined in the collection.

The 22nd and 23rd *Selected Papers* collections constitute an impressive body of innovative and generative scholarship in Woolf Studies. These essays remind us of the ability of Woolf's work to interact with both traditional lines of critical inquiry and new theoretical frameworks, as her work continues to extend points of contact between her literary, cultural, and political output and the multiple and multilayered discourses of our own age. I look forward to the conference's next installment. Yes, please. And, thank you.

—Jean Mills, *John Jay College-CUNY*

Critical Insights: Virginia Woolf & 20th Century Women Writers.
Ed. Kathyrn Stelmach Artuso (Ipswich, MA: Salem Press/
Grey House Publishing, 2014) 300 pp.

Designed as one of a series of volumes to aid undergraduate research, Kathryn Stelmach Artuso's anthology on Woolf and twentieth-century women writers is generally serviceable but falls rather short of Salem Press's stated mission to provide the "most up-to-date collection of scholarly thinking about authors and individual works from all standard critical perspectives" (www.salempress.com).

The book is composed of a brief introduction, followed by four "Critical Contexts" essays, three of which explore general topics associated with Woolf and a fourth on Woolf and Bowen. The bulk of the book consists of eleven essays which read Woolf in relation to a variety of twentieth-century commonwealth women writers including Katherine Mansfield, Rebecca West, Jean Rhys and Eavan Boland, as well as Americans Nella Larsen, Jessie Redmon Fauset, Eudora Welty, Sylvia Plath, Alice Walker, Sandra Cisneros, Maxine Hong Kingston, and Toni Morrison.

As the introduction, "About This Volume," makes clear, the collection of essays is somewhat haphazard, the only themes which reappear in more than one or two essays being a discussion of windows and mirrors as reflective/refractive devices and a concern with the fluidity of identity as it relates to spatial metaphors for autonomy. The lead essay by the editor focuses on windows and mirrors, and since it concentrates—like many others in the collection—largely on *A Room of One's Own*, it hardly works as a wholesale introduction to Woolf's work. Unfortunately, this first piece does not set a high standard for the rest of the volume. The author mistakenly refers to Woolf's famous passage about a pattern underlying the cotton wool of everyday reality as coming from the conclusion of *Moments of Being* rather than the beginning of "A Sketch of the Past"—an error perhaps explained by the fact that she quotes the passage from a Jane Marcus article instead of going to the primary source. Although her essay is one of the few that takes up current theoretical issues in Woolf studies, her summary of critical debates surrounding androgyny and post-structural approaches which attempts to bridge the gaps between Anglo-American and French feminism (a concern of the 1980s and 1990s) with a kind of multi-perspectivism drawn from work on the visual arts and transnationalism studies arrives at a rather bland synthesis of opposites that harkens back to traditional approaches to Woolf.

The quality of particular essays varies widely, depending mostly on the effort and ambition of individual authors, as there appears to have been little editorial intervention: some essays barely mention Woolf, others do extensive close readings, while still others mostly compare plot elements. There is also no attempt to enforce standard abbreviations or editions, some authors using long outdated versions which are no longer easily available. Bibliographic coverage is similarly spotty, with a few essays not quoting any scholarship published in the last decade.

The four essays establishing the Critical Contexts for Woolf are a case in point. Vincent Pecora's introduction to "The Woolf Era" contains so much information that it often reads like an encyclopedia article in hyperdrive; one page, for example, goes from "Die Brucke" to Dada to Freud, to Bataille, to Boas and Durkheim in the space of two sentences. Much of the content is rather tangential to Woolf, and the whole essay suffers from an uneasy sense of its audience, including a variety of references that strike me as too obscure for the kind of undergraduates who need a survey of political and cultural events before, during, and after the two world wars. Jean Mills's comprehensive and workmanlike survey of critical reactions to Woolf is, on the other hand, a model of what such overview essays should be. Copiously footnoted, the essay is nicely balanced between classic and recent treatments of Woolf; out of the 98 works cited in her bibliography (including primary works), 38 were published in 2000 or later, and there is quite a sprinkling of pieces published in the last year or two. Given the fact that she only has a page or so to devote to each major work, she does a laudable job of highlighting major debates and even manages to squeeze in the advent of digital approaches. Although narrower in scope, J. Ashley Foster's account of *Three Guineas* in the context of peace studies is similarly informative and competent. It is not really clear why Roberta White's essay on Elizabeth Bowen and Virginia Woolf is in the Critical Contexts section rather than with the other comparative essays in the Critical Readings section. Simply and clearly organized, it provides comparisons of novels with similar plot elements such as courtship, attention to the war, and families at a beach house.

The eleven essays in the Critical Readings section are arranged more or less chronologically, but only occasionally have any other relationship to each other. Beginning with a brief but useful summary of the two women's interests in contemporary theories of art and the work of Chekhov, Angela Smith does a nice job of explicating the painterly qualities linking Woolf's writing to that of Katherine Mansfield. Bernard Schweizer's article on Rebecca West is one of several where there is only a perfunctory mention of Woolf; mostly dedicated to describing West's "heretical humanism," the only sustained comparison is of the two writers' posthumous reputations. Mich Yonah Nywaldo's treatment of postcolonial themes in Rhys's *Wide Sargasso Sea* and Woolf's *The Voyage Out* is one of the outstanding essays in the volume. Based on an informed awareness of previous criticism, it provides a sophisticated analysis of how both novels undercut their critiques of imperialism by reproducing the colonial gaze. Using the metaphor of Woolf's room of one's own to discuss racial indeterminacy in novels by Nella Larsen and Jessie Redmon Fauset, Christopher Allen Varlack's piece is less satisfying since it neither establishes any real connection nor works out any sustained comparison with Woolf. While Emily Daniel Magruder's essay on Eudora Welty's inheritance from Woolf also begins with *A Room of One's Own*, it goes on to a fairly systematic coverage of the influence of several Woolf novels and short stories, based on a good review of traditional scholarship up to 2003.

The next two essays offer an example of the potential webs of influence linking Woolf's literary daughters. The only essay to delve into manuscript sources, Amanda Golden's account of Sylvia Plath's annotations to Woolf, offers a helpfully comprehensive picture of the poet's reading of Woolf, chasing down not only the marginalia in her personal copies of the novels, but also mentions of Woolf in Plath's journals and letters as well as traces of influences in Plath's own early fiction and later poetry. Plath reoccurs as an avatar of Judith Shakespeare in the next essay, Helen Emmitt's account of Irish poet Eavan Boland's debt to Woolf in her prose accounts of the life of the woman poet. Unlike other essays that simply evoke the generic idea of autonomy in Woolf's *Room*, Emmitt teases out a number of imagistic parallels between Woolf's text and Boland's, convincingly arguing that Boland carries many of the key insights of Woolf's feminist classic into a more contemporary context.

The last four essays bring the volume more or less up to date, returning to deal with the way women of color have negotiated their affiliation to and critiques of Woolf. Sarah Skripsky's survey of Alice Walker's re-readings of Woolf does a good job of citing much of the previous scholarship, using it to outline the thematic areas where Walker challenges the limited vision of Woolf's privileged perspective, but with only one article cited since 1995 the piece does not break any new ground. Using Homi Bhahba's theorization of the unhomed subject and Gloria Anzaldua's concepts of the mestiza consciousness of the borderlands, Shanna M. Salinas's treatment of how homes function in forming the identity of the heroine in *The House on Mango Street* is one of the more critically sophisticated essays in the volume, but has so little to say about Woolf that she is not even cited. Equally critically sophisticated, Quyuh Nhu Le reads *Orlando*'s deconstruction of the objective narrator, linear history, and the sexually unitary self into the subversion of the premises of ethnic life writing in Maxine Hong Kingston's *Woman Warrior* and *China Men*. The volume ends with Sandra Cox's intertextual reading of Woolf and Toni Morrison. Taking her cue from Barbara Christian's brilliant and delicate construction of a conversation between the two writers, Cox differentiates between influence and affinity in her analysis of the relationships between the rhetorical metaphors of *Three Guineas* and those deployed in *Playing in the Dark* and in a discussion of the treatment of motherhood in *To the Lighthouse* and *A Mercy*.

This Critical Insights volume is laudable in its inclusion of a wide range of Anglophone women writers, including a number of women of various ethnic and racial backgrounds, though most of them are from the expected canonical pantheon. But aside from a few nods to postcolonial perspectives, the book as a whole seems fairly undertheorized. One might expect that a book so centered on *A Room of One's Own* would engage with space/place theory or that a collection of works on women writers would at least acknowledge the existence of lesbian and queer perspectives.

At $95.00, the volume is priced for libraries and indeed is part of a series apparently designed for academic collections as it comes as part of a package including access to a database, which does not seem to be included in the purchase price for individuals. The best of the essays make this book worth checking out.

—Elisa Kay Sparks, *Clemson University*

Modernist Fiction and Vagueness: Philosophy, Form, and Language. Megan Quigley (New York: Cambridge UP, 2015) xi + 219 pp.

Speaking of truth, reality and objectivity in humanistic studies in the early 1990s, Richard Rorty imagines a "heyday of the fuzzy" in which the oppositions between subject and object would gradually fade away, along with the disciplinary oppositions within the humanities. In a 2005 review of Scott Soames's history of analytic philosophy, however, Rorty is surprised to find that vagueness has emerged as a "hot topic" in professional Anglophone philosophy at the end of the twentieth century, and dismayed that the boom in investigations of vague predicates marks not the breakdown of disciplinary boundaries he foresaw in his synoptic vision, but the increasing hyper-specialization of philosophical inquiry within that discipline.

It is to the porousness of the boundaries between philosophy and literature (and the issues of subject, object and the nature of reality explored within them) that Megan Quigley attends in *Modernist Fiction and Vagueness*, offering a rich scholarly examination of the modernist period, in which developments in both fiction and philosophy were shaped by the mutually influential obsession with language's imprecision that marks the linguistic turn. As Quigley points out, the problem of vagueness is hardly new. For if its explosion in analytic philosophy since the 1970s originates in the sorites paradox (how many grains of sand constitute a heap?), it finds a more immediate source in the founding figures of analytic philosophy, specifically Frege and Russell (who sought to eradicate vague predicates by creating a logically precise language) and Wittgenstein (who sought to bring clarification about the relation between language and world). Quigley attends equally to the parallel philosophical interest in what Henry James called the "positive saving virtue of vagueness" (5) that stimulated Peirce's and William James's pragmatism, and seeks to correct the impression that analytic philosophy influenced literary modernist theories of language any more than did William James's "reinstatement of the vague" (9), which sought to enlist this inevitable aspect of ordinary language as a tool rather than strive to banish it as a linguistic aberration to be rectified or overcome.

With its focus on the under-examined problem of vagueness that becomes such a pressing philosophical and aesthetic concern in the early twentieth century, Quigley's book fills a gap in modernist studies. By regarding vagueness as a defining attribute of modernism's formal experiments and situating modernist literature within the debate between analytic and pragmatist philosophers over the question of language's imprecision, *Modernist Fiction and Vagueness* offers a compelling new interdisciplinary approach through which to account for the relationship between English language literary modernism and the two predominant countervailing forces in twentieth-century Anglo-American philosophy. Quigley traces the fascination with vagueness that surges across disciplinary boundaries in the early 1920s, looking at a range of vague stylistics that modernist fiction deploys in deliberate opposition to the move in logico-philosophical circles to reform ordinary language. Her analysis of this array of modernist modes of vagueness moves from Henry James's long indeterminate clauses and interest in ineffable secrets to Woolf's attention to gendered language, dissolution of direct discourse, and impressionistic rendering of subjectivity to James Joyce's postcolonial verbal coinages and investigations of radical uncertainty and inconclusive answers. Quigley concludes with an examination of the philosophical influences on Eliot's notion of impersonality and embrace of vagueness in his later criticism. By arguing that modernist fiction's reconceptualization of realism derives not only from a desire to break with the "appalling narrative business" of an earlier tradition in literary realism, but also from an effort to respond to new theories in philosophical realism and the revolt against positivism in the philosophy of language, Quigley's study recasts the central question of modernism and mimesis (59). *Modernism and Vagueness* adds conceptual and intellectual-historical nuance to our understanding of the interplay between these experimental developments in philosophy and literature in their different attempts to mount a more faithful representation of the real.

In her effort to show the discursive evolution of the philosophical linguistic turn's influence on modernist literature's embrace of the uncertainty and contingency of everyday life (and the longing for objectivity and order with which it is so often met), Quigley pairs a philosopher with a novelist in each chapter: Henry James with Peirce and William James; Woolf with Russell; Joyce and Wittgenstein triangulated through Ogden, all the while accounting for the salient influence of each member. It is Quigley's treatment of Woolf in the second chapter that will appeal most to readers of this journal.

Taking seriously the impact of Henry James's commitment to the nebulous (along with the negative capability of the "vagulous" character of Forster's writing [79]) on Woolf's efforts to explode the realist conventions of the nineteenth-century novel by inaugurating a literary linguistic turn of her own, Quigley concentrates on how Woolf's "philosophy" also seeks to challenge the ideal of precision upheld in the new analytic philosophy embodied in the work of Bertrand Russell. She begins by reading Woolf's 1937 radio broadcast, "Craftsmanship," alongside Russell's 1921 lecture, "Vagueness," pointing to the ways in which Woolf's writerly philosophy of language and representation is antithetical to, even parodic of, Russell's. Indeed, as Quigley suggests, Woolf's portrayal in *To the Lighthouse* of Mr. Ramsay (a philosopher who eschews vagueness in gendered terms and prefers logical precision to elusive questions) seems to draw upon what she knew of Russell. While he seeks to pass from "vague, ambiguous things" to "something precise, clear, definite" in order to speak to the "real truth of which the vague thing is sort of shadow" (15), Woolf sees in the philosophical questions and linguistic formulations Russell aims to correct a salutary means of speaking to what she called in "Modern Fiction" the "vague general confusion" of modern life (qtd. Quigley 43).

In her reading of *Night and Day*, Quigley is keen to subvert the influence of Katherine Mansfield's standard-setting criticism of the novel (which Mansfield disparages as an overly traditional anachronism in in a modern "age of experiment"). Quigley argues that the developmental narrative arc of this comparatively traditional novel sets the stage for the lessons about the power of vagueness that become a mainstay in Woolf's later works. Katharine's defining devotion to mathematical exactitude and distrust of ordinary language in *Night and Day* ultimately gives way to an acceptance of "the confusion, agitation, and vagueness of the finest prose" (*ND* 34) and fragments of "the unfinished, the unfulfilled, the unwritten" (*ND* 432). By emphasizing the central shift in outlook upon which the structure of the novel depends, Quigley links *Night and Day* to the meditations on the issues of vagueness and vision that famously preoccupy later more experimental (and generically complex) works *Jacob's Room* and *The Waves*: the perennially unanswered questions of meaning; self, impersonality and community; shadow and substance.

Quigley's carefully researched book is rife with passages from her central authors that powerfully attest to literary modernism's interest in the philosophical question of vagueness, and Quigley does an especially thorough job of showing that Woolf's endeavors to convey the "crepuscular" haziness of life's transparent envelope was something she elaborated within (and also against) the context of a cultural moment in which a search for precision was the order of the day. Quigley reminds us that although Woolf described her own thinking as a "philosophy" she was, of course, a novelist and essayist, not a professional philosopher. It makes sense, then, to emphasize, as Quigley does, that Woolf's acquaintance with Russell, though it sparked an important exchange between one influential cultural presence and another, was nonetheless one of a personal nature. It is for this reason, perhaps, that Quigley refrains from reading Woolf in terms of Russell's more philosophically rigorous papers on the problem of acquaintance or description, for example. In her discussion of how Woolf's literature responds to a prevailing philosophical desire to create a perfect atomistic language, Quigley attends in a broader fashion to the influence on Woolf's thinking of Russell's popular literature and lectures. It is possible that the excellent case Quigley makes about the vagueness that becomes a central concern in the early twentieth century, as a variety of different aesthetic spheres simultaneously consider similar questions about language, meaning and world, would only be derailed by a myopic scrutiny of the influence on Woolf of works that marked Russell's most important philosophical interventions. Nonetheless, some readers may crave a more sustained analysis of the two figures that limns the bearing of the particulars of Russell's philosophy upon Woolf. Others will wish for a more extended discussion of the relationship between Quigley's views and those of formidable critics of Woolf and philosophy, Ann Banfield and S. P. Rosenbaum. Though Quigley cites both as foundational to her own divergent views on philosophical realism in relation to modernist literature, she mentions them only in passing, thus unfortunately foregoing the chance to engage in deeper discussion with two of the chapter's most important interlocutors.

Quigley nonetheless presents us with an excellent book that makes an important contribution to Woolf studies and to studies in modernism more generally.

—Karen Zumhagen-Yekplé, *Tulane University*

International Notes

The Virginia Woolf Society of Korea

The Virginia Woolf Society of Korea gave weekly lectures for common readers at Seoul National University in the Spring of 2015. We have held two one-day conferences in April and December biannually since 2003. The Society has published several translations of Woolf's novels and short stories into Korean, and our second collection of the translations of Woolf's essays has been published this year. Our current monthly meetings revolve around the reading and discussion of Woolf's essays, and preparing further publications of translations of Woolf's essays. Furthermore, the Society organized the collection and publishing of selected papers written by our members in 2010 and in 2013, with the 3rd collection scheduled to be issued in 2016. The Society's upcoming event is the third Korea-Japan joint conference scheduled on August 25th-26th, 2016 at Kookmin University in Seoul, Korea. We cordially invite you to this two-day conference, with the theme of "Virginia Woolf and Her Legacy in the Age of Globalization." For more information, visit us at http://www.woolf.or.kr/.

Notes on Contributors

Emily Dalgarno is Emeritus Professor of English, Boston University. She has written *Virginia Woolf and the Migrations of Language* (2012), *Virginia Woolf and the Visible World* (2001), as well as articles on the work of Conrad, Faulkner, Woolf and Hurston.

J. Ashley Foster is Visiting Assistant Professor of Writing and Fellow in the Writing Program at Haverford College. She has published articles on Virginia Woolf, modernist pacifist networks, and radical artistic and literary responses to the Spanish Civil War. Ashley and the students from her spring and fall 2015 "Peace Testimonies in Literature & Art" Writing Seminar are the curators of the interactive student digital humanities and special collections exhibition *Testimonies in Art & Action: Igniting Pacifism in the Face of Total War*, which ran in Haverford College's Magill Library. Ashley's work examines the intersections between pacifism, modernism, and war, and recuperates the lost threads of modernism's pacifist history.

Christine Fouirnaies is a doctoral candidate at Wolfson College, University of Oxford. Her work examines intersections of photography, life-writing and the novel in the twentieth and twenty-first centuries.

Clara Jones is a Lecturer in Modern Literature at King's College London. She is the author of *Virginia Woolf: Ambivalent Activist*, published by Edinburgh University Press.

Submission Guidelines

Woolf **S**tudies **A**nnual invites articles on the work and life of Virginia Woolf and her milieu. The *Annual* intends to represent the breadth and eclecticism of critical approaches to Woolf and particularly welcomes new perspectives and contexts of inquiry. Articles discussing relations between Woolf and other writers and artists are also welcome.

Articles are sent for review anonymously to a member of the Editorial Board and at least one other reader. Manuscripts should not be under consideration elsewhere or have been previously published. It is strongly advised that those submitting work to *WSA* be familiar with the journal's content. Among criteria on which evaluation of submissions depends are whether an article demonstrates familiarity with scholarship already published in the field, whether the article is written clearly and effectively, and whether it makes a genuine contribution to Woolf studies.

Preparation of Copy

1. Articles are typically between 25 and 30 pages, and do not exceed 8,000 words. This is a guide rather than a stipulation, and inquiries about significantly shorter or longer submissions should be sent to the Editor at woolfstudiesannual@gmail.com.

2. A separate file should include the article's title, author's name, address, phone number, and email address. The author's name and any other identifying references should not appear on the manuscript to preserve anonymity for our readers.

3. All submissions must include an abstract of no more than 250 words.

4. Manuscripts should conform to the most recent MLA style.

5. Submissions should be sent as Word files by email to woolfstudiesannual@gmail.com.

6. Authors of accepted manuscripts are responsible for any necessary permissions fees and for securing any necessary permissions.

All editorial inquiries should be addressed to woolfstudiesannual@gmail.com.

Inquiries concerning orders, advertising, reviews, etc. should be addressed to PaceUP@pace.edu.

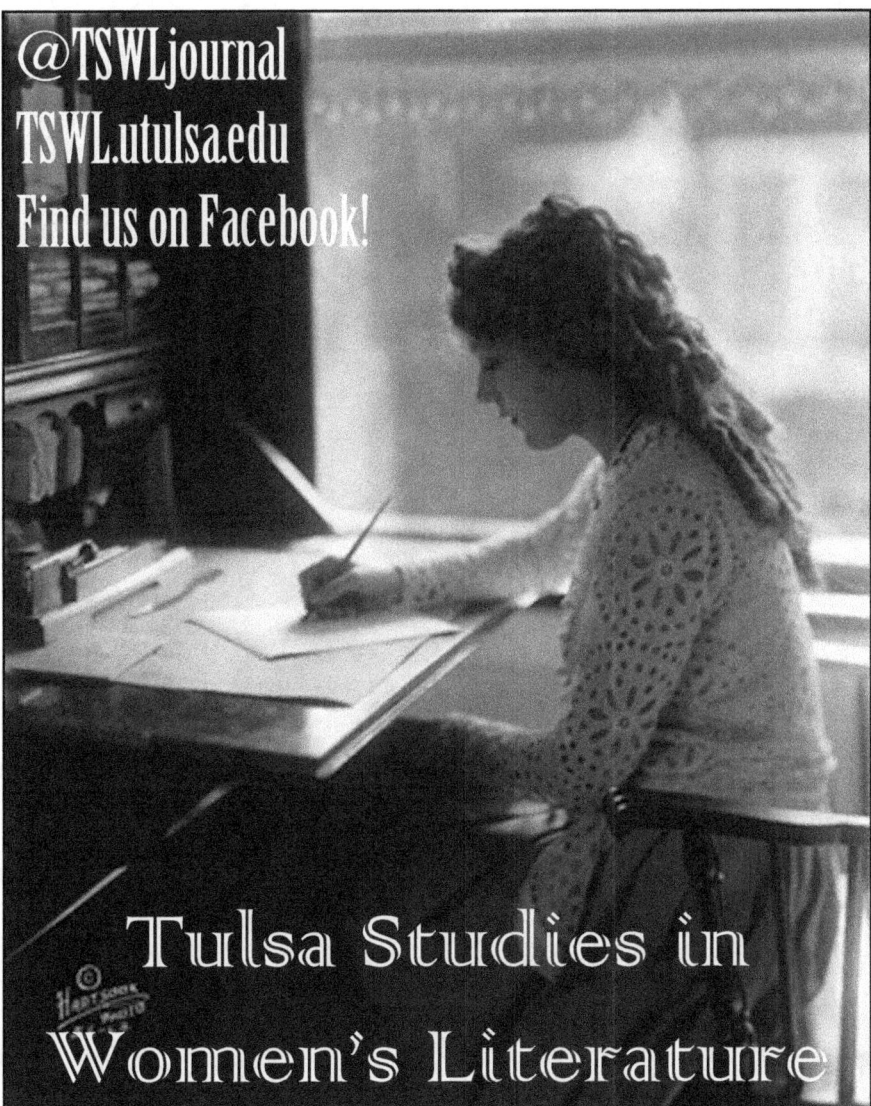

A journal dedicated to scholarship on women's literature of all nationalities and time periods

Subscribe now for Spring 2016 Vol. 35 No. 1

Other Woolf titles available:

"The Hours": The British Museum Manuscript of Mrs. Dalloway, transcribed and edited by Helen M. Wussow (paper 2010)

Virginia Woolf, Jacob's Room: *The Holograph Draft*, transcribed and edited by Edward L. Bishop (paper 2010)

Women in the Milieu of Leonard and Virginia Woolf: Peace, Politics and Education Ed. Wayne K. Chapman and Janet M. Manson (1998)

Virginia Woolf and Trauma: Embodied Texts Ed. Suzette Henke & David Eberly (2007)

Woolf Across Cultures Ed. Natalya Reinhold (2004)

Woolf Studies Annual 5 (1999)

Woolf Studies Annual 6 (2000): The *Three Guineas* Correspondence, edited by Anna Snaith

Woolf Studies Annual 7 (2001)

Woolf Studies Annual 8 (2002): The Fawcett Library Correspondence, edited by Merry Pawlowski

Woolf Studies Annual 9 (2003): *Virginia Woolf and Literary History Part 1*, edited by Jane Lilienfeld, Jeffrey Oxford, and Lisa Low

Woolf Studies Annual 10 (2004): *Virginia Woolf and Literary History Part 2*, edited by Jane Lilienfeld, Jeffrey Oxford, and Lisa Low

Woolf Studies Annual 11 (2005) - *Woolf Studies Annual* 21 (2015)

Woolf Studies Annual 19 (2013): *Special Focus: Virginia Woolf and Jews*, edited by Mark Hussey

Virginia Woolf and Communities: Selected Papers from the Eighth Annual Conference on Virginia Woolf, edited by Jeanette McVicker and Laura Davis

Virginia Woolf Turning the Centuries: Selected Papers from the Ninth Annual Conference on Virginia Woolf, edited by Ann Ardis and Bonnie Kime Scott

Virginia Woolf Out of Bounds: Selected Papers from the Tenth Annual Conference on Virginia Woolf, edited by Jessica Berman and Jane Goldman

The twenty-second volume of *Woolf Studies Annual*
was published in Spring 2016
by Pace University Press

Cover Design by Mary Katherine Cornfield
Interior Design by Angela Taldone
The journal was typeset in Times New Roman and Arial
and printed by Lightning Source in La Vergne, Tennessee

Pace University Press

Director: Sherman Raskin
Associate Director: Manuela Soares
Marketing Manager: Patricia Hinds
Design Consultant: Sara Yager

Graduate Assistants: Mary Katherine Cornfield and Angela Taldone
Student Aide: Kelsey O'Brien-Enders

www.ingramcontent.com/pod-product-compliance
Lightning Source LLC
Chambersburg PA
CBHW061449300426
44114CB00014B/1897